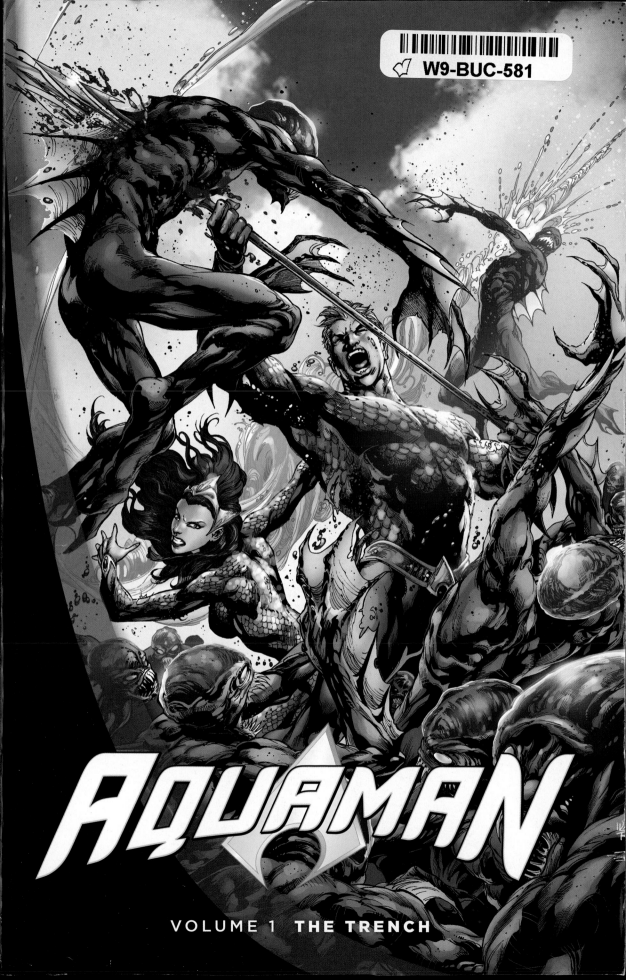

AQUAMAN

VOLUME 1 THE TRENCH

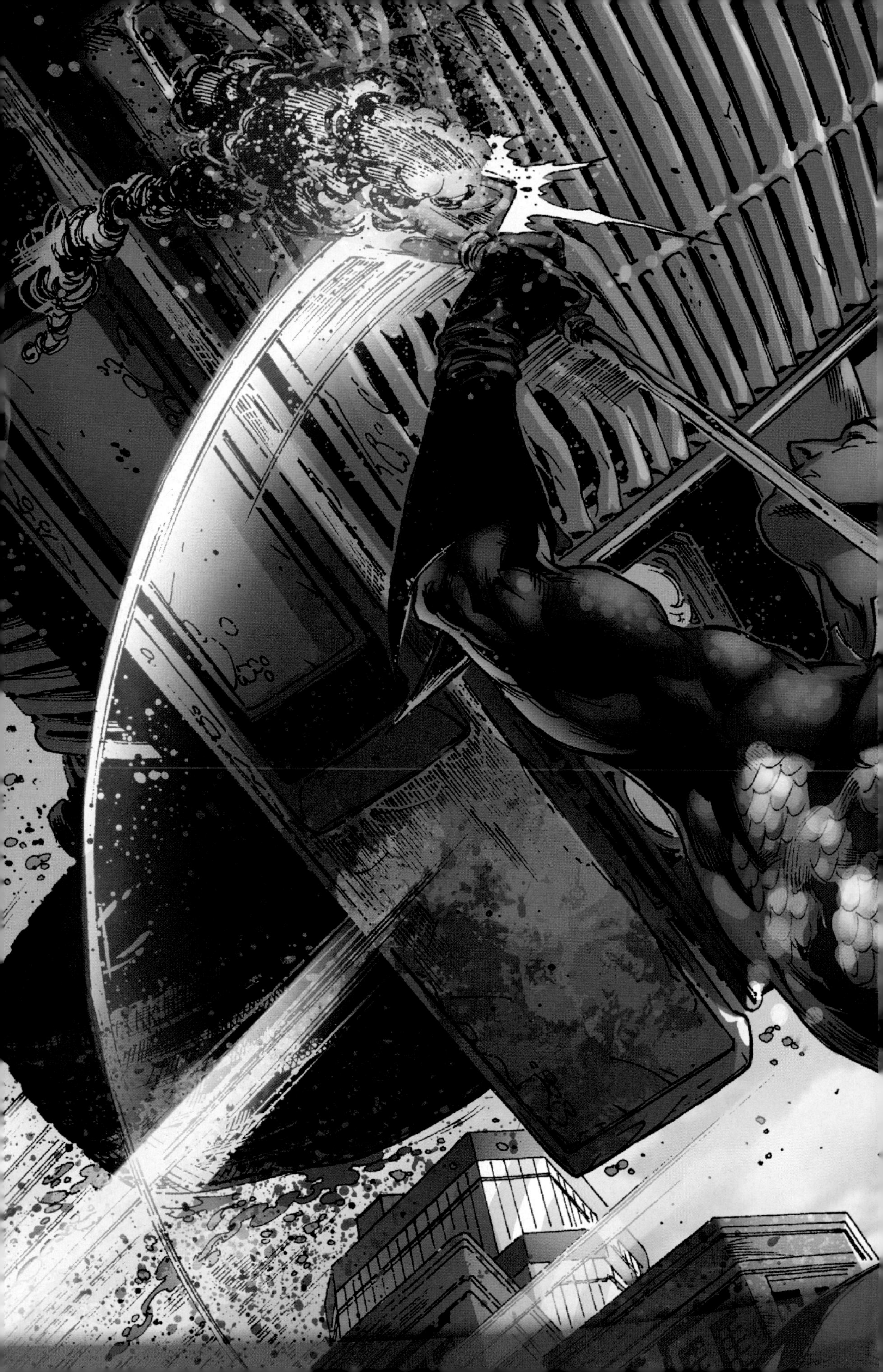

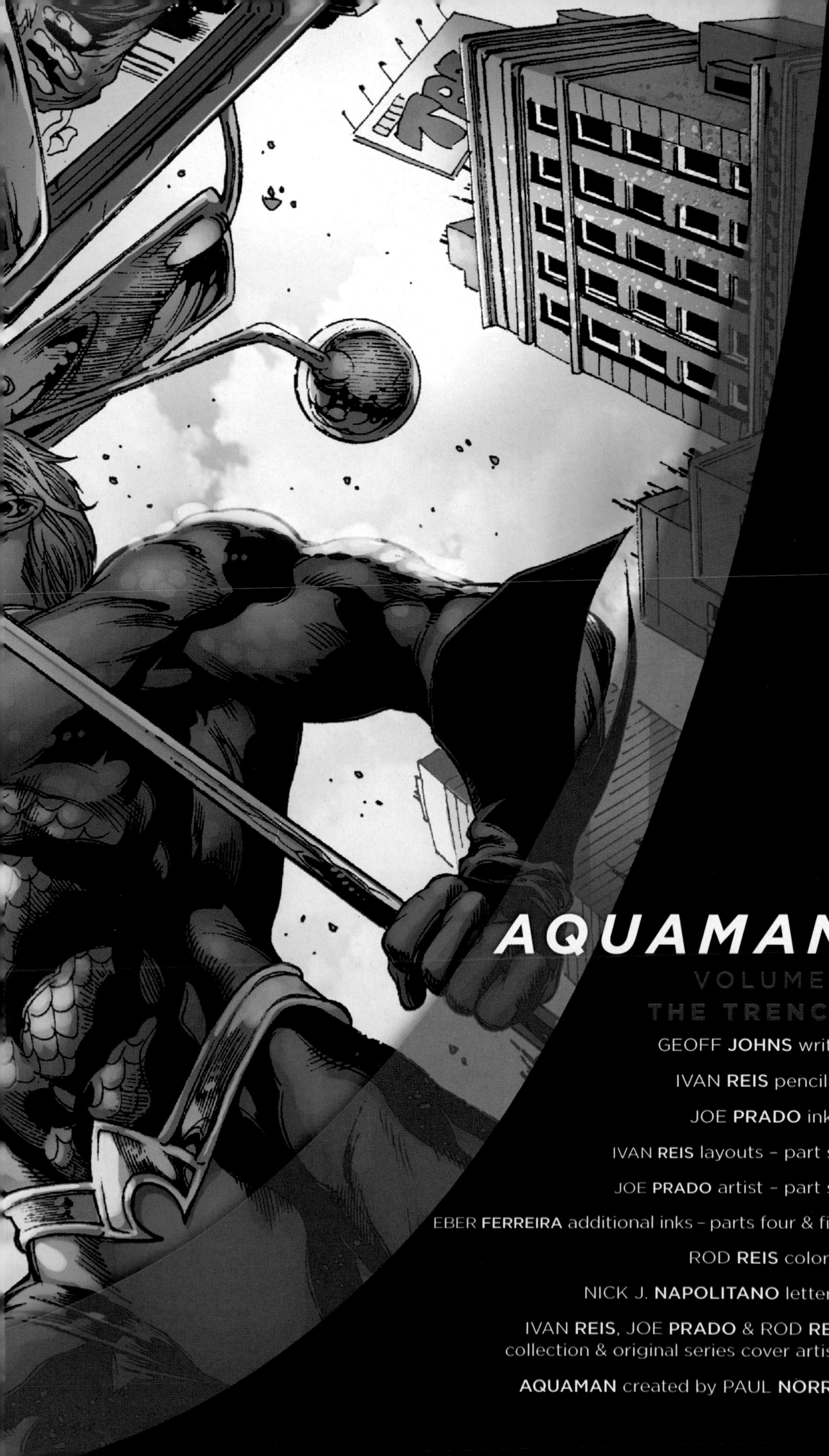

AQUAMAN

VOLUME 1
THE TRENCH

GEOFF **JOHNS** writer

IVAN **REIS** penciller

JOE **PRADO** inker

IVAN **REIS** layouts – part six

JOE **PRADO** artist – part six

EBER **FERREIRA** additional inks – parts four & five

ROD **REIS** colorist

NICK J. **NAPOLITANO** letterer

IVAN **REIS**, JOE **PRADO** & ROD **REIS**
collection & original series cover artists

AQUAMAN created by PAUL **NORRIS**

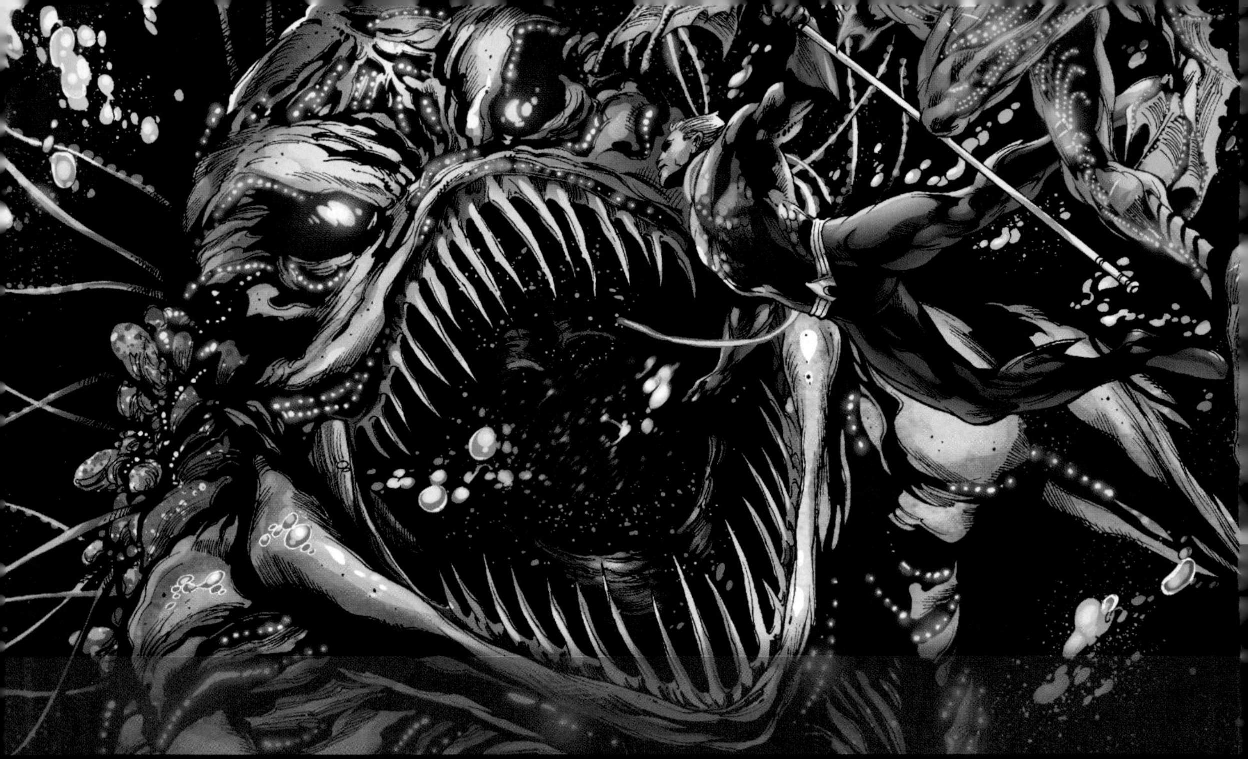

PAT McCALLUM Editor - Original Series SEAN MACKIEWICZ Assistant Editor - Original Series
JEB WOODARD Group Editor - Collected Editions PETER HAMBOUSSI Editor - Collected Edition ROBBIE BIEDERMAN Publication Design

BOB HARRAS Senior VP - Editor-in-Chief, DC Comics

DIANE NELSON President DAN DIDIO and JIM LEE Co-Publishers
GEOFF JOHNS Chief Creative Officer
AMIT DESAI Senior VP - Marketing & Global Franchise Management
NAIRI GARDINER Senior VP - Finance SAM ADES VP - Digital Marketing BOBBIE CHASE VP - Talent Development
MARK CHIARELLO Senior VP - Art, Design & Collected Editions JOHN CUNNINGHAM VP - Content Strategy
ANNE DEPIES VP - Strategy Planning & Reporting DON FALLETTI VP - Manufacturing Operations
LAWRENCE GANEM VP - Editorial Administration & Talent Relations
ALISON GILL Senior VP - Manufacturing & Operations HANK KANALZ Senior VP - Editorial Strategy & Administration
JAY KOGAN VP - Legal Affairs DEREK MADDALENA Senior VP - Sales & Business Development
DAN MIRON VP - Sales Planning & Trade Development NICK NAPOLITANO VP - Manufacturing Administration
CAROL ROEDER VP - Marketing EDDIE SCANNELL VP - Mass Account & Digital Sales
SUSAN SHEPPARD VP - Business Affairs COURTNEY SIMMONS Senior VP - Publicity & Communications
JIM (SKI) SOKOLOWSKI VP - Comic Book Specialty & Newsstand Sales

AQUAMAN VOLUME 1: THE TRENCH

DC Comics, 4000 Warner Blvd., Burbank, CA 91522
A Warner Bros. Entertainment Company.
Printed by RR Donnelley, Salem, VA, USA. 8/28/15. Fifth Printing.

SC ISBN: 978-1-4012-3710-3

Library of Congress Cataloging-in-Publication Data

Johns, Geoff, 1973-
Aquaman. Volume 1, The trench / Geoff Johns, Ivan Reis, Joe Prado.
p. cm.
"Originally published in single magazine form in AQUAMAN 1-6."
ISBN 978-1-4012-3551-2
1. Graphic novels. I. Reis, Ivan. II. Prado, Joe. III. Title. IV. Title: Trench.
PN6728.A68J64 2012
741.5'973—dc23
2012018771

PEFC Certified
Printed on paper from sustainably managed forests and controlled sources
PEFC
PEFC/29-31-75
www.pefc.org

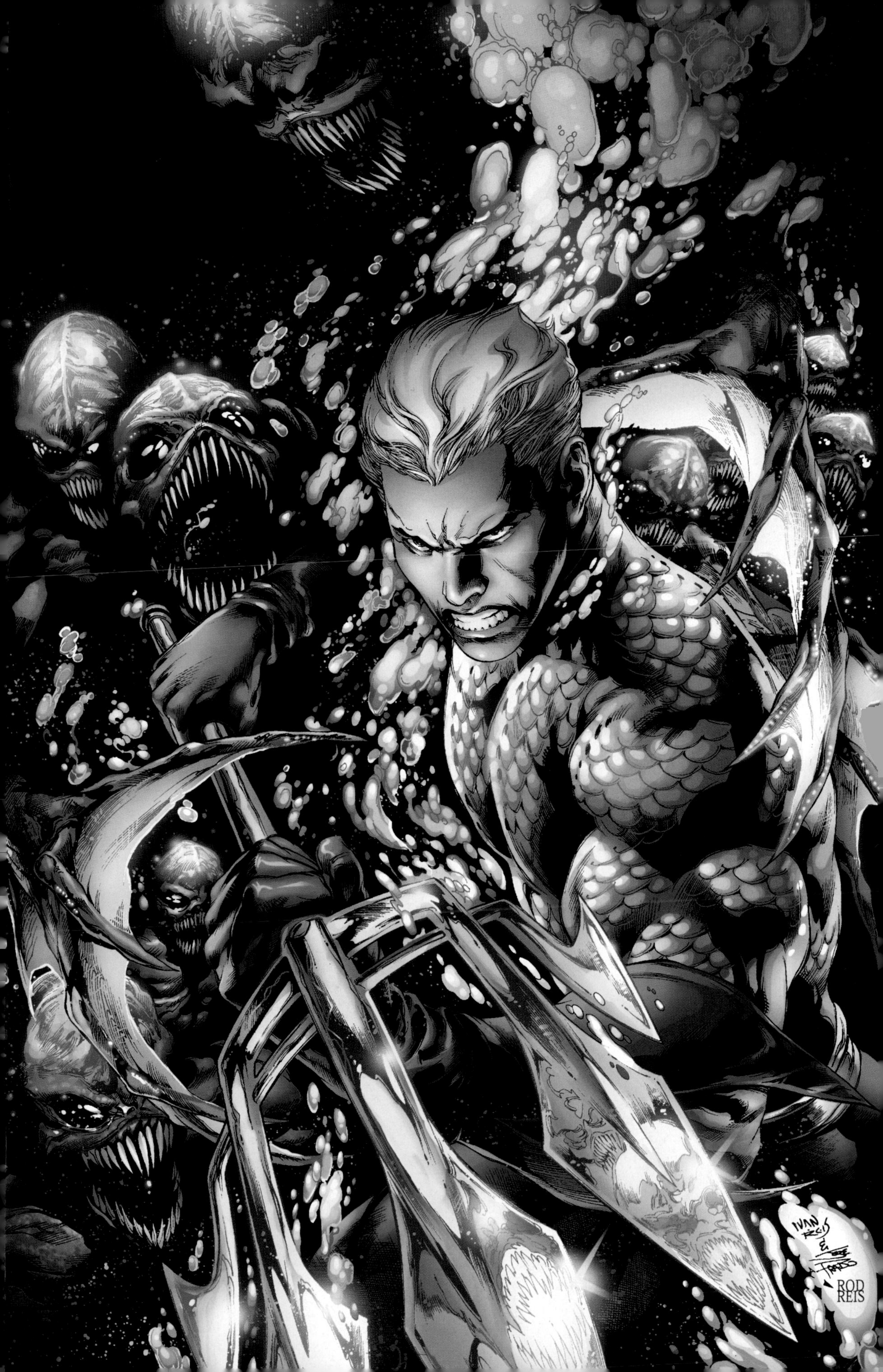
ROD REIS

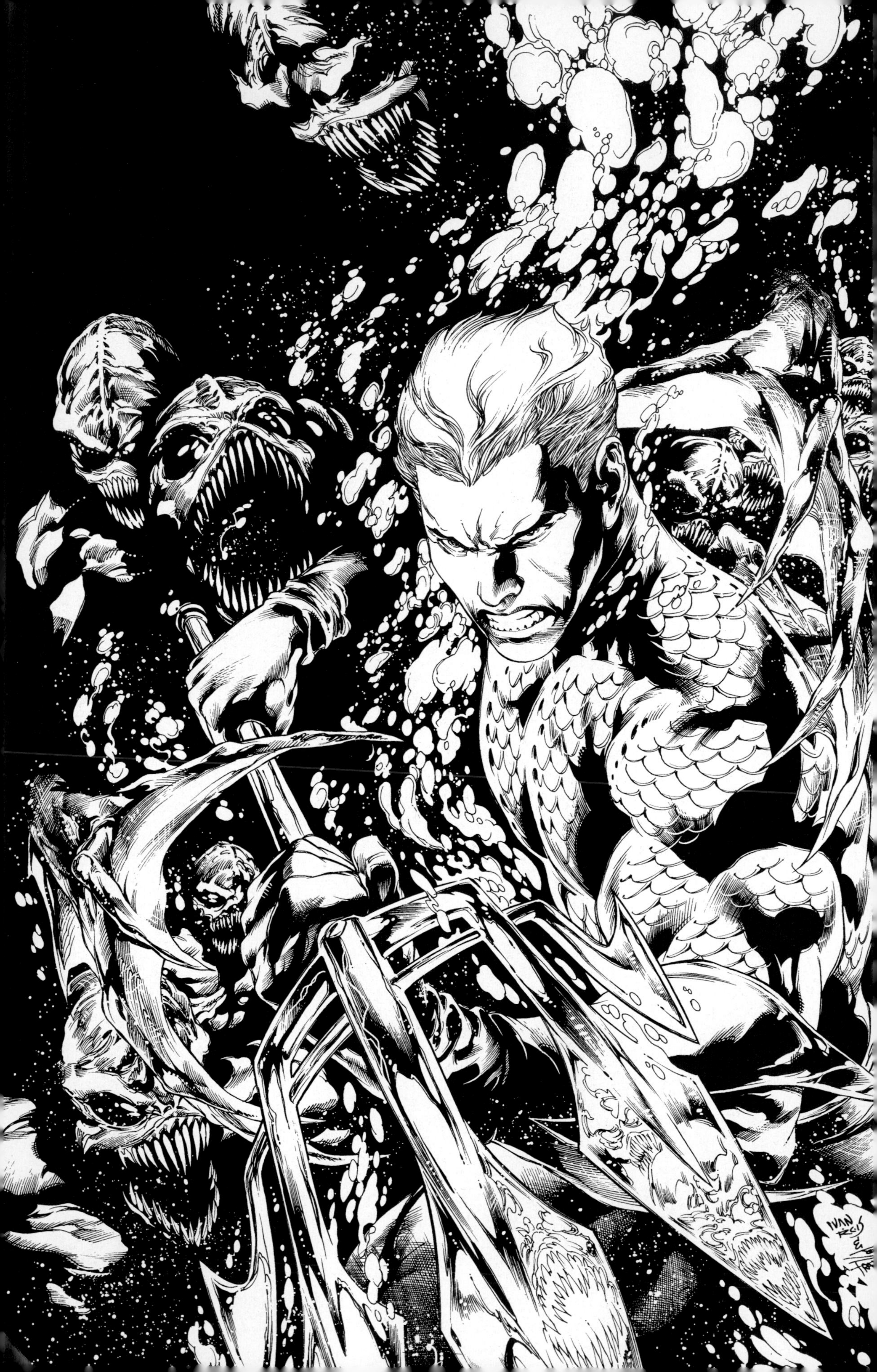
IVAN REIS
&

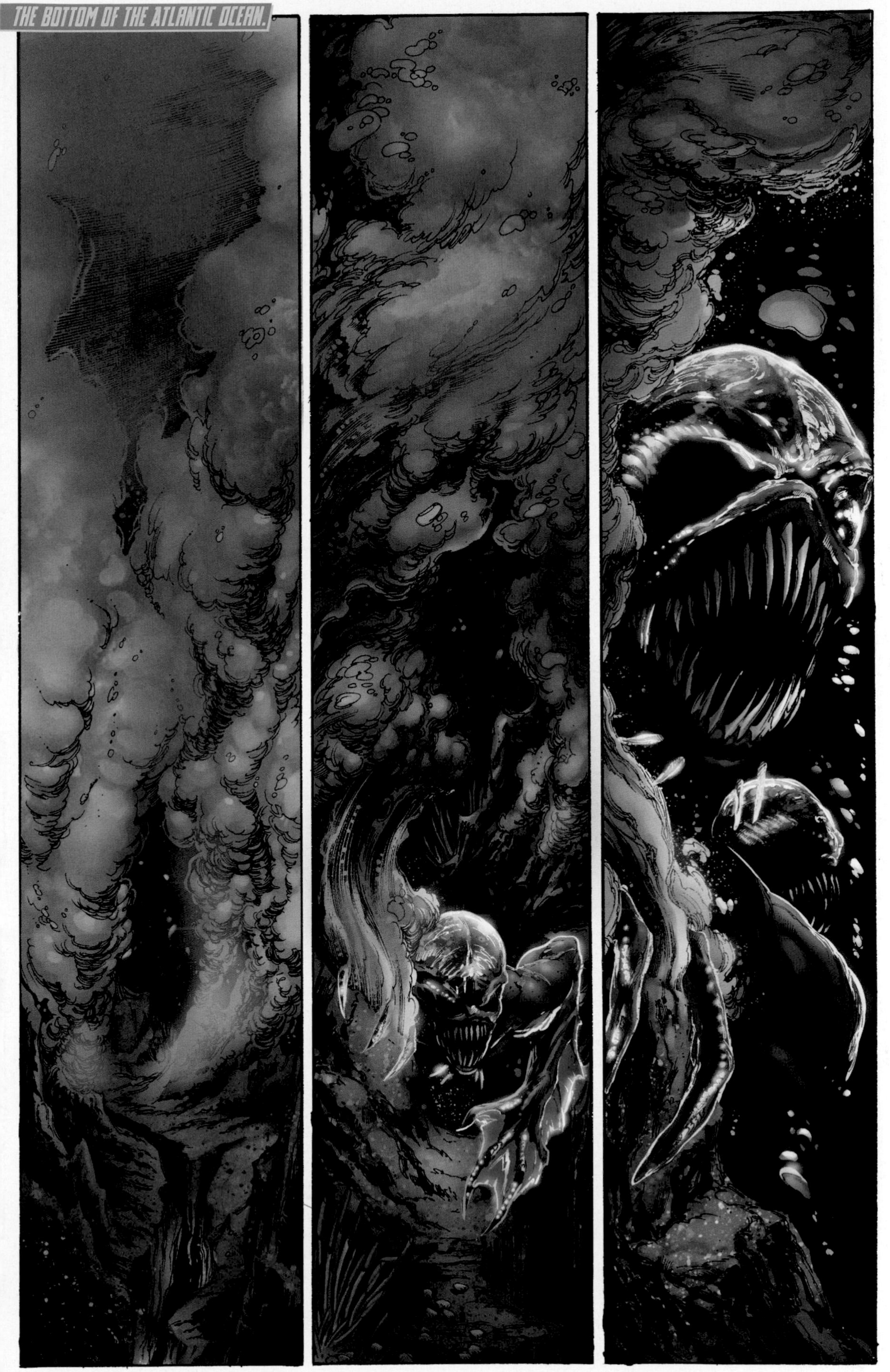
THE BOTTOM OF THE ATLANTIC OCEAN.

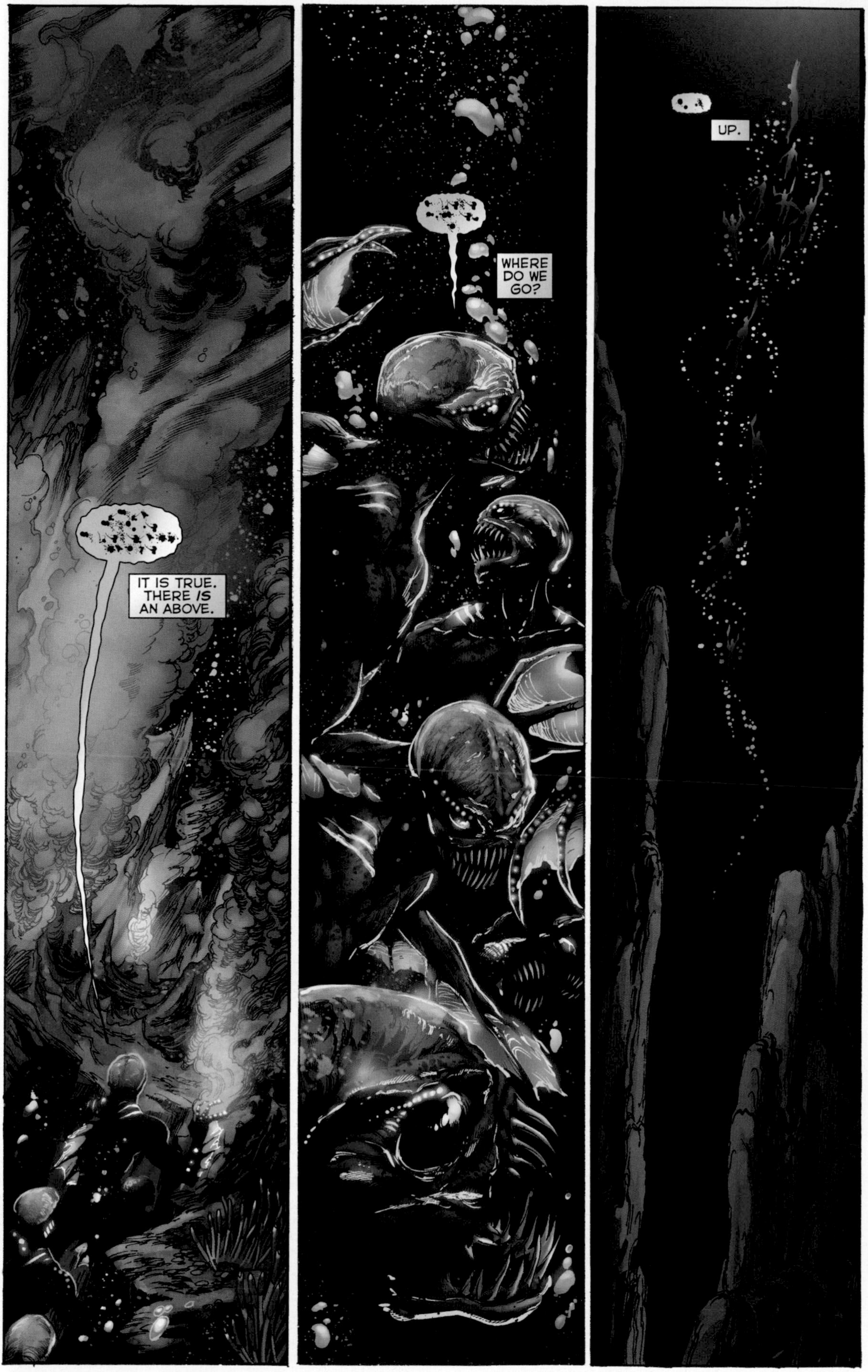
IT IS TRUE. THERE IS AN ABOVE.
WHERE DO WE GO?
UP.

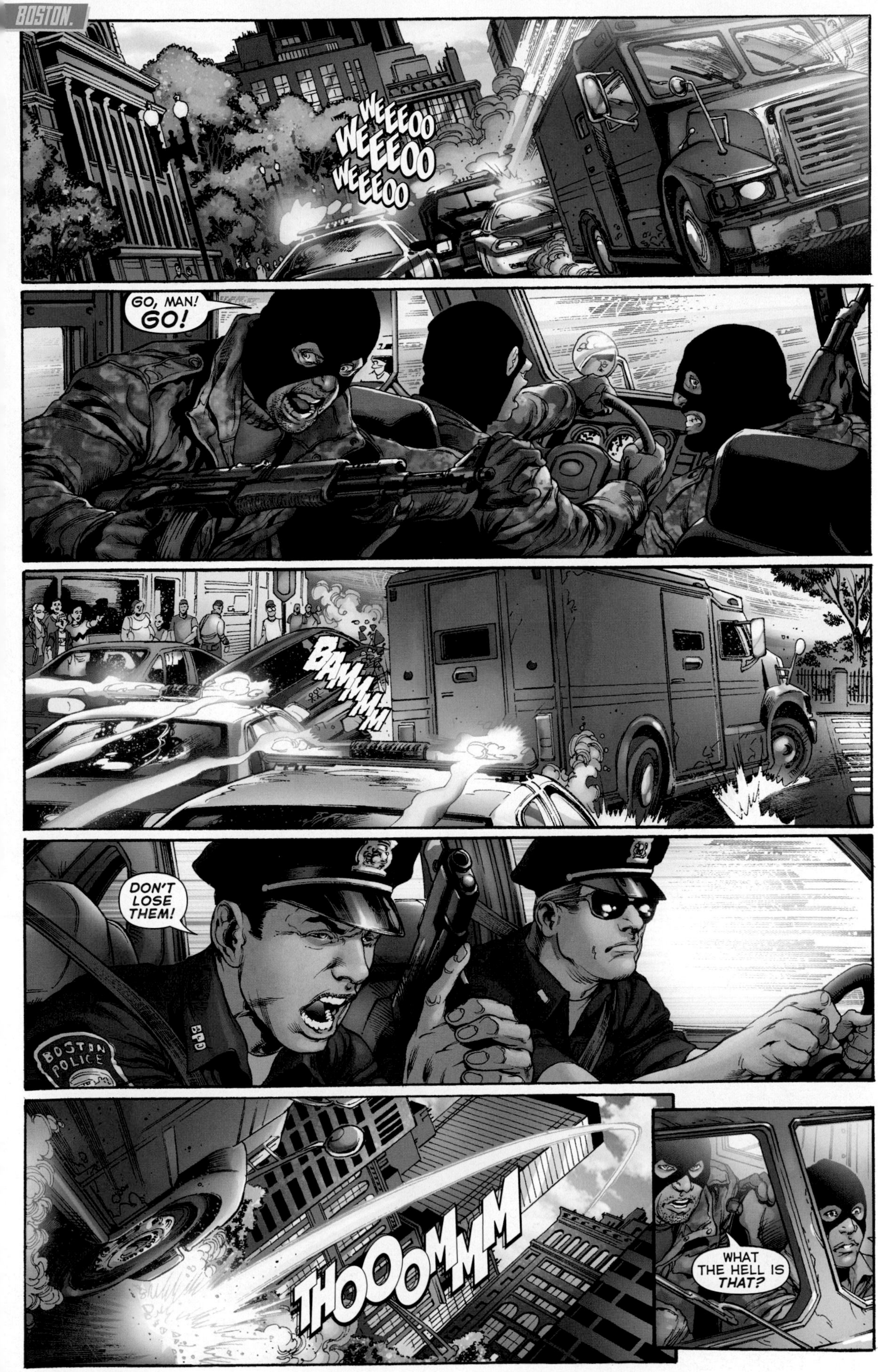
BOSTON.
WEEEOO WEEEOO WEEEOO
GO, MAN! GO!
BAMMMM
DON'T LOSE THEM!
BOSTON POLICE
BPD
THOOOMMM
WHAT THE HELL IS THAT?

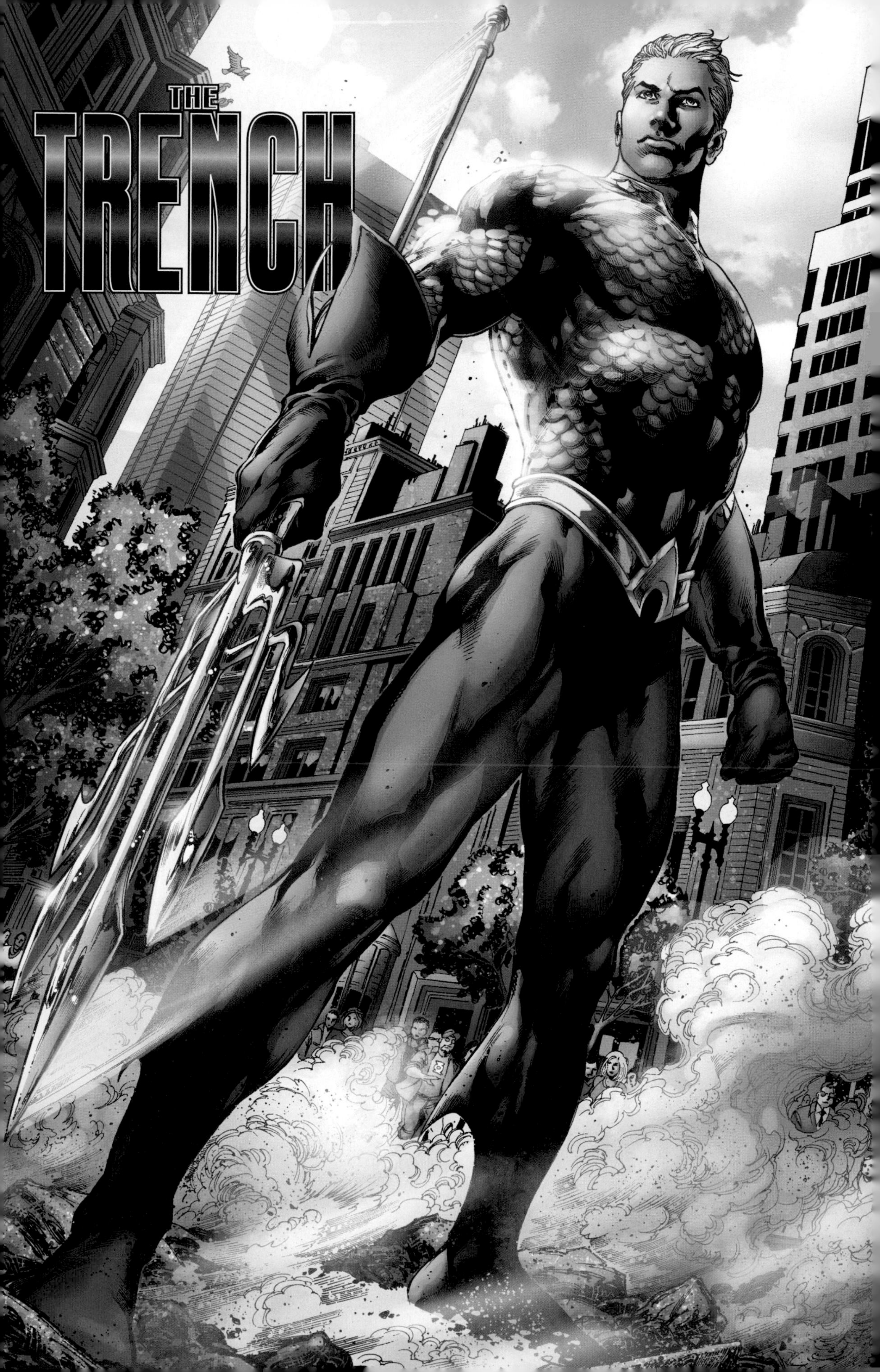
THE
TRENCH

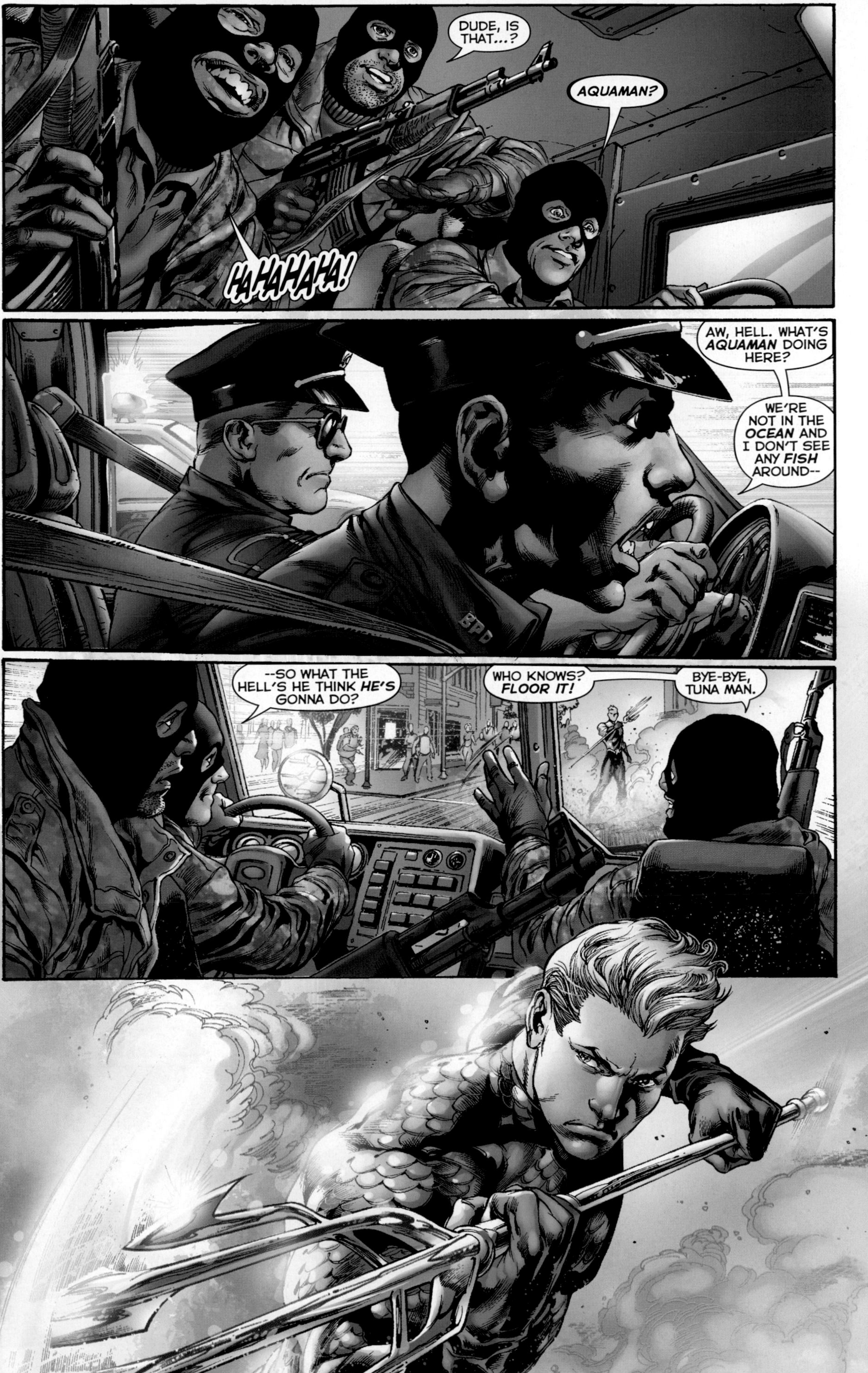
DUDE, IS THAT...?
AQUAMAN?
HAHAHAHA!
AW, HELL. WHAT'S AQUAMAN DOING HERE?
WE'RE NOT IN THE OCEAN AND I DON'T SEE ANY FISH AROUND--
--SO WHAT THE HELL'S HE THINK HE'S GONNA DO?
WHO KNOWS? FLOOR IT!
BYE-BYE, TUNA MAN.

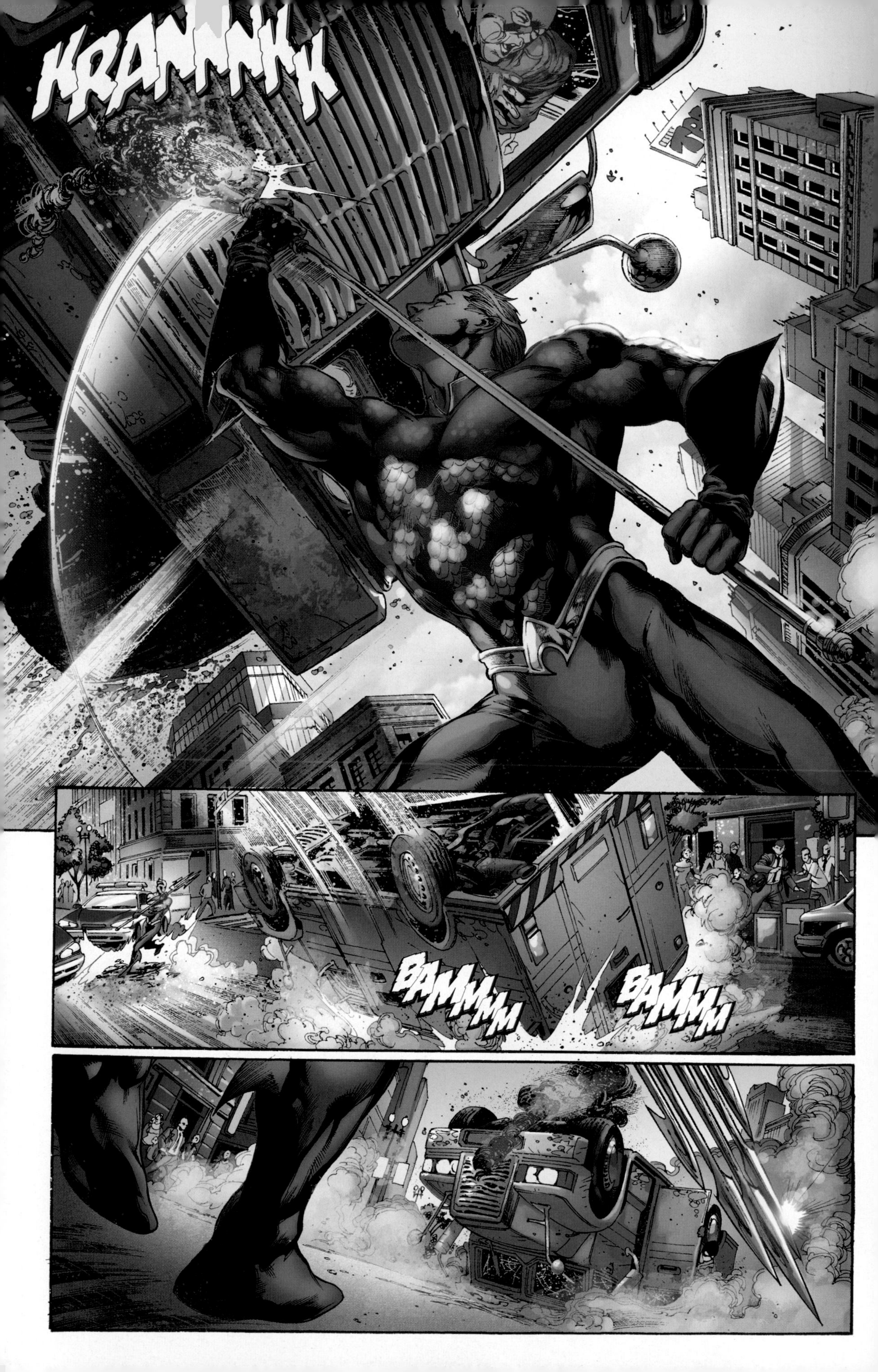
KRANNNKK
BAMMMM
BAMMMM

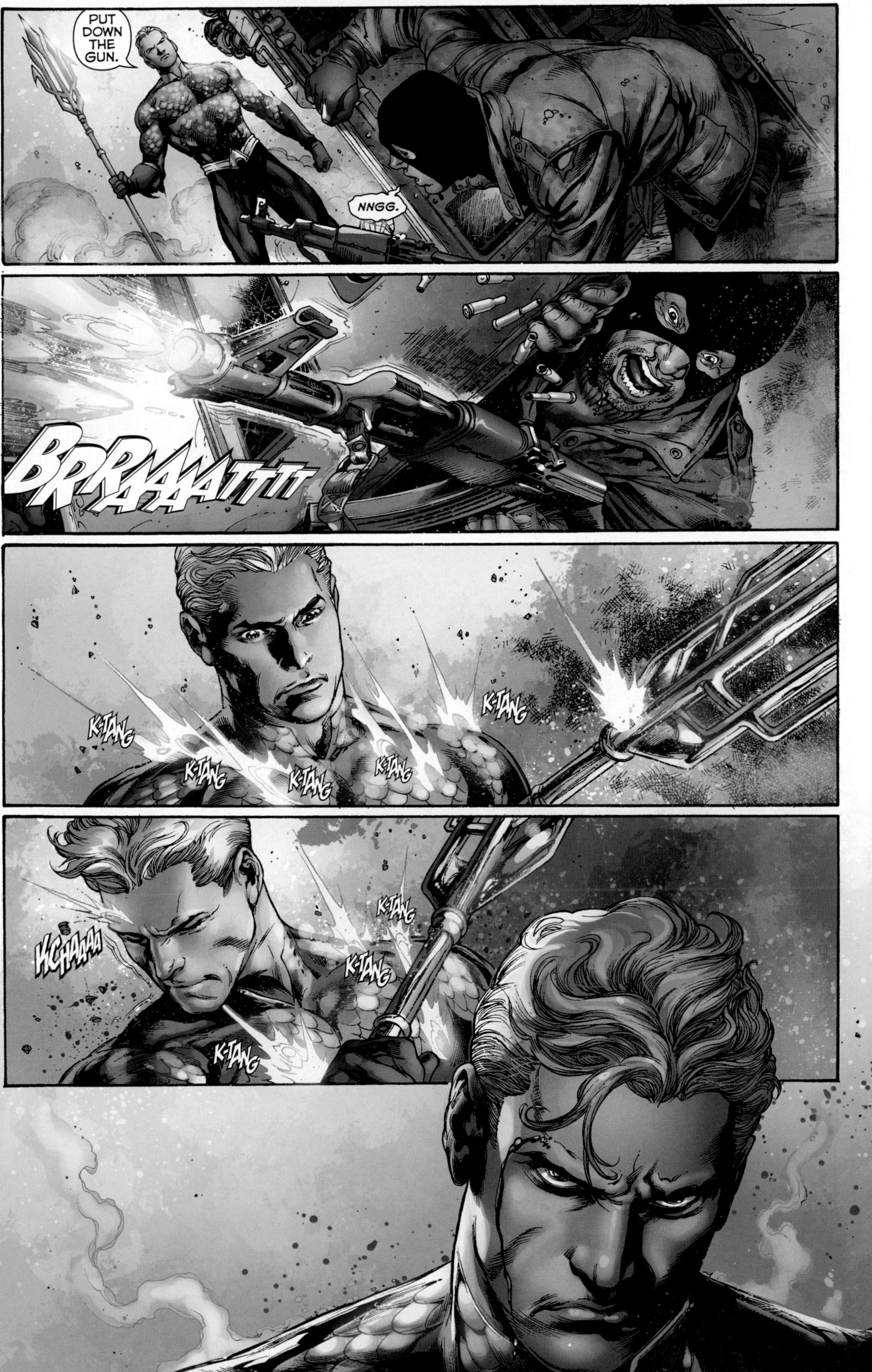
PUT DOWN THE GUN.
NNGG.
BRRAAAATTTT
K-TANG
K-TANG
K-TANG
K-TANG
K-TANG
KCHAAAA
K-TANG
K-TANG
K-TANG

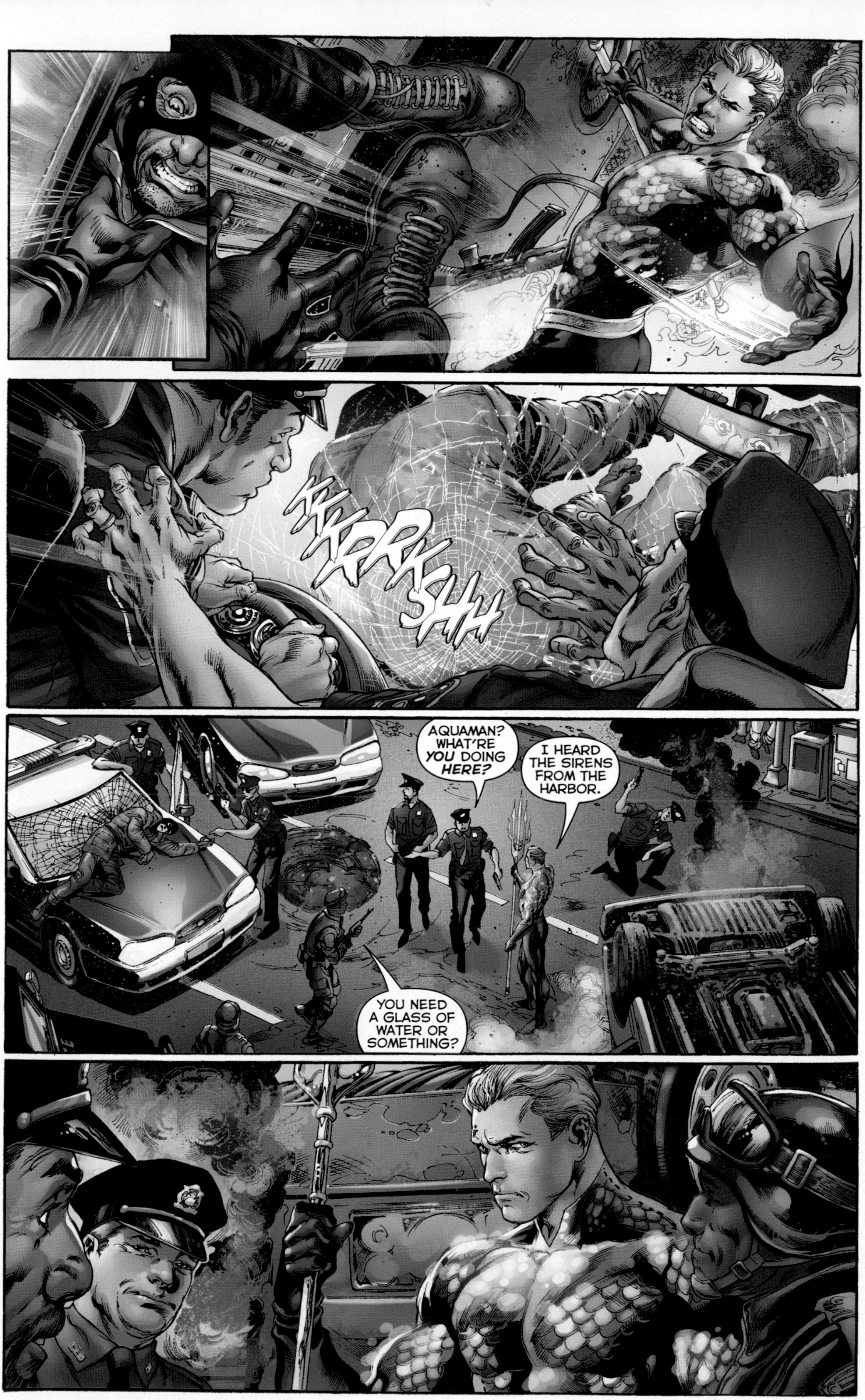
KKKRRKSHH
AQUAMAN? WHAT'RE *YOU* DOING *HERE?*
I HEARD THE SIRENS FROM THE HARBOR.
YOU NEED A GLASS OF WATER OR SOMETHING?

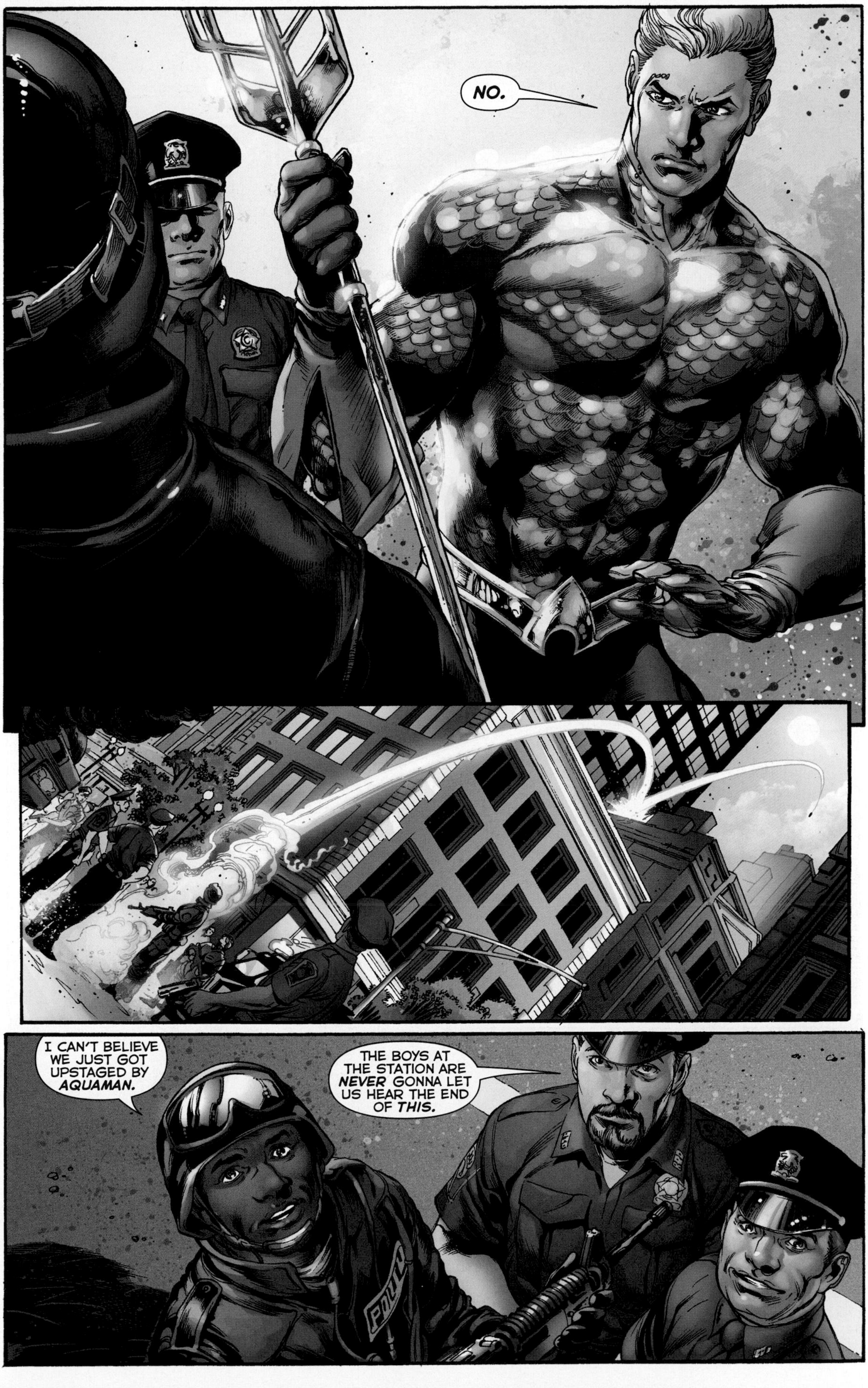
NO.
I CAN'T BELIEVE WE JUST GOT UPSTAGED BY *AQUAMAN.*
THE BOYS AT THE STATION ARE *NEVER* GONNA LET US HEAR THE END OF *THIS.*

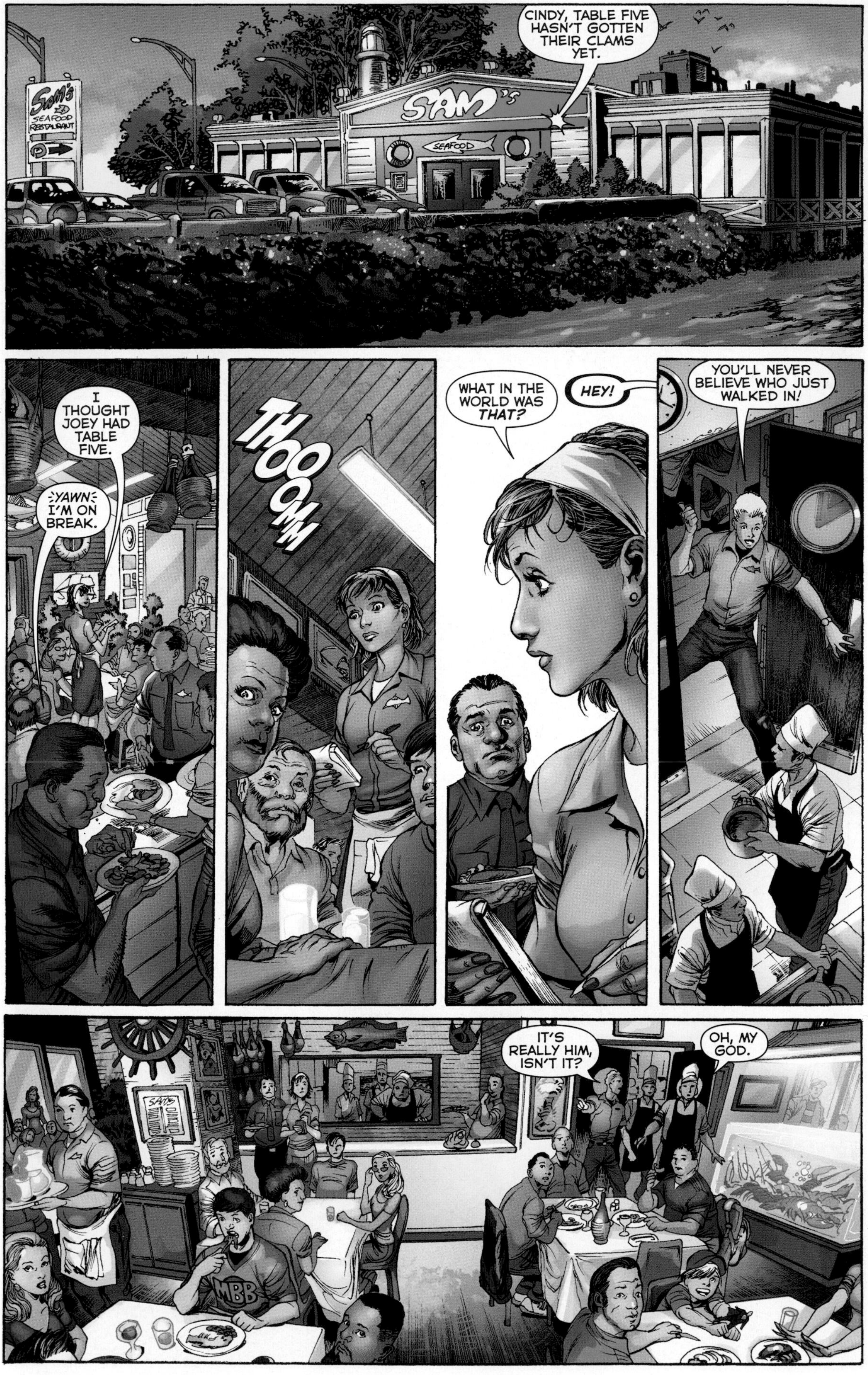
CINDY, TABLE FIVE HASN'T GOTTEN THEIR CLAMS YET.
SAM'S SEAFOOD RESTAURANT
SAM'S
SEAFOOD
I THOUGHT JOEY HAD TABLE FIVE.
YAWN
I'M ON BREAK.
THOOOMM
WHAT IN THE WORLD WAS THAT?
HEY!
YOU'LL NEVER BELIEVE WHO JUST WALKED IN!
IT'S REALLY HIM, ISN'T IT?
OH, MY GOD.
MBB

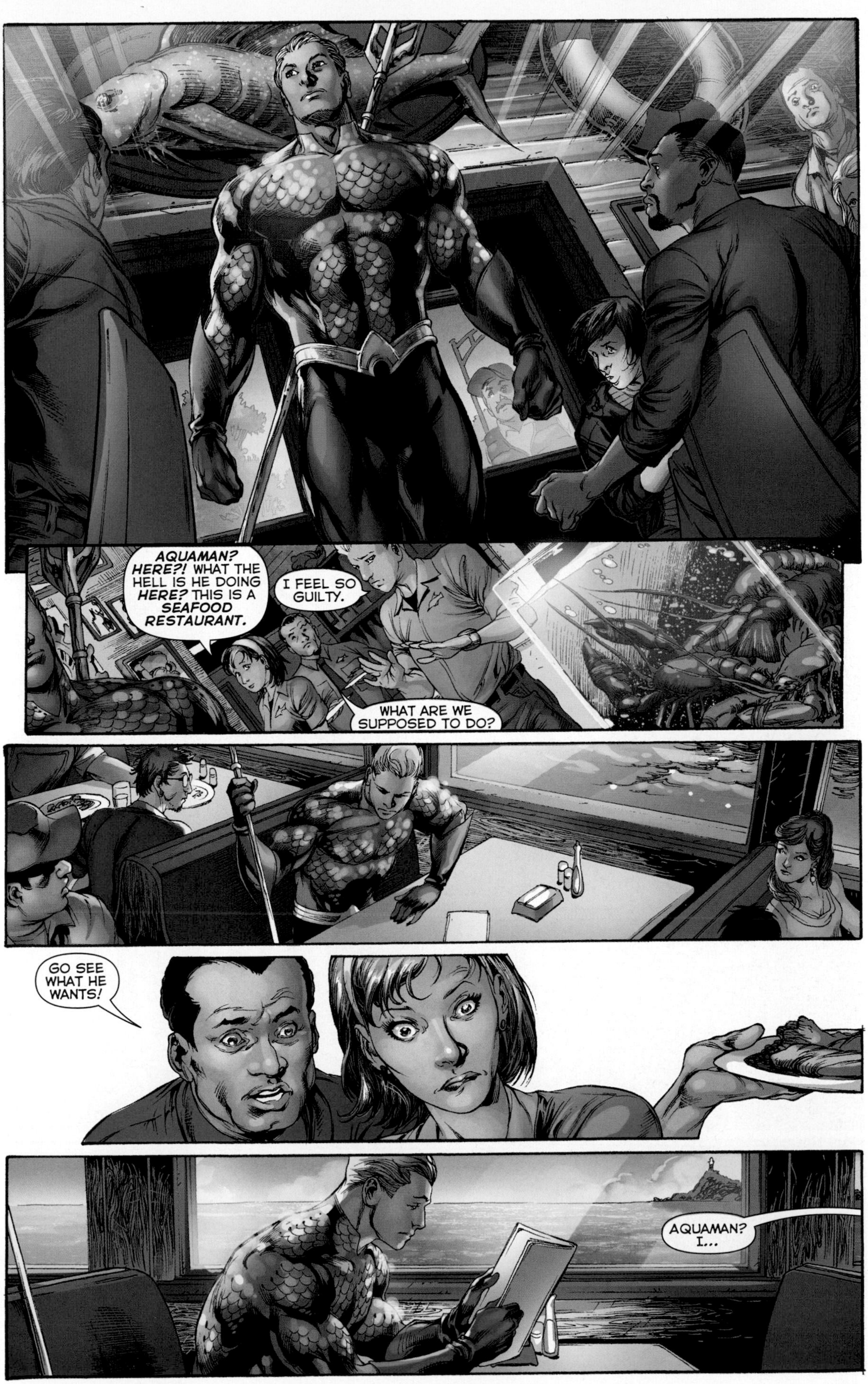
AQUAMAN? HERE?! WHAT THE HELL IS HE DOING HERE? THIS IS A SEAFOOD RESTAURANT.
I FEEL SO GUILTY.
WHAT ARE WE SUPPOSED TO DO?
GO SEE WHAT HE WANTS!
AQUAMAN? I...

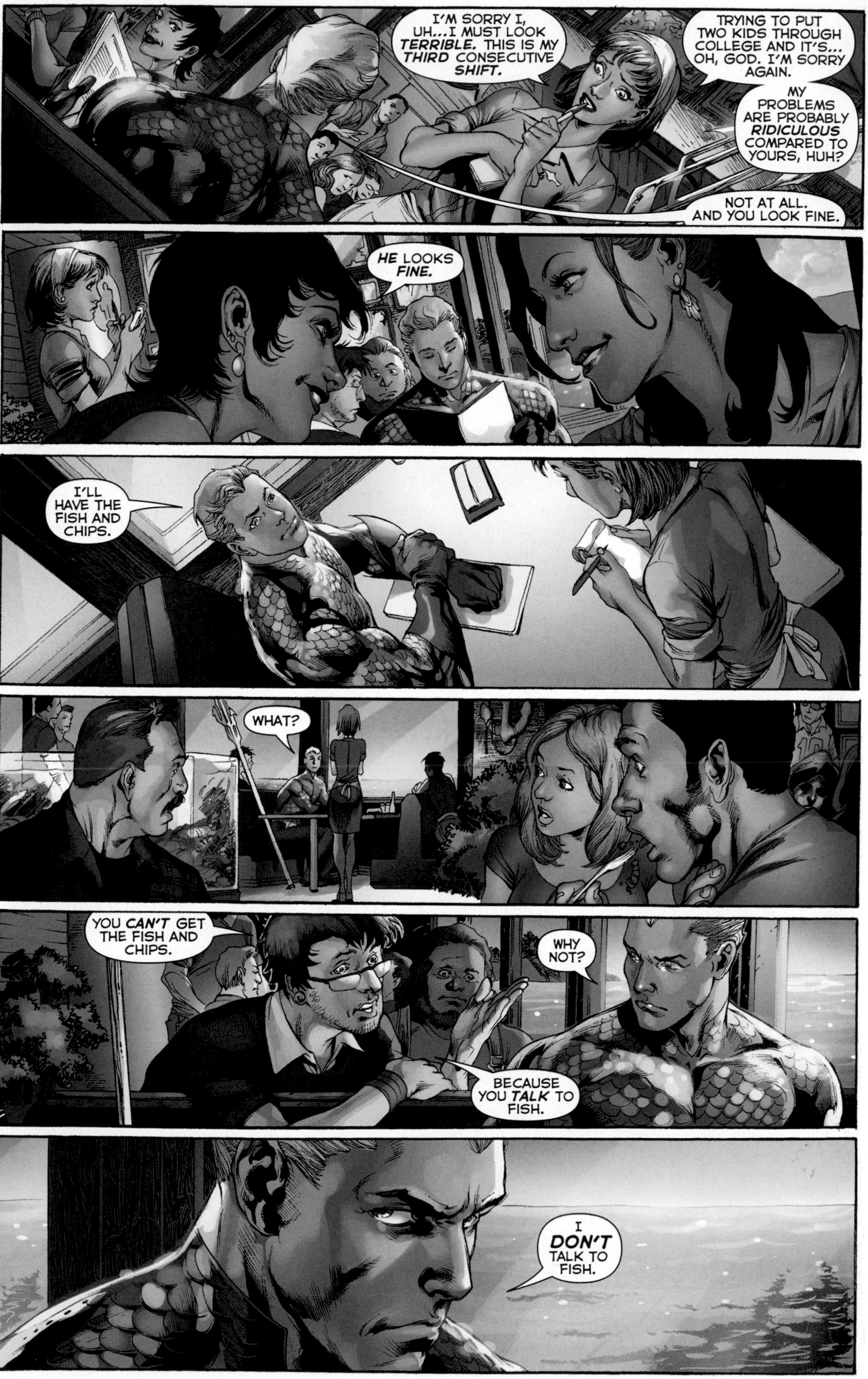

I'M SORRY I, UH...I MUST LOOK *TERRIBLE.* THIS IS MY *THIRD* CONSECUTIVE *SHIFT.*
TRYING TO PUT TWO KIDS THROUGH COLLEGE AND IT'S... OH, GOD. I'M SORRY AGAIN.
MY PROBLEMS ARE PROBABLY *RIDICULOUS* COMPARED TO YOURS, HUH?
NOT AT ALL. AND YOU LOOK FINE.
HE LOOKS *FINE.*
I'LL HAVE THE FISH AND CHIPS.
WHAT?
YOU *CAN'T* GET THE FISH AND CHIPS.
WHY NOT?
BECAUSE YOU *TALK* TO FISH.
I *DON'T* TALK TO FISH.

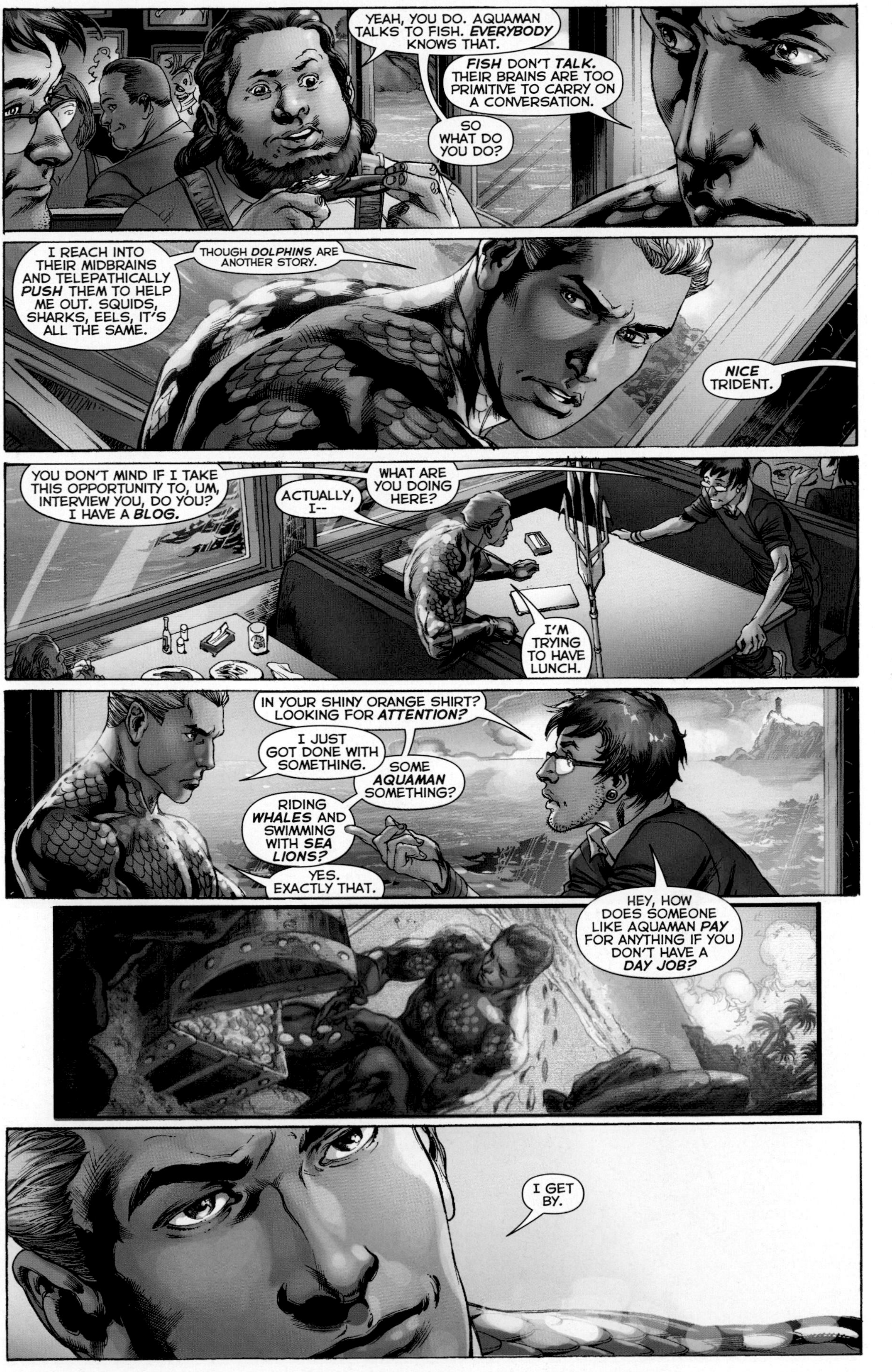
YEAH, YOU DO. AQUAMAN TALKS TO FISH. EVERYBODY KNOWS THAT.
FISH DON'T TALK. THEIR BRAINS ARE TOO PRIMITIVE TO CARRY ON A CONVERSATION.
SO WHAT DO YOU DO?
I REACH INTO THEIR MIDBRAINS AND TELEPATHICALLY PUSH THEM TO HELP ME OUT. SQUIDS, SHARKS, EELS, IT'S ALL THE SAME.
THOUGH DOLPHINS ARE ANOTHER STORY.
NICE TRIDENT.
YOU DON'T MIND IF I TAKE THIS OPPORTUNITY TO, UM, INTERVIEW YOU, DO YOU? I HAVE A BLOG.
WHAT ARE YOU DOING HERE?
ACTUALLY, I--
I'M TRYING TO HAVE LUNCH.
IN YOUR SHINY ORANGE SHIRT? LOOKING FOR ATTENTION?
I JUST GOT DONE WITH SOMETHING.
SOME AQUAMAN SOMETHING?
RIDING WHALES AND SWIMMING WITH SEA LIONS?
YES. EXACTLY THAT.
HEY, HOW DOES SOMEONE LIKE AQUAMAN PAY FOR ANYTHING IF YOU DON'T HAVE A DAY JOB?
I GET BY.

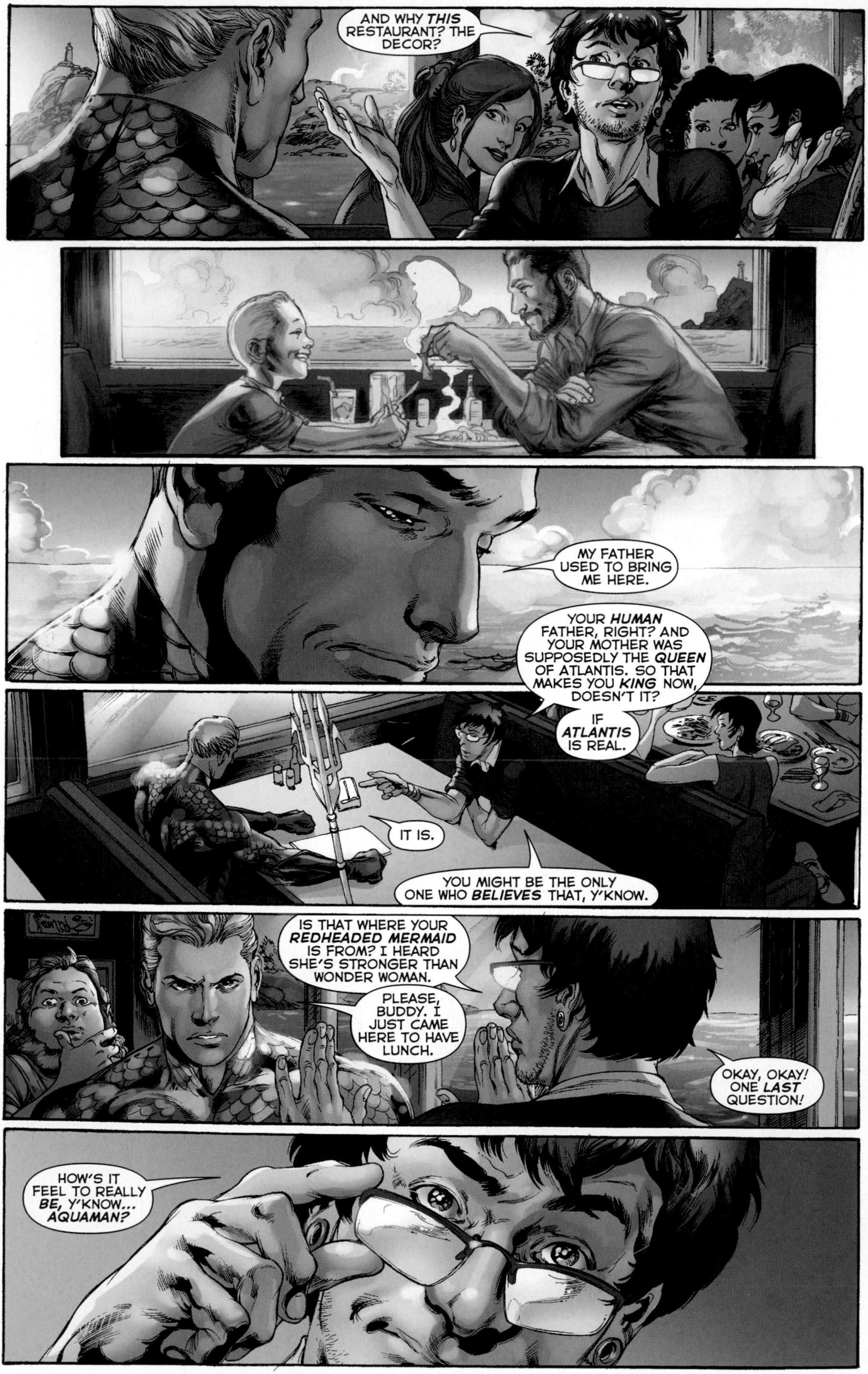
AND WHY THIS RESTAURANT? THE DECOR?
MY FATHER USED TO BRING ME HERE.
YOUR HUMAN FATHER, RIGHT? AND YOUR MOTHER WAS SUPPOSEDLY THE QUEEN OF ATLANTIS. SO THAT MAKES YOU KING NOW, DOESN'T IT?
IF ATLANTIS IS REAL.
IT IS.
YOU MIGHT BE THE ONLY ONE WHO BELIEVES THAT, Y'KNOW.
IS THAT WHERE YOUR REDHEADED MERMAID IS FROM? I HEARD SHE'S STRONGER THAN WONDER WOMAN.
PLEASE, BUDDY. I JUST CAME HERE TO HAVE LUNCH.
OKAY, OKAY! ONE LAST QUESTION!
HOW'S IT FEEL TO REALLY BE, Y'KNOW... AQUAMAN?

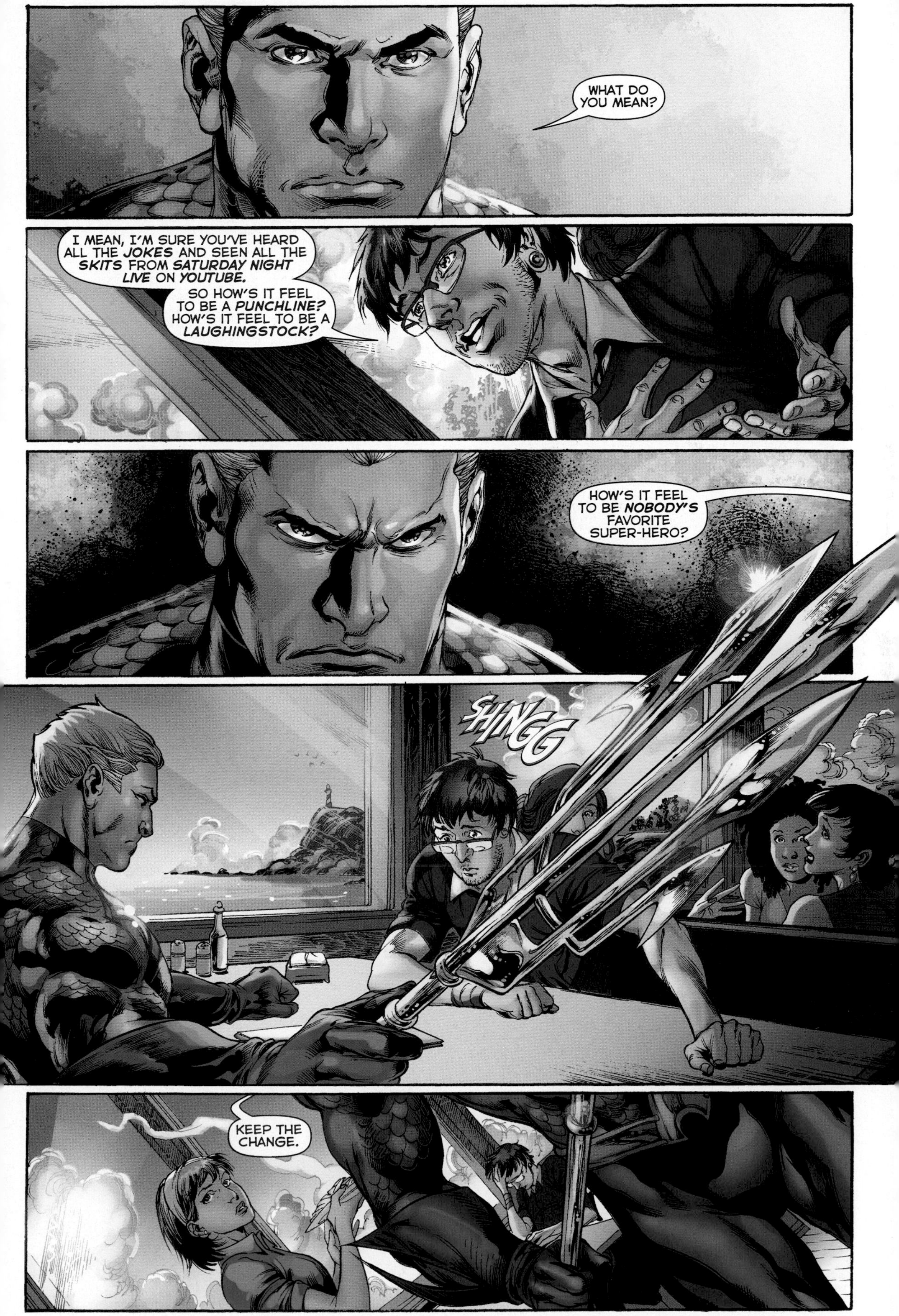
WHAT DO YOU MEAN?
I MEAN, I'M SURE YOU'VE HEARD ALL THE JOKES AND SEEN ALL THE SKITS FROM SATURDAY NIGHT LIVE ON YOUTUBE.
SO HOW'S IT FEEL TO BE A PUNCHLINE? HOW'S IT FEEL TO BE A LAUGHINGSTOCK?
HOW'S IT FEEL TO BE NOBODY'S FAVORITE SUPER-HERO?
SHINGG
KEEP THE CHANGE.

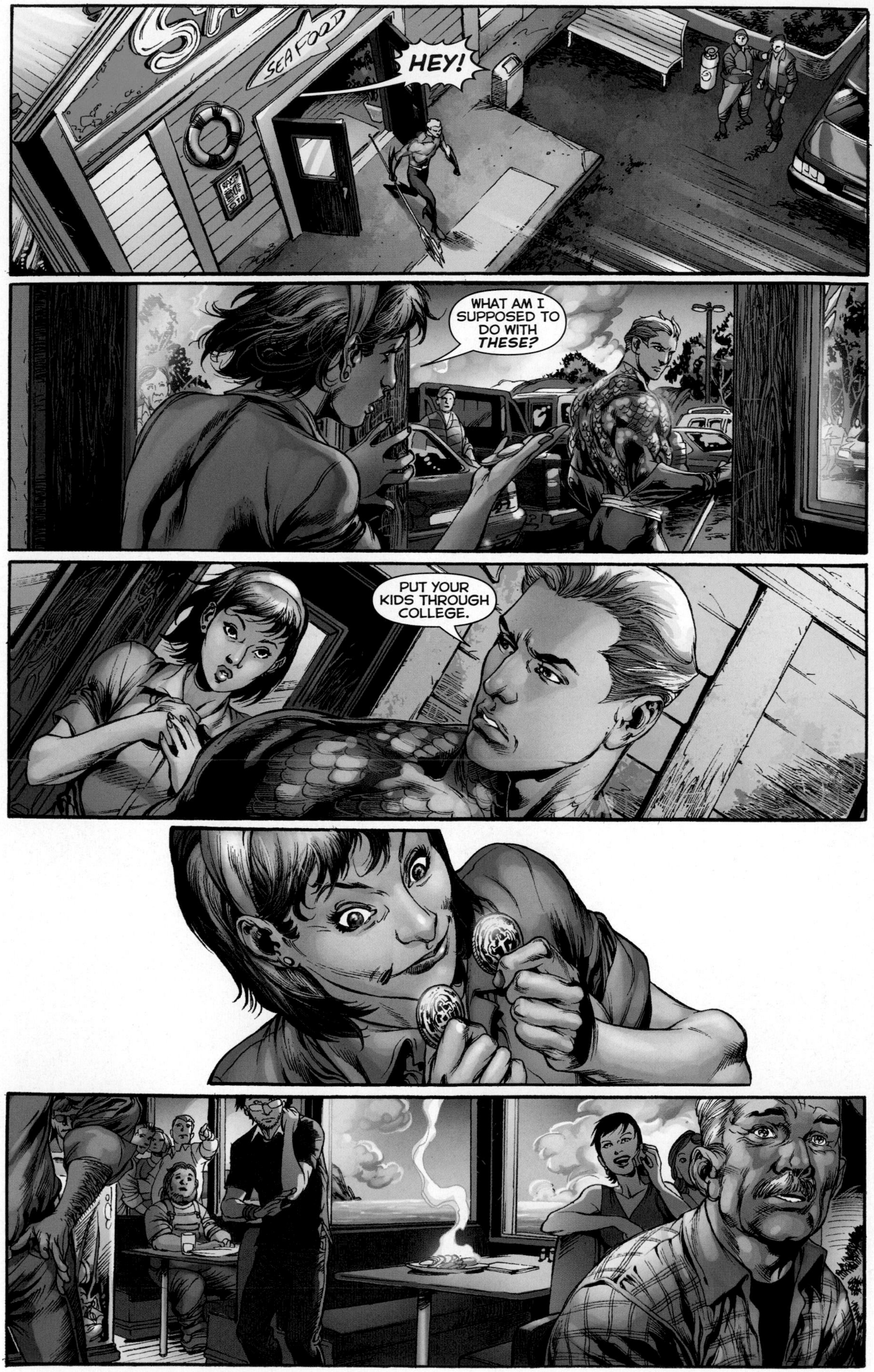
SEA FOOD
HEY!
WHAT AM I SUPPOSED TO DO WITH THESE?
PUT YOUR KIDS THROUGH COLLEGE.

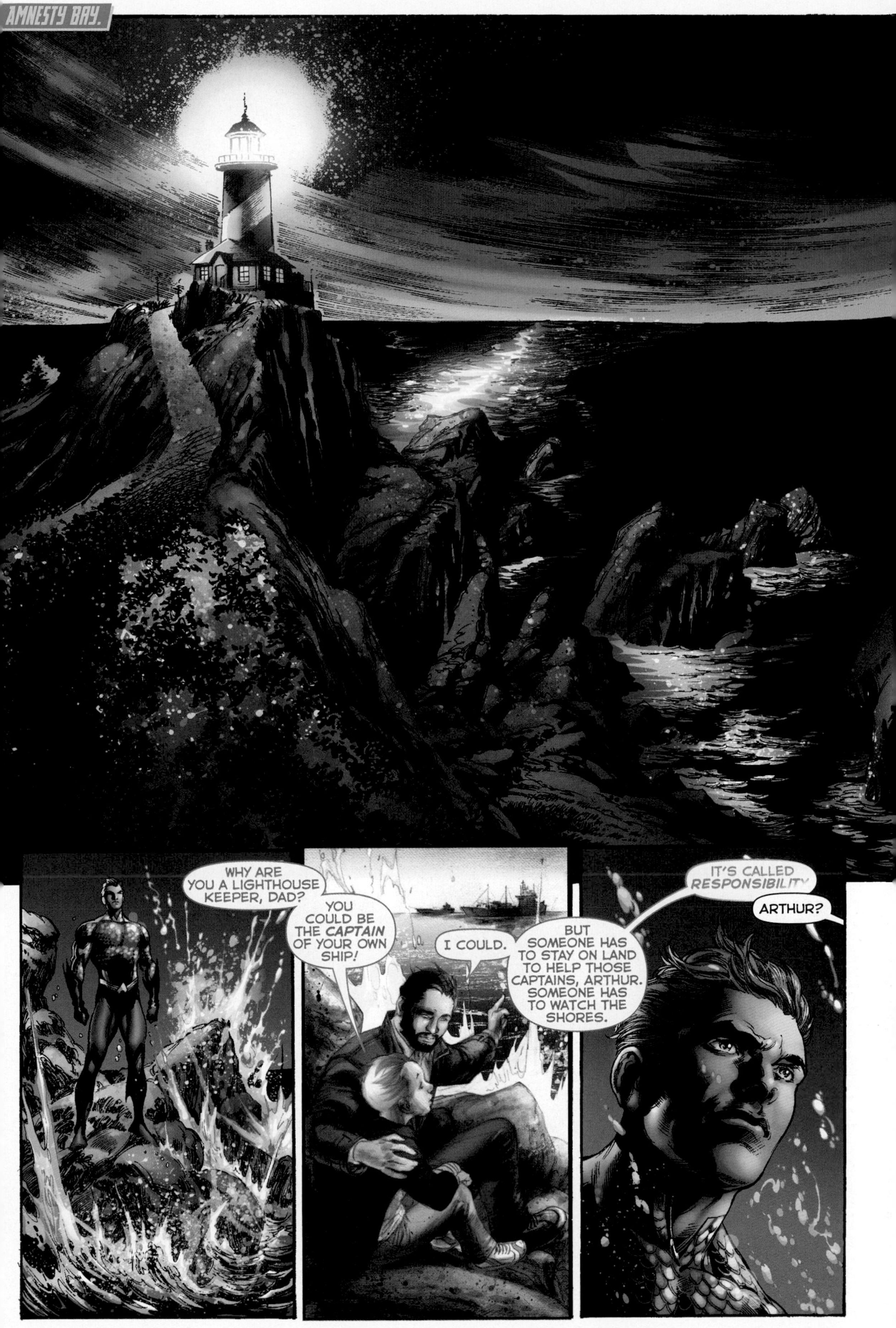
AMNESTY BAY.
WHY ARE YOU A LIGHTHOUSE KEEPER, DAD?
YOU COULD BE THE CAPTAIN OF YOUR OWN SHIP!
I COULD.
BUT SOMEONE HAS TO STAY ON LAND TO HELP THOSE CAPTAINS, ARTHUR. SOMEONE HAS TO WATCH THE SHORES.
IT'S CALLED RESPONSIBILITY
ARTHUR?

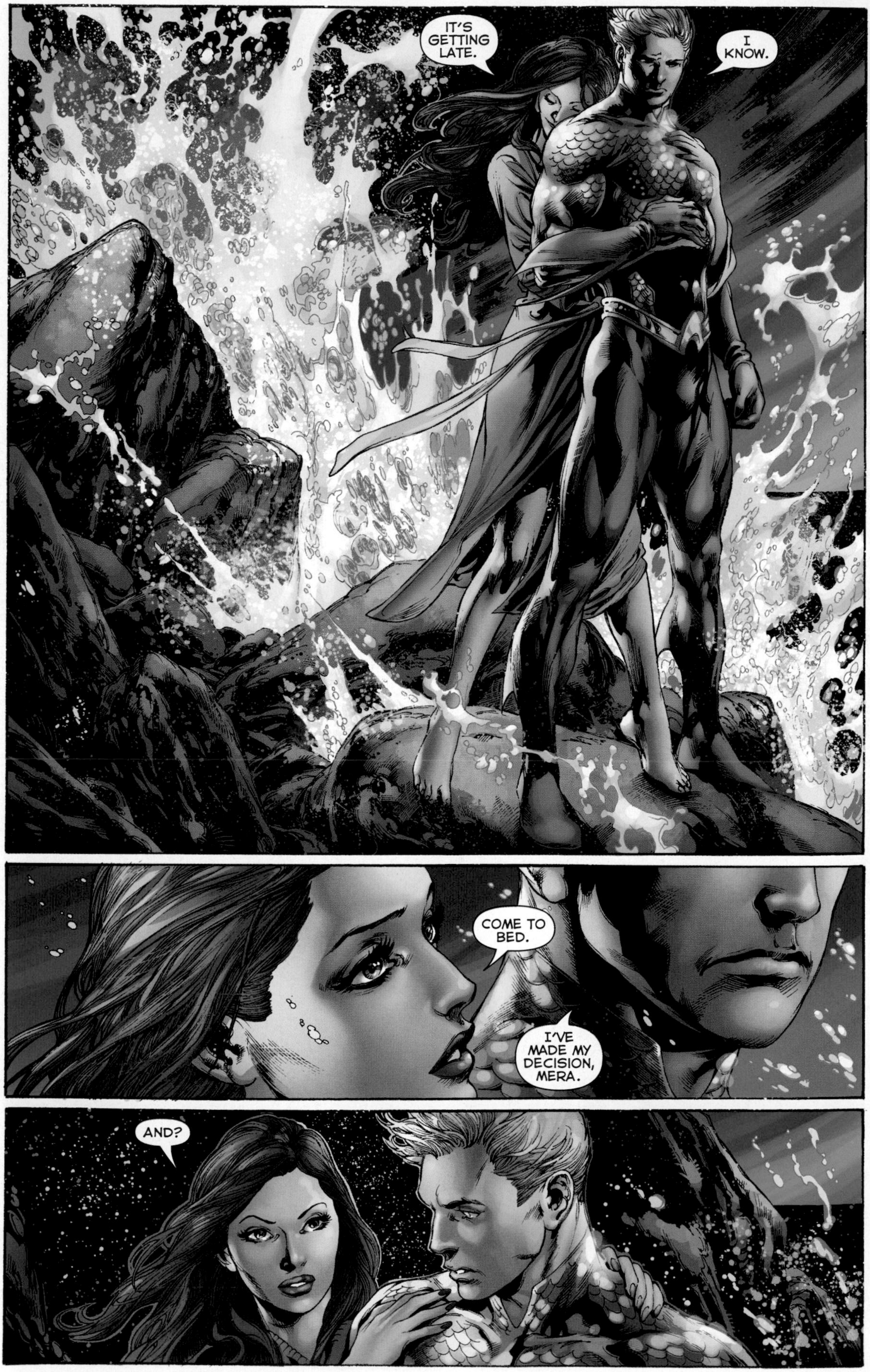
IT'S GETTING LATE.
I KNOW.
COME TO BED.
I'VE MADE MY DECISION, MERA.
AND?

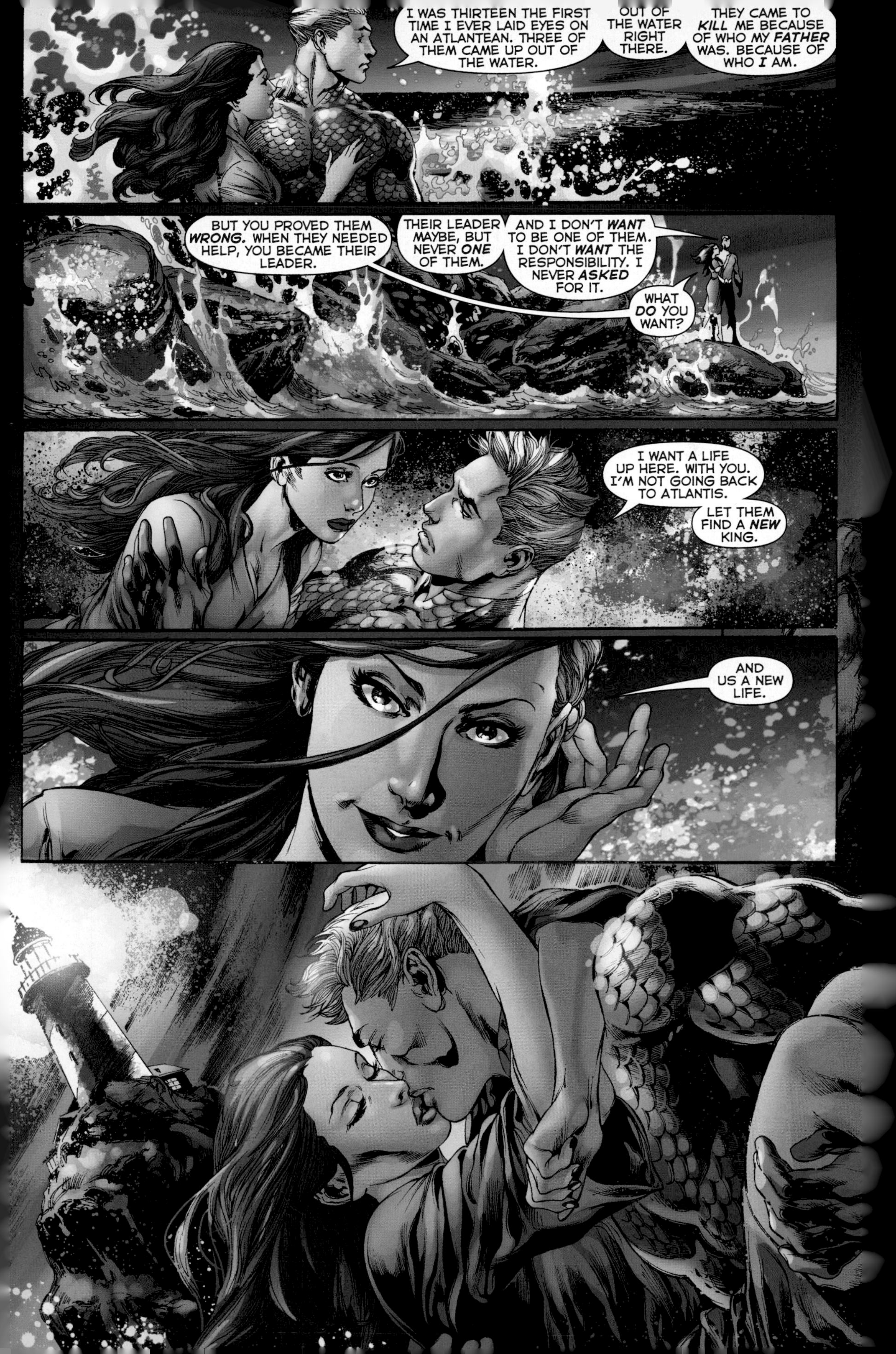
I WAS THIRTEEN THE FIRST TIME I EVER LAID EYES ON AN ATLANTEAN. THREE OF THEM CAME UP OUT OF THE WATER.
OUT OF THE WATER RIGHT THERE.
THEY CAME TO KILL ME BECAUSE OF WHO MY FATHER WAS. BECAUSE OF WHO I AM.
BUT YOU PROVED THEM WRONG. WHEN THEY NEEDED HELP, YOU BECAME THEIR LEADER.
THEIR LEADER MAYBE, BUT NEVER ONE OF THEM.
AND I DON'T WANT TO BE ONE OF THEM. I DON'T WANT THE RESPONSIBILITY. I NEVER ASKED FOR IT.
WHAT DO YOU WANT?
I WANT A LIFE UP HERE. WITH YOU. I'M NOT GOING BACK TO ATLANTIS.
LET THEM FIND A NEW KING.
AND US A NEW LIFE.

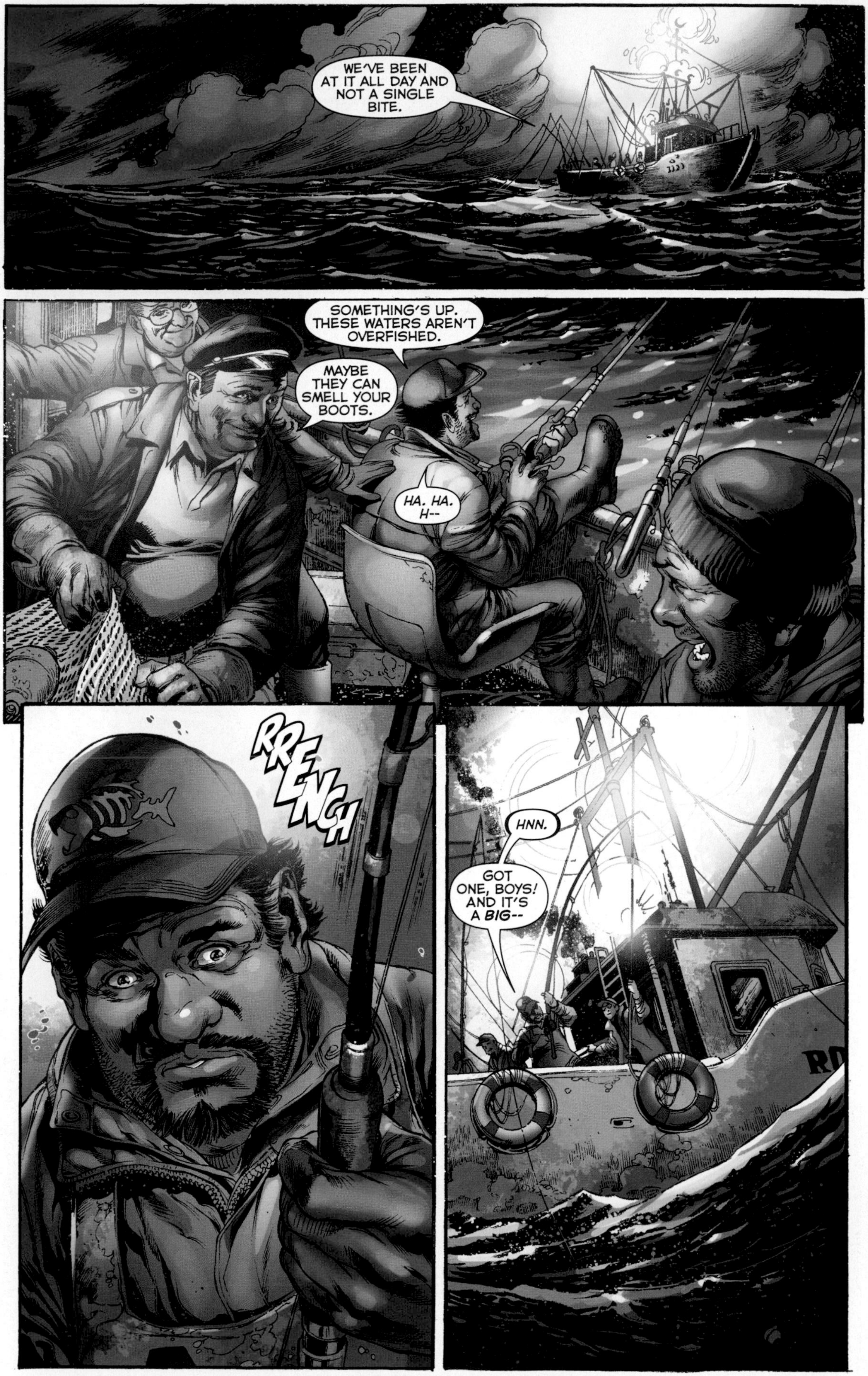
WE'VE BEEN AT IT ALL DAY AND NOT A SINGLE BITE.
SOMETHING'S UP. THESE WATERS AREN'T OVERFISHED.
MAYBE THEY CAN SMELL YOUR BOOTS.
HA. HA. H--
RRENCH
HNN.
GOT ONE, BOYS! AND IT'S A BIG--

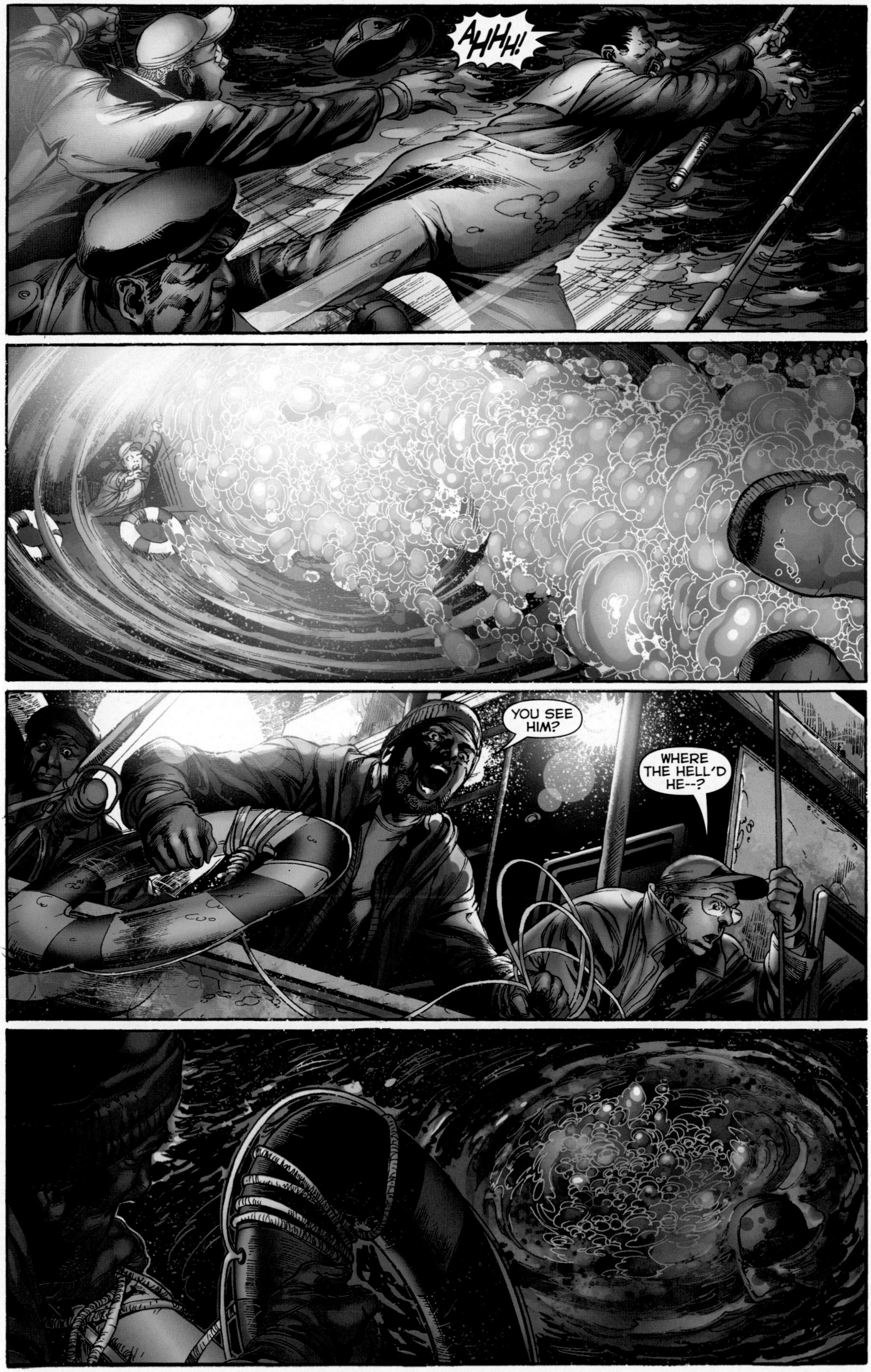
AHHH!
YOU SEE HIM?
WHERE THE HELL'D HE--?

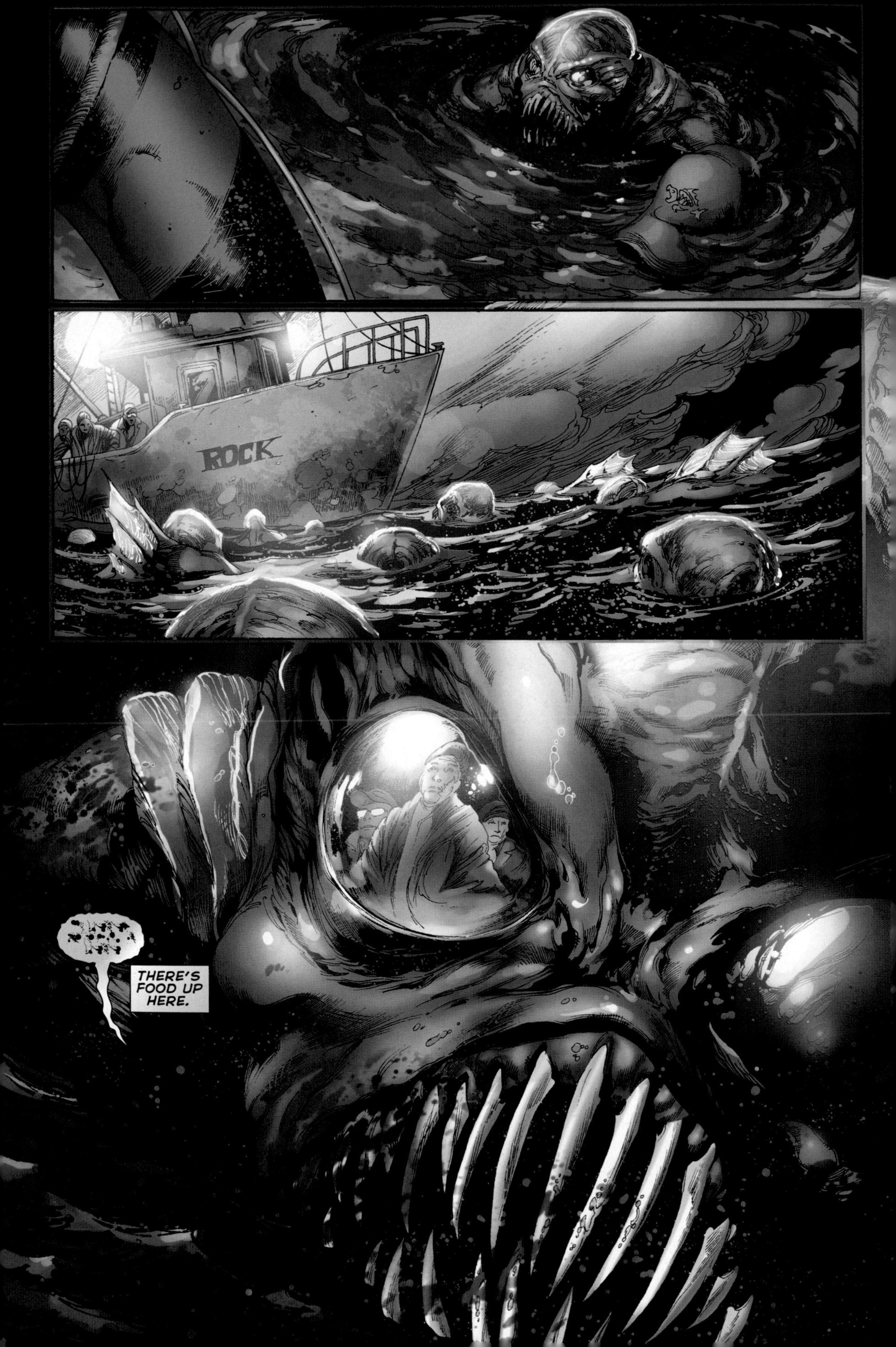
ROCK
THERE'S FOOD UP HERE.

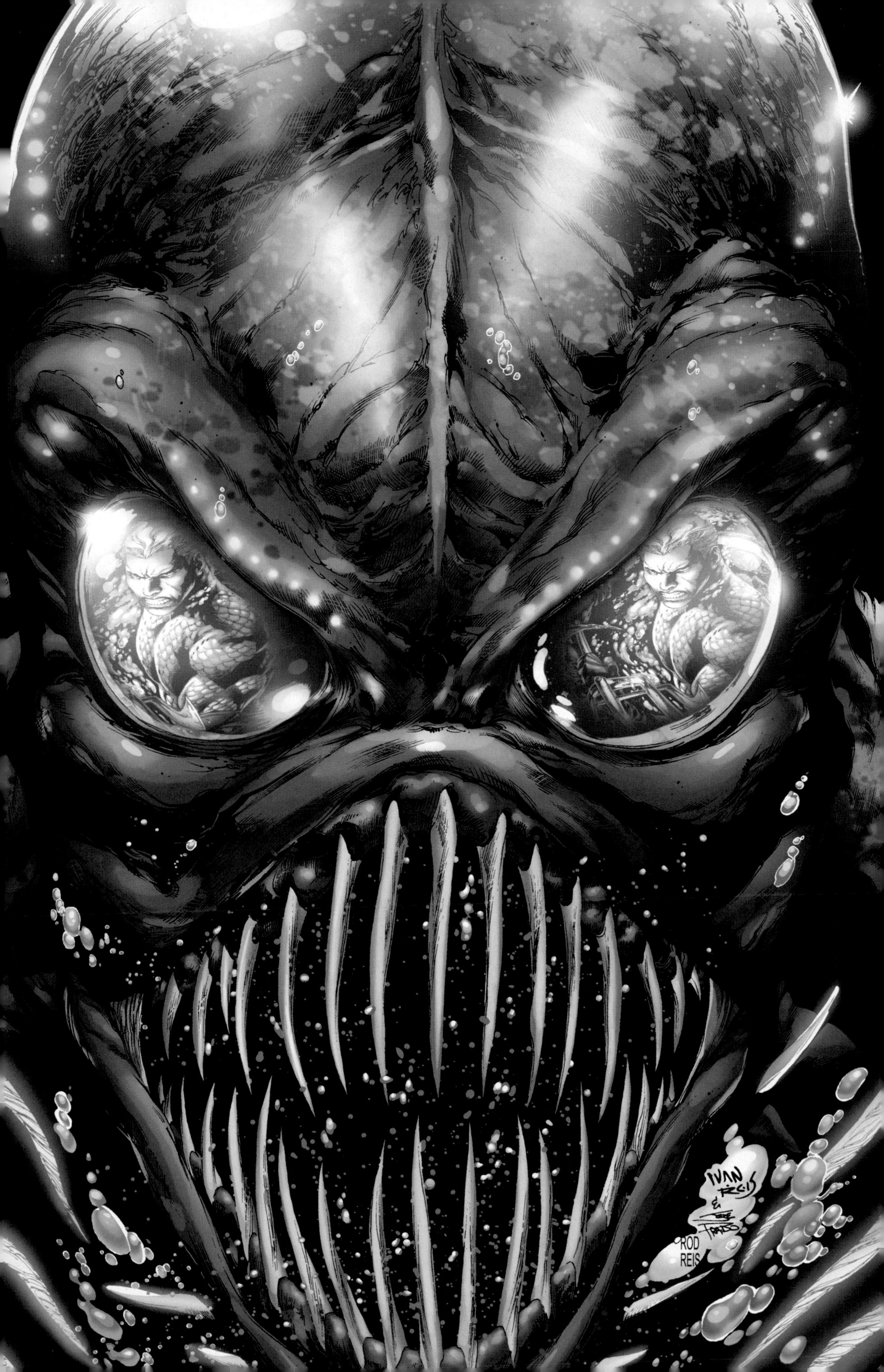
ROD
REIS

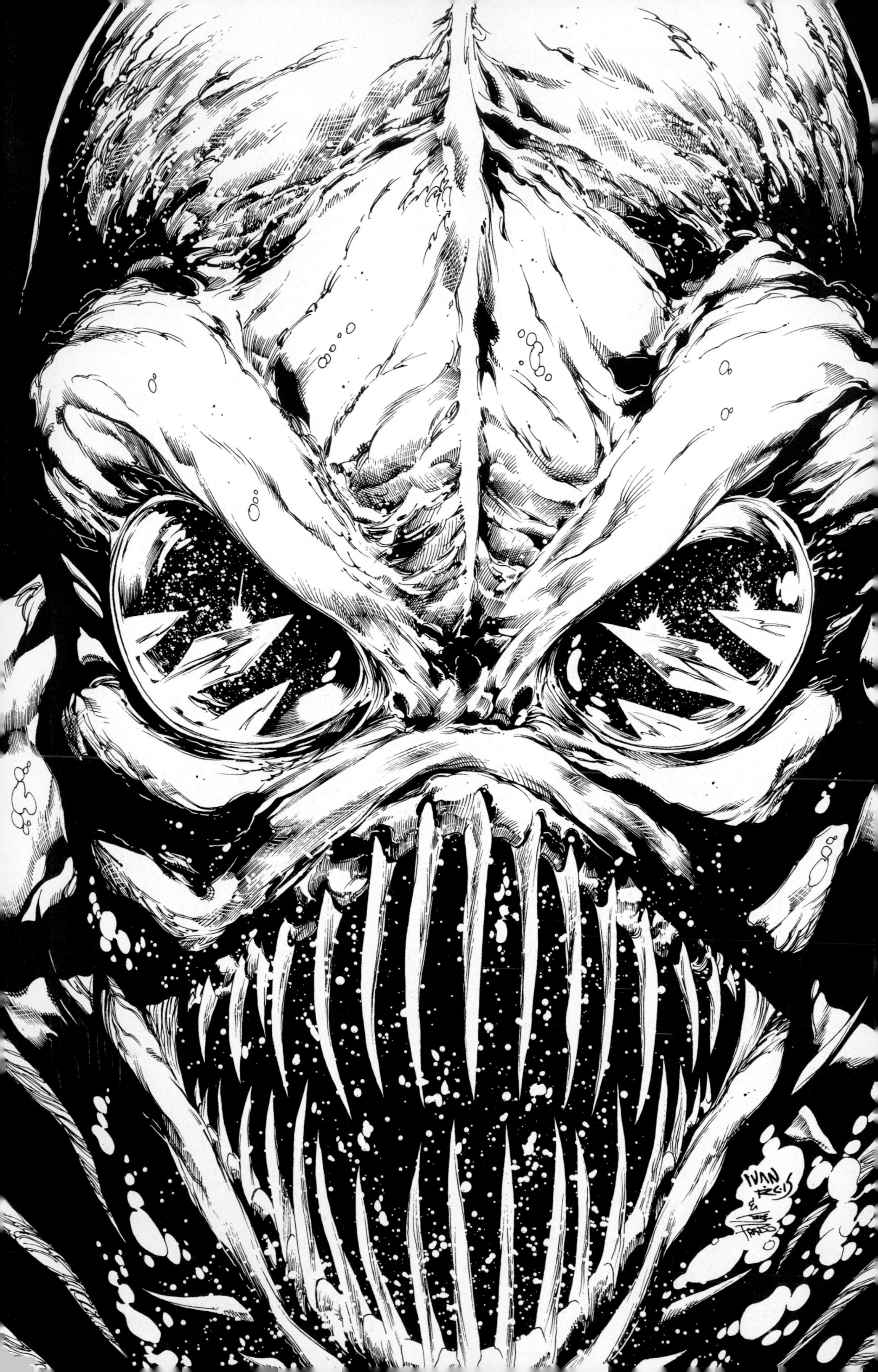

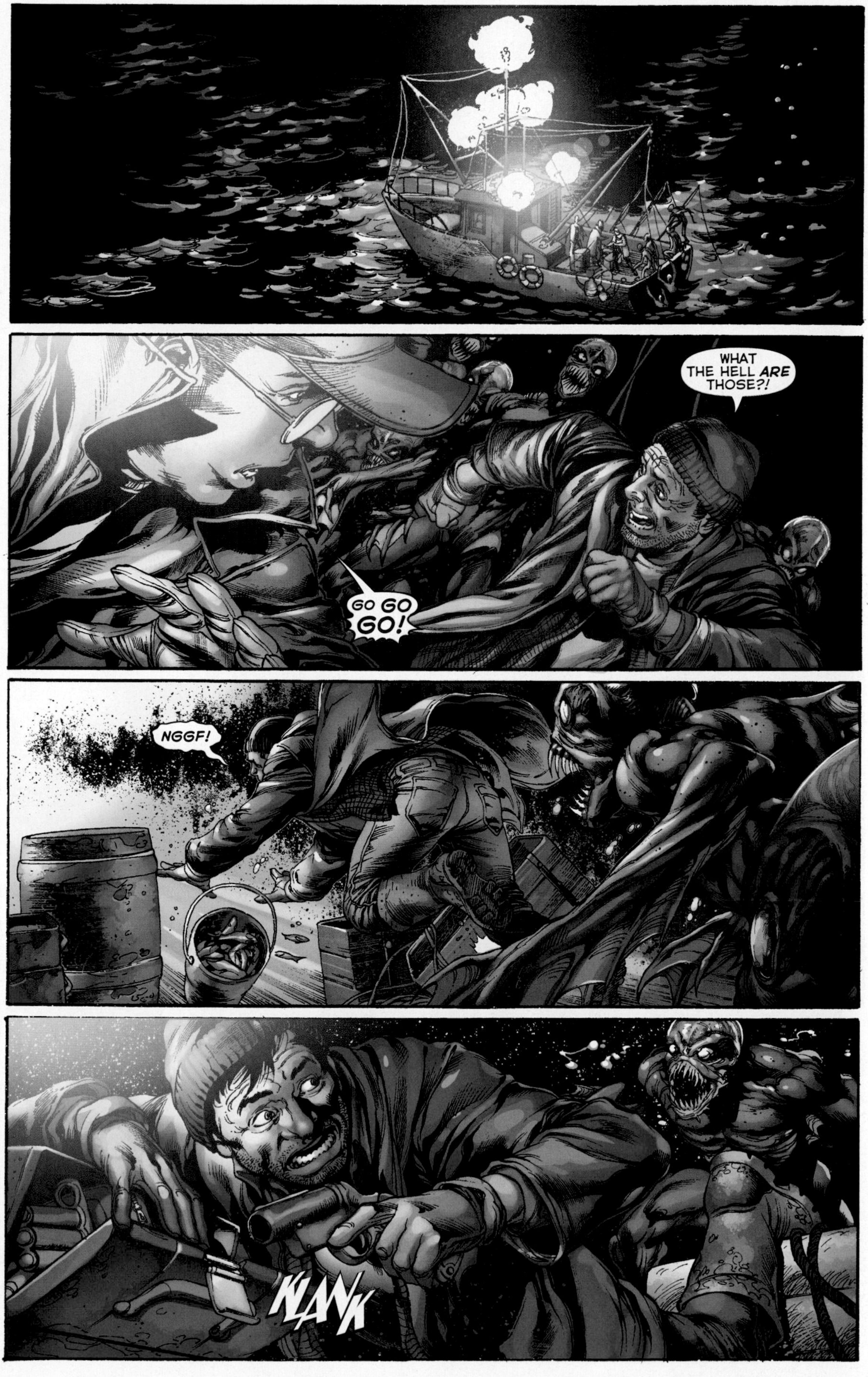
WHAT THE HELL ARE THOSE?!
GO GO GO!
NGGF!
KLANK

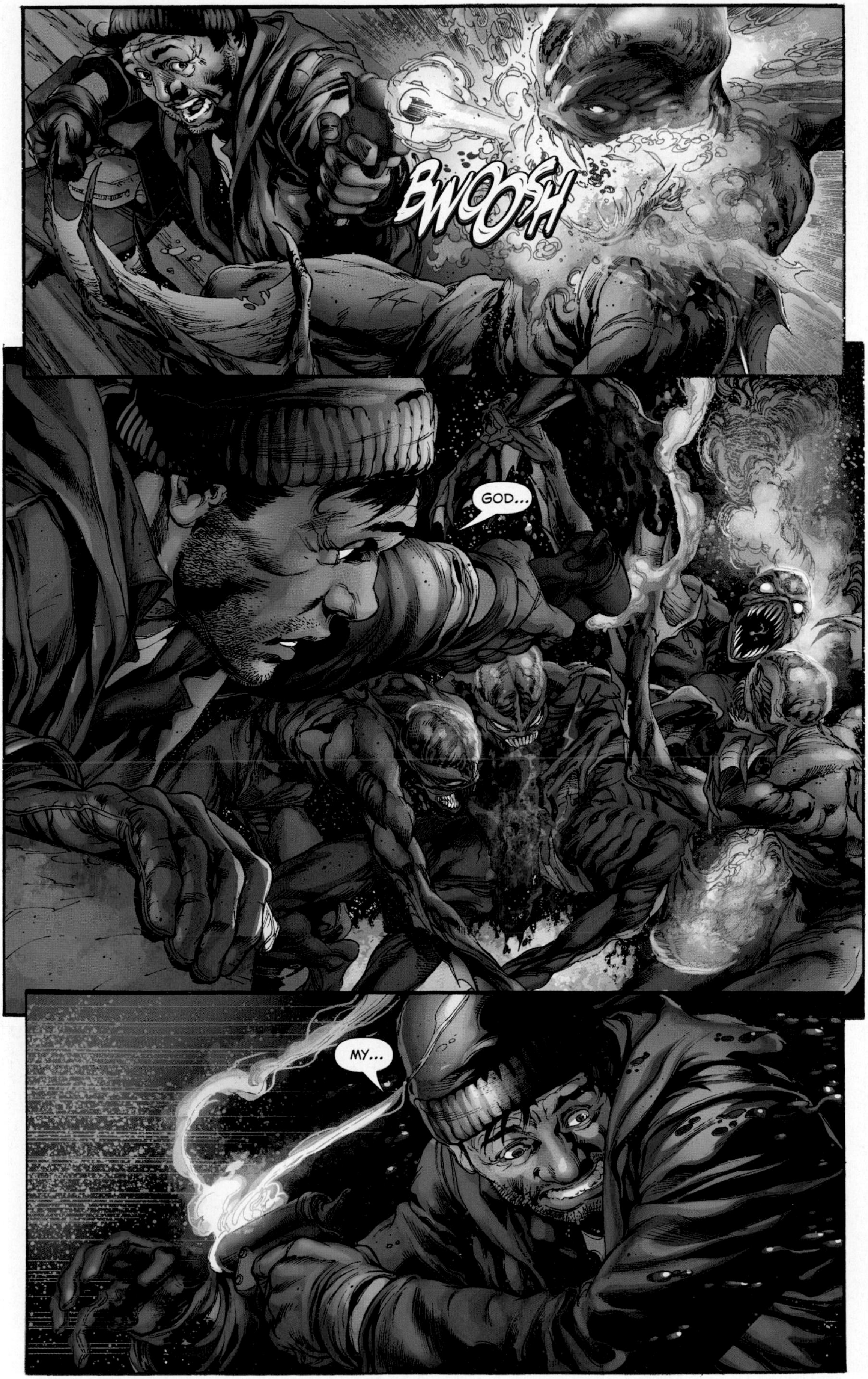
BWOOSH
GOD...
MY...

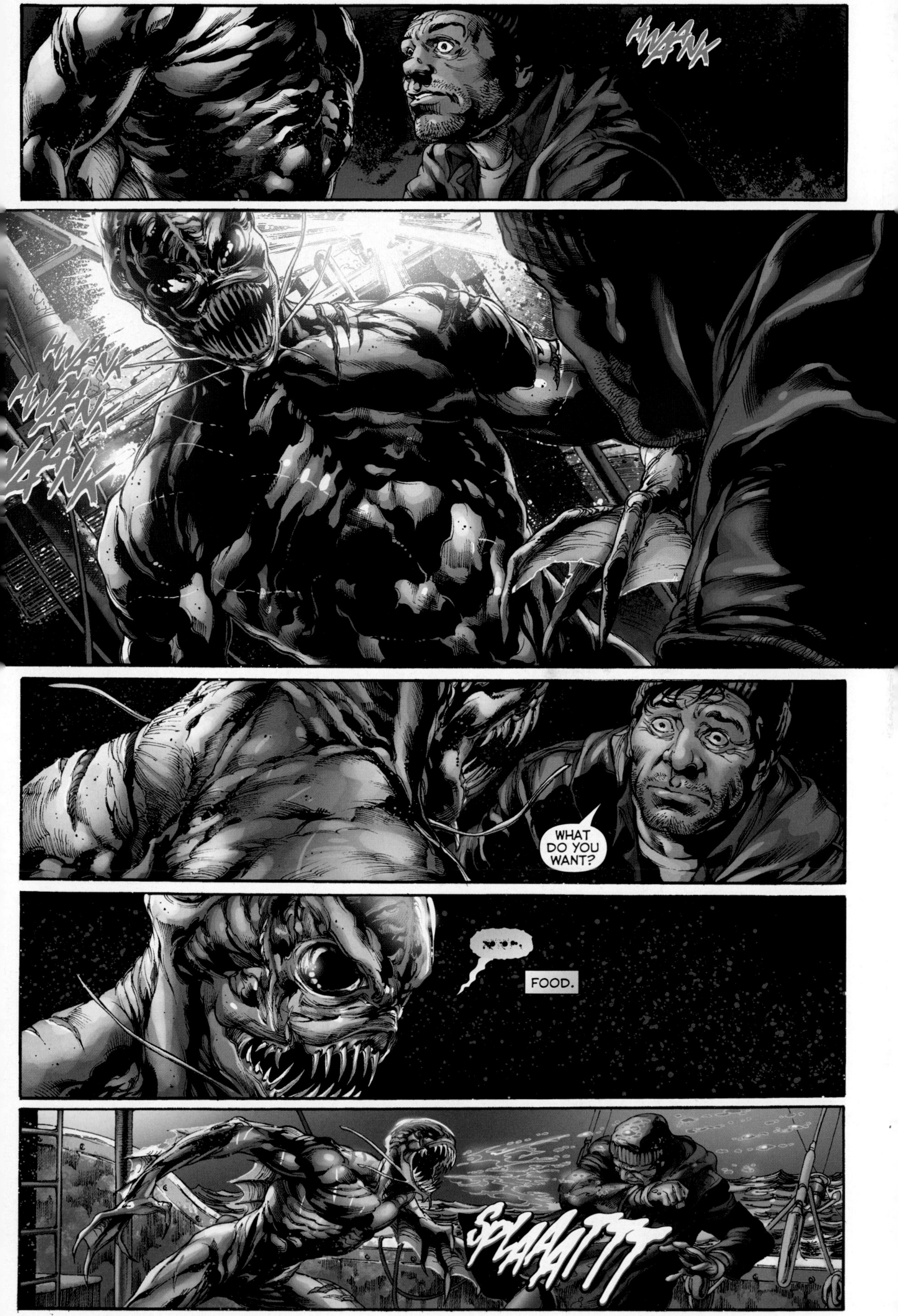
HWANK
HWANK
HWANK
WANK
WHAT DO YOU WANT?
FOOD.
SPLAAAITTT

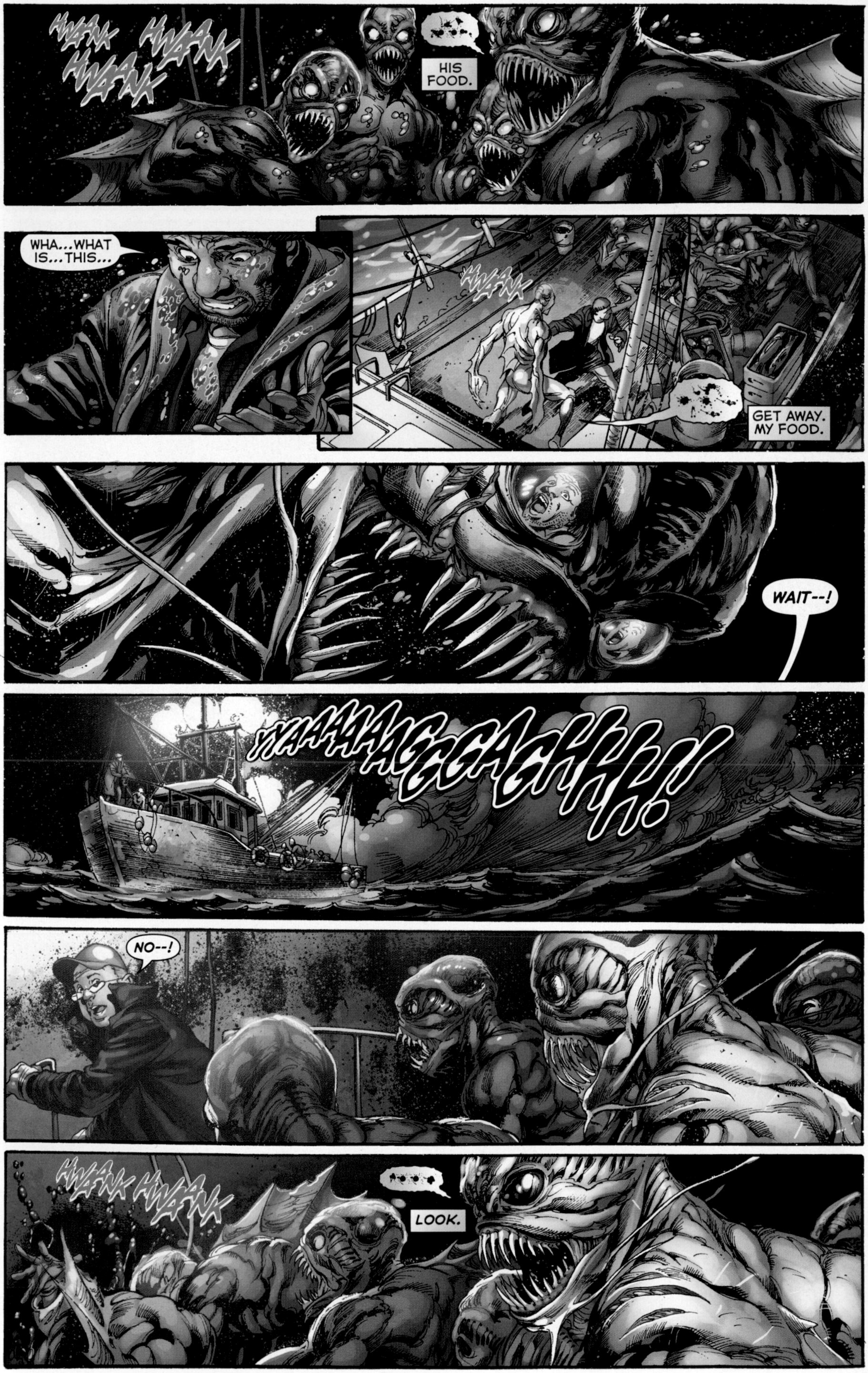
HWANK HWANK HWANK HWANK
HIS FOOD.
WHA...WHAT IS...THIS...
HWANK
GET AWAY. MY FOOD.
WAIT--!
YYAAAAAAGGGACHHH!!
NO--!
HWANK HWANK HWANK
LOOK.

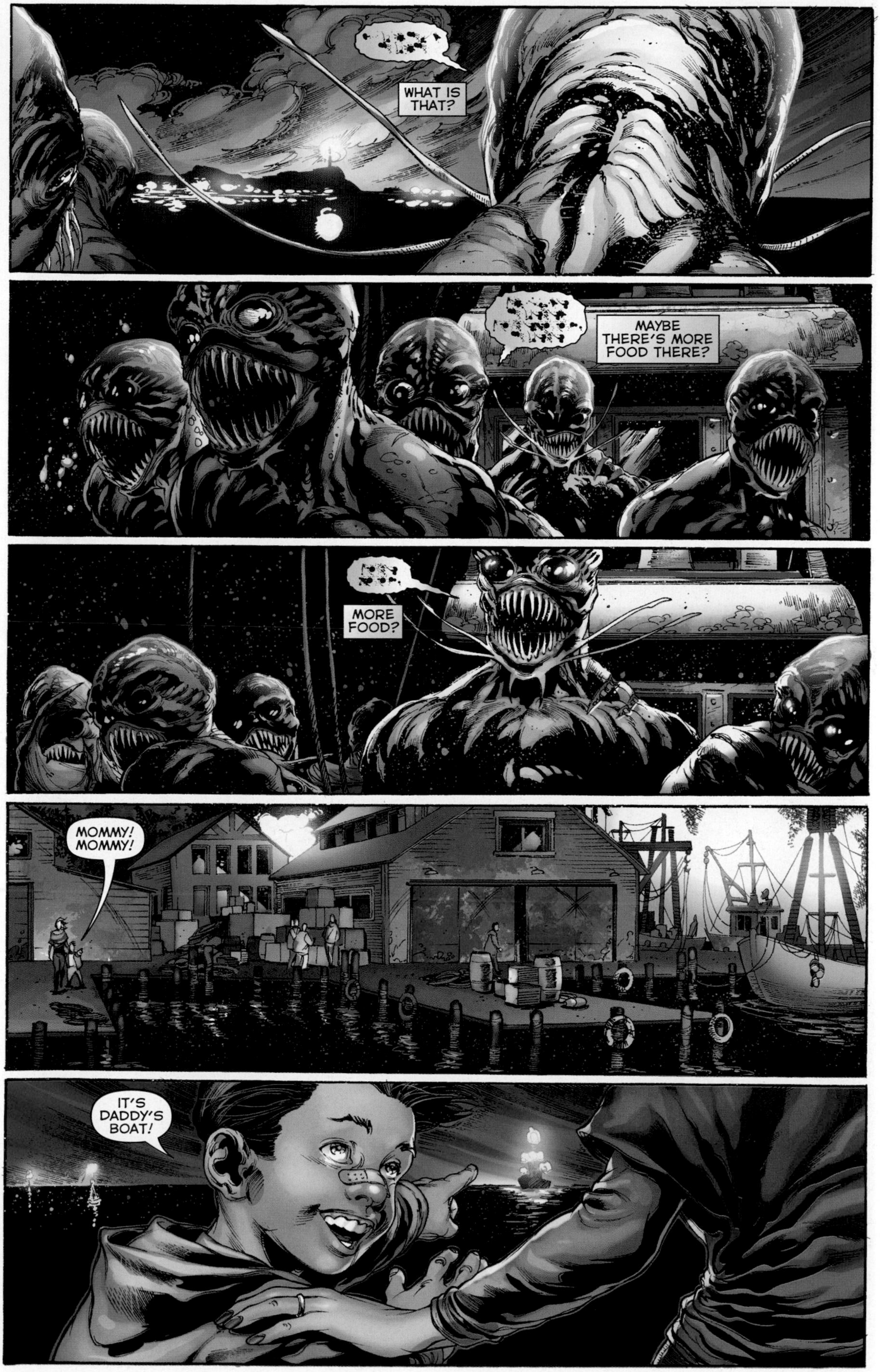
WHAT IS THAT?
MAYBE THERE'S MORE FOOD THERE?
MORE FOOD?
MOMMY! MOMMY!
IT'S DADDY'S BOAT!

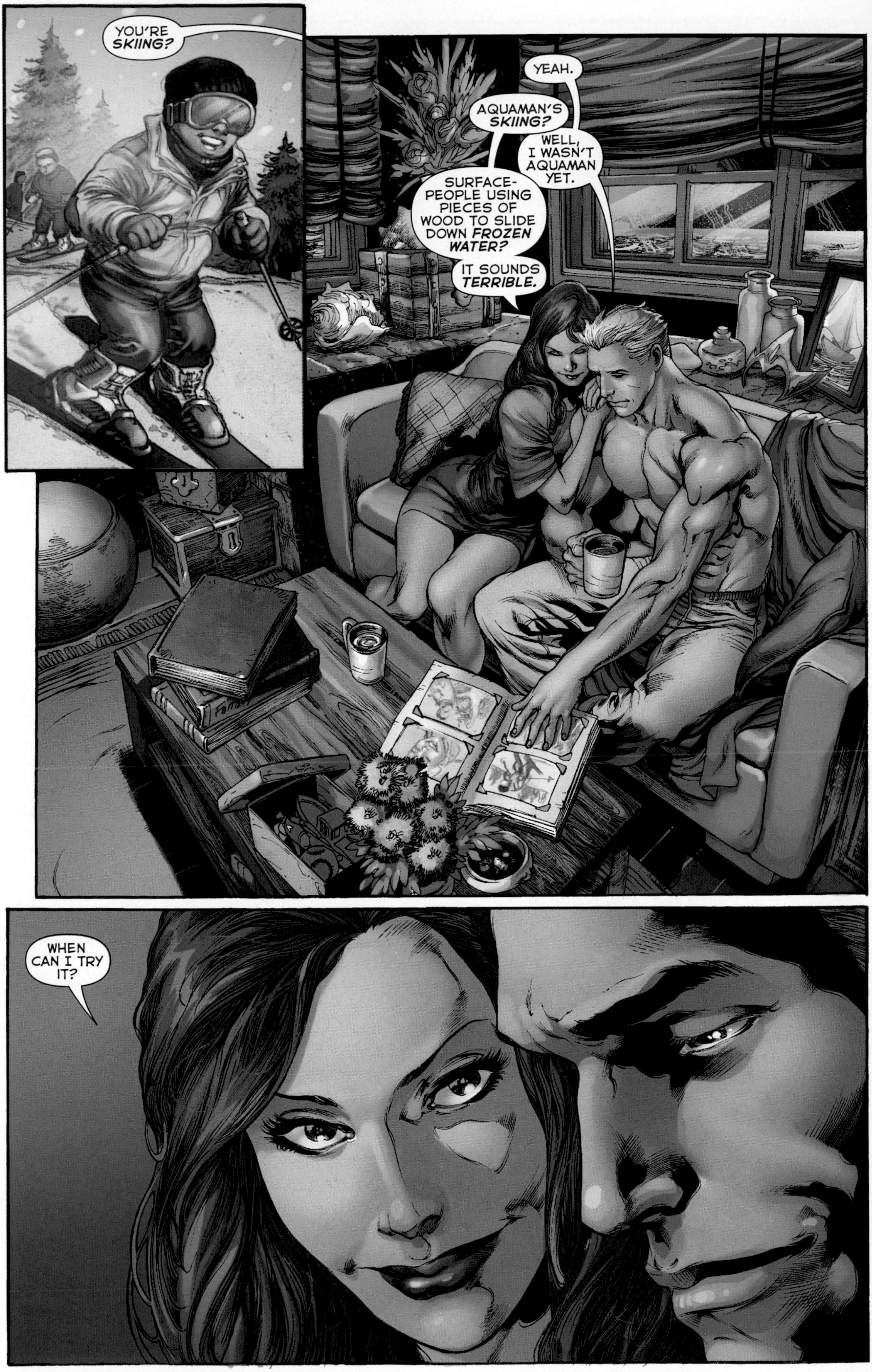
YOU'RE SKIING?
YEAH.
AQUAMAN'S SKIING?
WELL, I WASN'T AQUAMAN YET.
SURFACE-PEOPLE USING PIECES OF WOOD TO SLIDE DOWN FROZEN WATER?
IT SOUNDS TERRIBLE.
WHEN CAN I TRY IT?

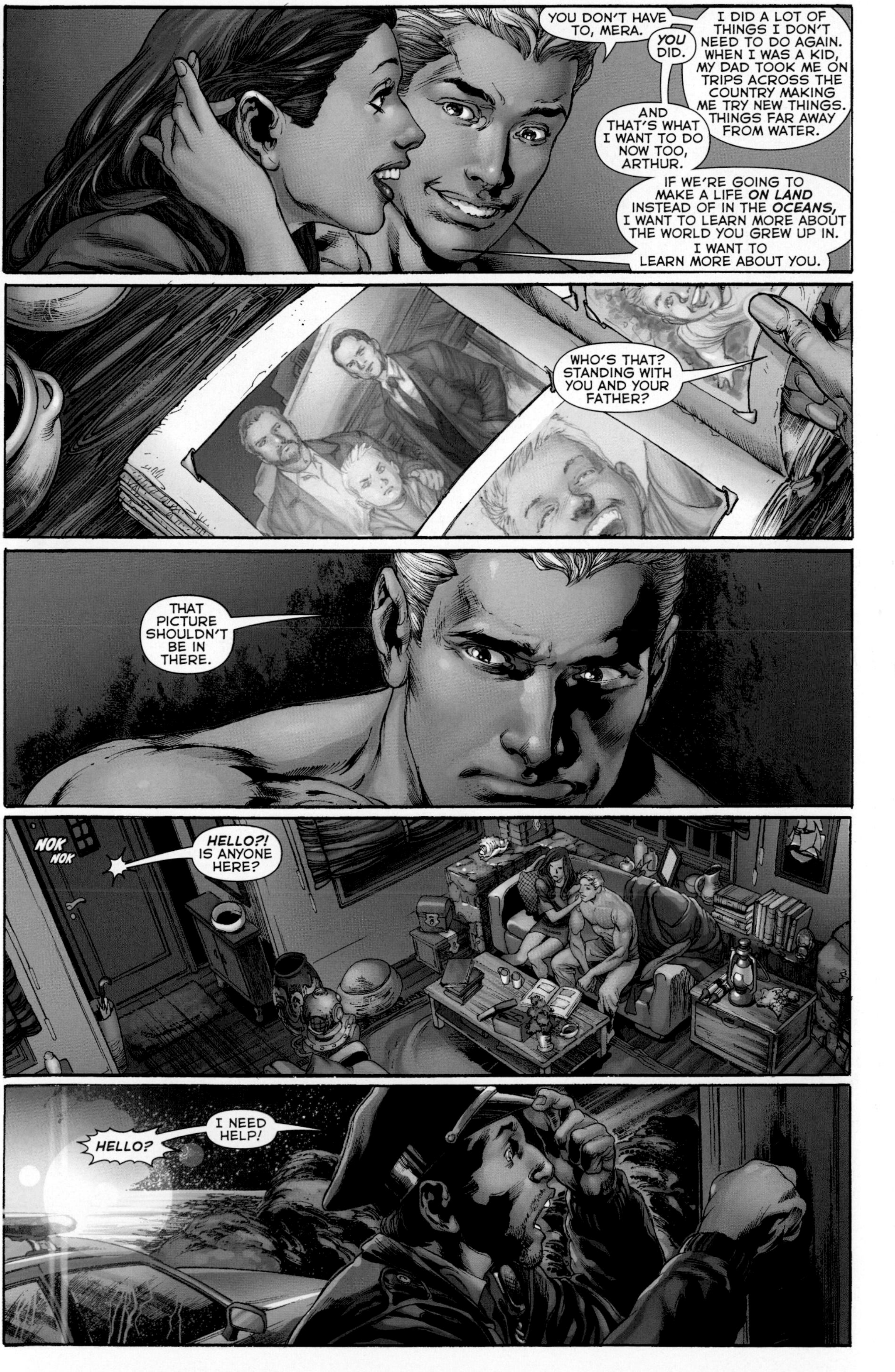
YOU DON'T HAVE TO, MERA.
YOU DID.
I DID A LOT OF THINGS I DON'T NEED TO DO AGAIN. WHEN I WAS A KID, MY DAD TOOK ME ON TRIPS ACROSS THE COUNTRY MAKING ME TRY NEW THINGS. THINGS FAR AWAY FROM WATER.
AND THAT'S WHAT I WANT TO DO NOW TOO, ARTHUR.
IF WE'RE GOING TO MAKE A LIFE ON LAND INSTEAD OF IN THE OCEANS, I WANT TO LEARN MORE ABOUT THE WORLD YOU GREW UP IN.
I WANT TO LEARN MORE ABOUT YOU.
WHO'S THAT? STANDING WITH YOU AND YOUR FATHER?
THAT PICTURE SHOULDN'T BE IN THERE.
NOK NOK
HELLO?! IS ANYONE HERE?
HELLO?
I NEED HELP!

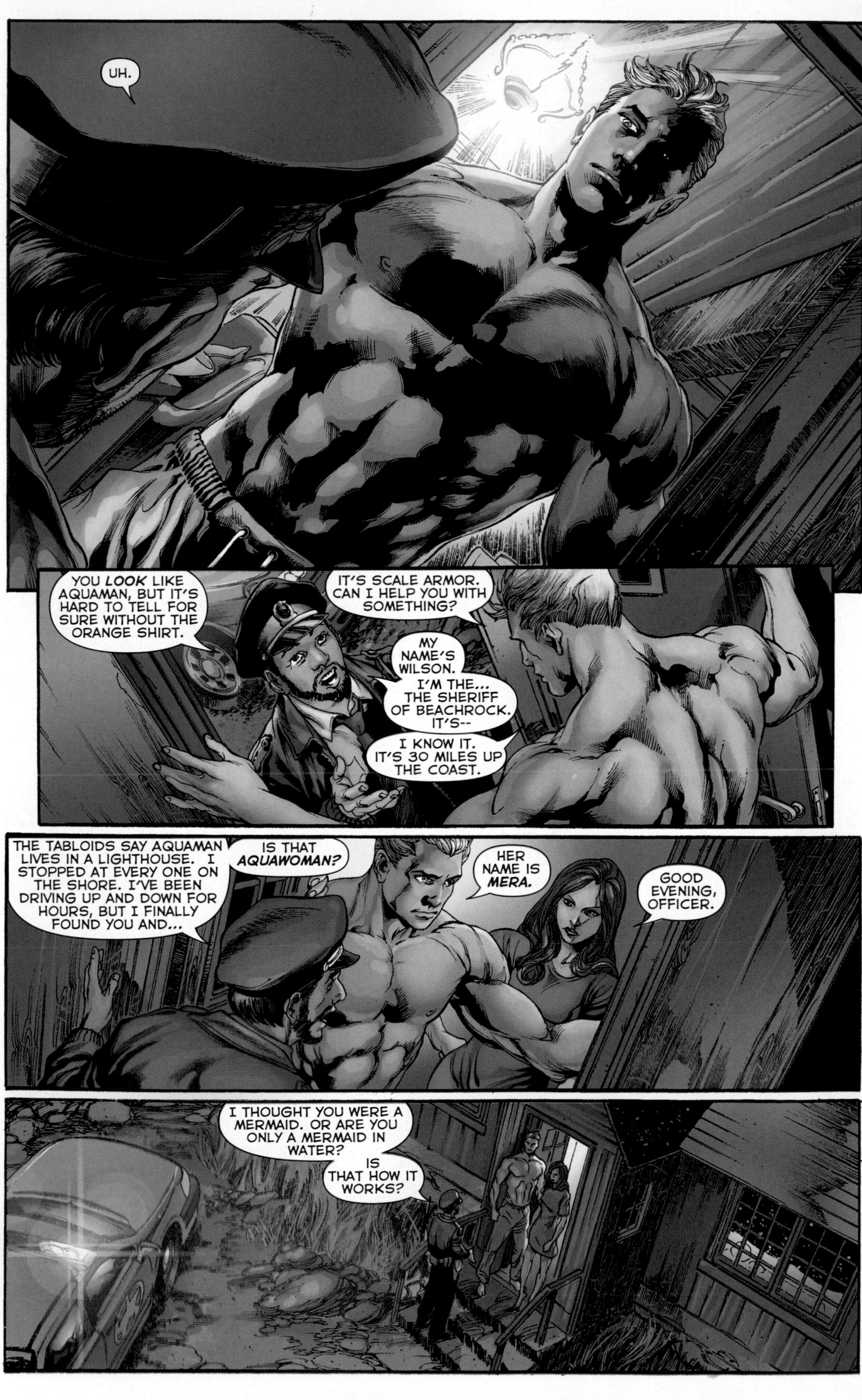
UH.
YOU LOOK LIKE AQUAMAN, BUT IT'S HARD TO TELL FOR SURE WITHOUT THE ORANGE SHIRT.
IT'S SCALE ARMOR. CAN I HELP YOU WITH SOMETHING?
MY NAME'S WILSON.
I'M THE... THE SHERIFF OF BEACHROCK. IT'S--
I KNOW IT. IT'S 30 MILES UP THE COAST.
THE TABLOIDS SAY AQUAMAN LIVES IN A LIGHTHOUSE. I STOPPED AT EVERY ONE ON THE SHORE. I'VE BEEN DRIVING UP AND DOWN FOR HOURS, BUT I FINALLY FOUND YOU AND...
IS THAT AQUAWOMAN?
HER NAME IS MERA.
GOOD EVENING, OFFICER.
I THOUGHT YOU WERE A MERMAID. OR ARE YOU ONLY A MERMAID IN WATER?
IS THAT HOW IT WORKS?

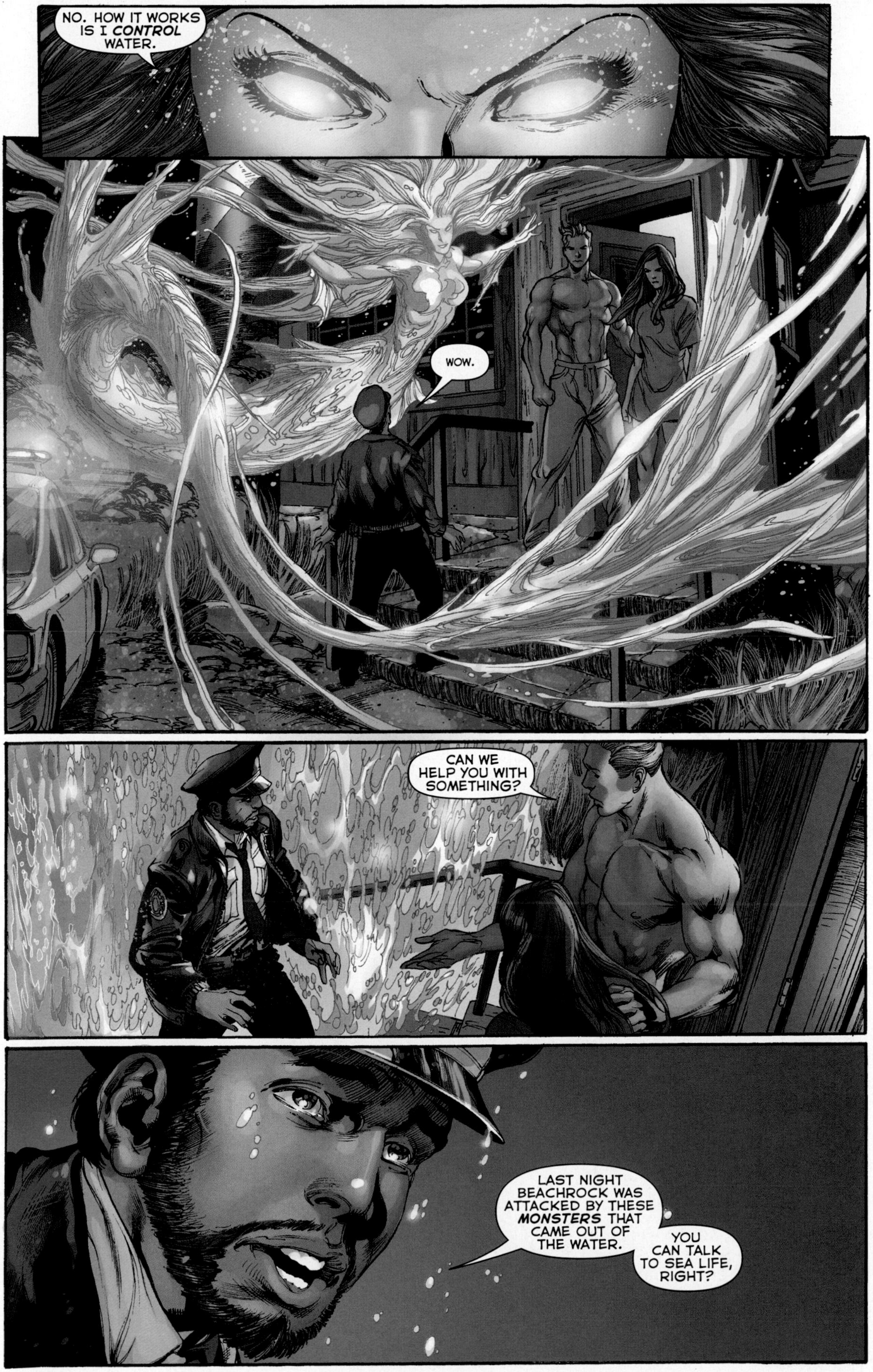
NO. HOW IT WORKS IS I CONTROL WATER.
WOW.
CAN WE HELP YOU WITH SOMETHING?
LAST NIGHT BEACHROCK WAS ATTACKED BY THESE MONSTERS THAT CAME OUT OF THE WATER.
YOU CAN TALK TO SEA LIFE, RIGHT?

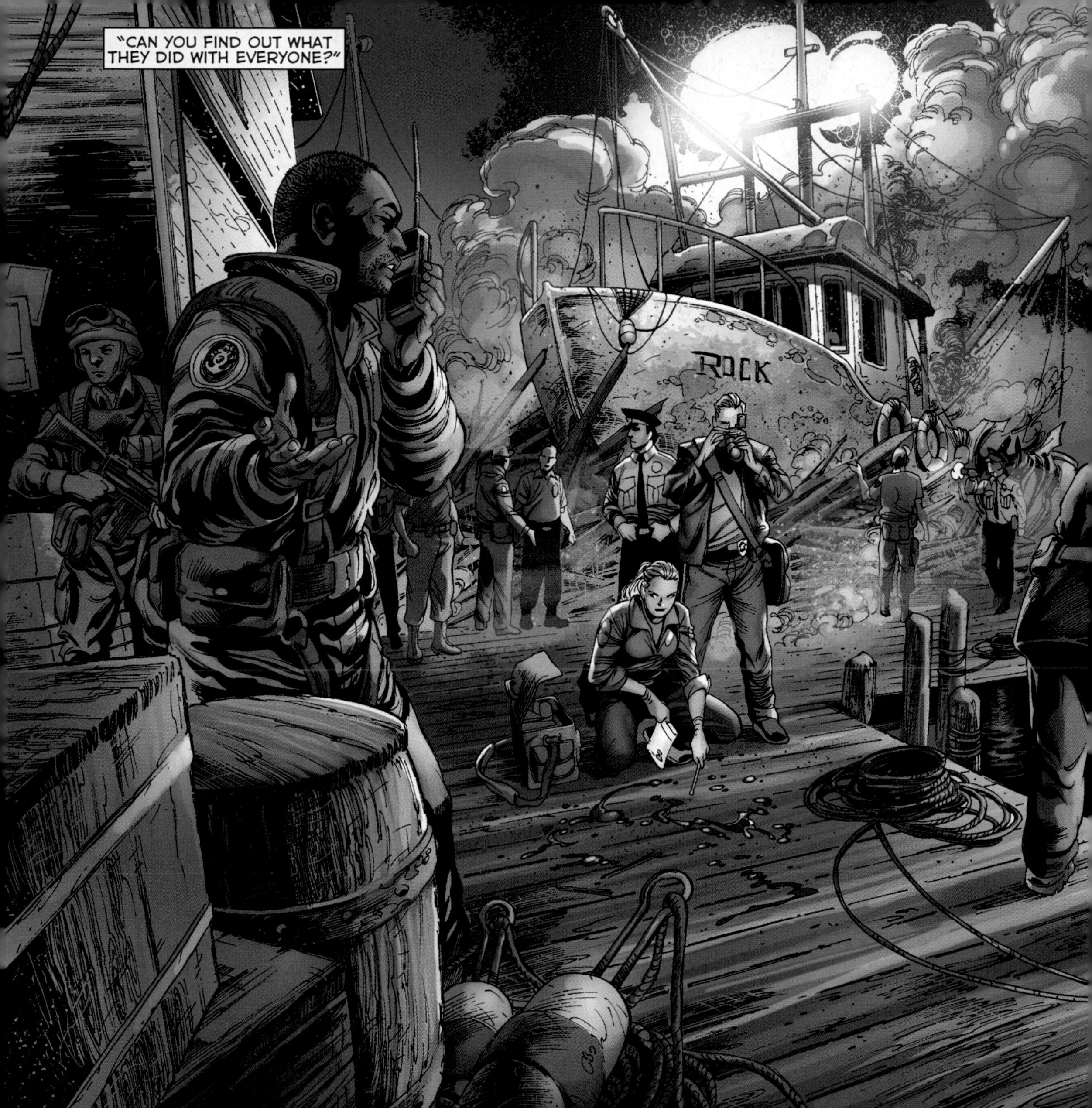
"CAN YOU FIND OUT WHAT THEY DID WITH EVERYONE?"
ROCK

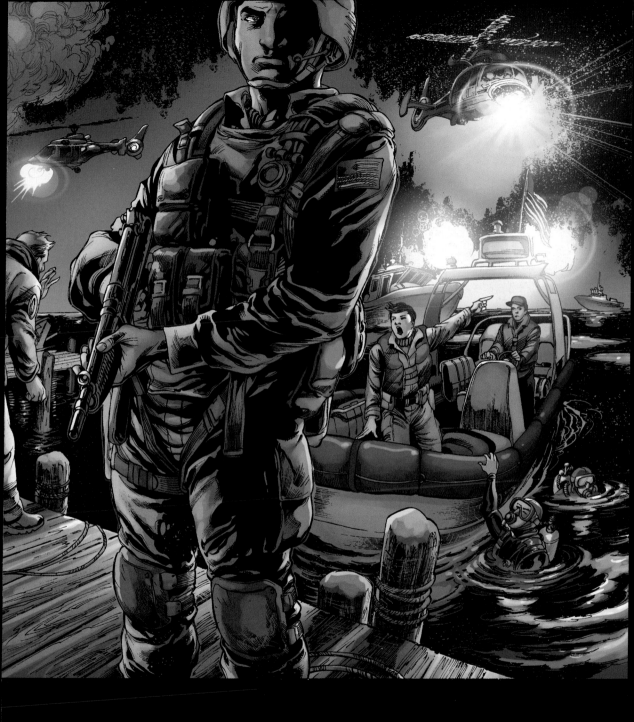

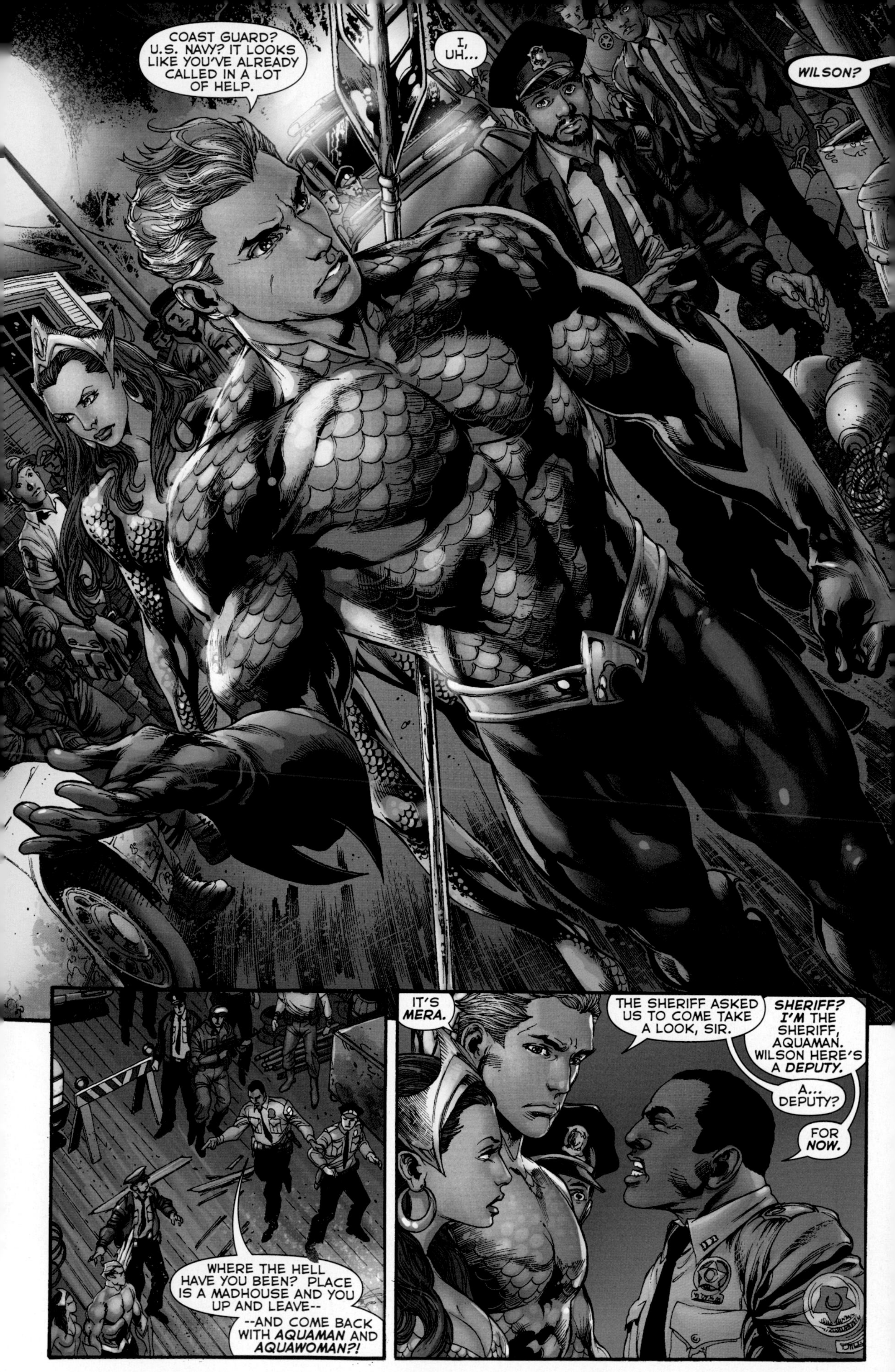
COAST GUARD? U.S. NAVY? IT LOOKS LIKE YOU'VE ALREADY CALLED IN A LOT OF HELP.
I, UH...
WILSON?
WHERE THE HELL HAVE YOU BEEN? PLACE IS A MADHOUSE AND YOU UP AND LEAVE--
--AND COME BACK WITH AQUAMAN AND AQUAWOMAN?!
IT'S MERA.
THE SHERIFF ASKED US TO COME TAKE A LOOK, SIR.
SHERIFF? I'M THE SHERIFF, AQUAMAN. WILSON HERE'S A DEPUTY.
A... DEPUTY?
FOR NOW.

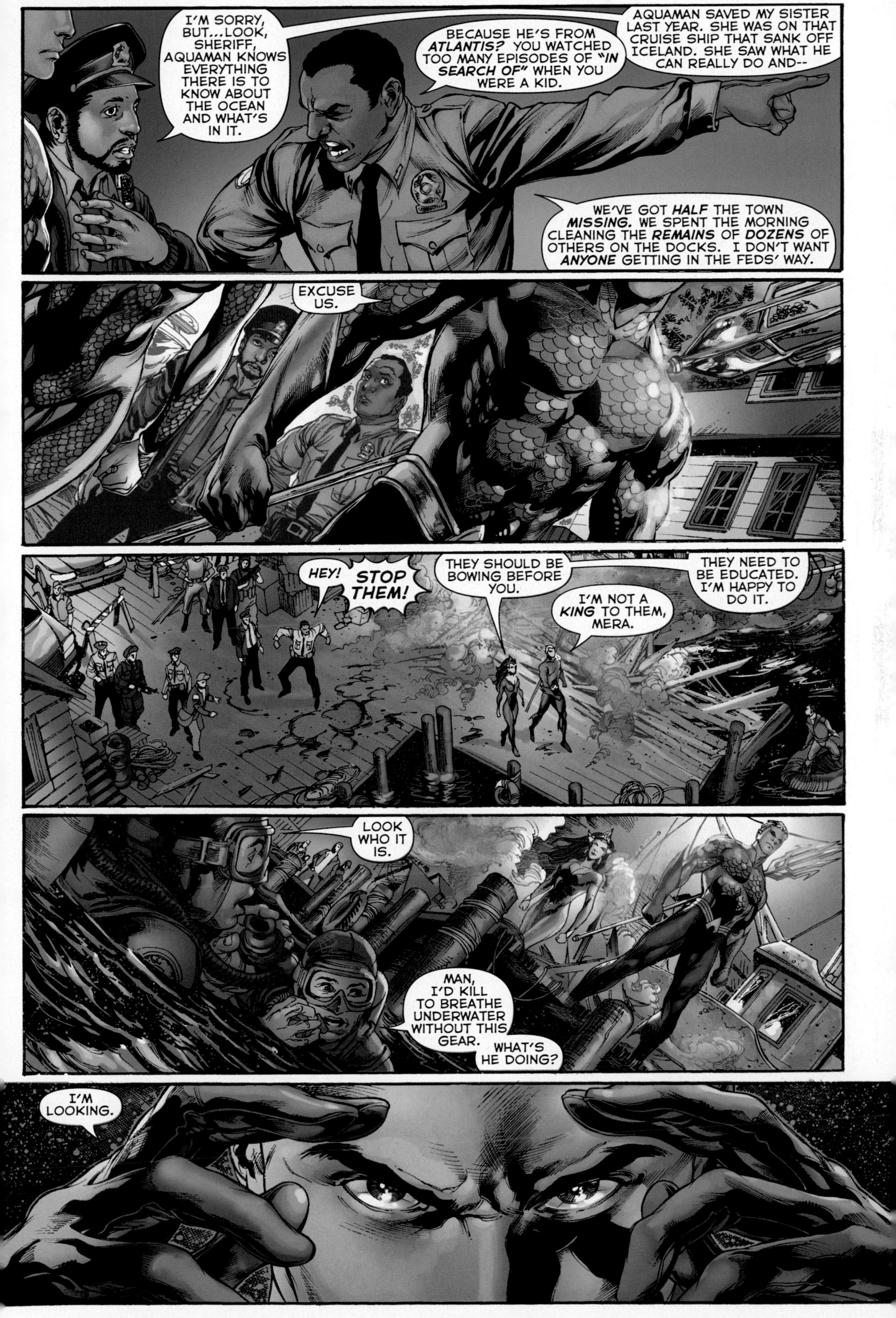

I'M SORRY, BUT...LOOK, SHERIFF, AQUAMAN KNOWS EVERYTHING THERE IS TO KNOW ABOUT THE OCEAN AND WHAT'S IN IT.
BECAUSE HE'S FROM ATLANTIS? YOU WATCHED TOO MANY EPISODES OF "IN SEARCH OF" WHEN YOU WERE A KID.
AQUAMAN SAVED MY SISTER LAST YEAR. SHE WAS ON THAT CRUISE SHIP THAT SANK OFF ICELAND. SHE SAW WHAT HE CAN REALLY DO AND--
WE'VE GOT HALF THE TOWN MISSING. WE SPENT THE MORNING CLEANING THE REMAINS OF DOZENS OF OTHERS ON THE DOCKS. I DON'T WANT ANYONE GETTING IN THE FEDS' WAY.
EXCUSE US.
HEY!
STOP THEM!
THEY SHOULD BE BOWING BEFORE YOU.
I'M NOT A KING TO THEM, MERA.
THEY NEED TO BE EDUCATED. I'M HAPPY TO DO IT.
LOOK WHO IT IS.
MAN, I'D KILL TO BREATHE UNDERWATER WITHOUT THIS GEAR.
WHAT'S HE DOING?
I'M LOOKING.

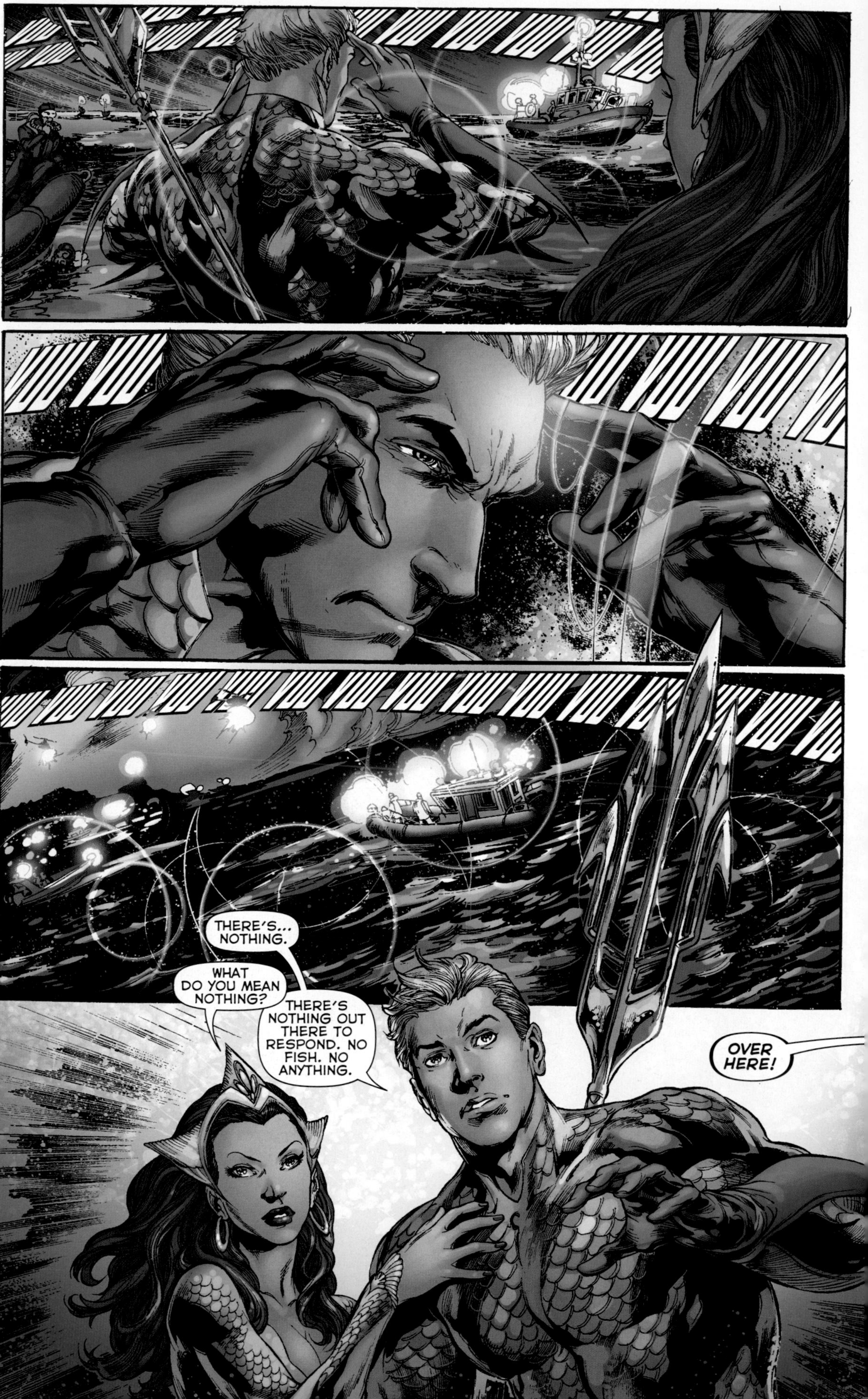
THERE'S... NOTHING.
WHAT DO YOU MEAN NOTHING?
THERE'S NOTHING OUT THERE TO RESPOND. NO FISH. NO ANYTHING.
OVER HERE!

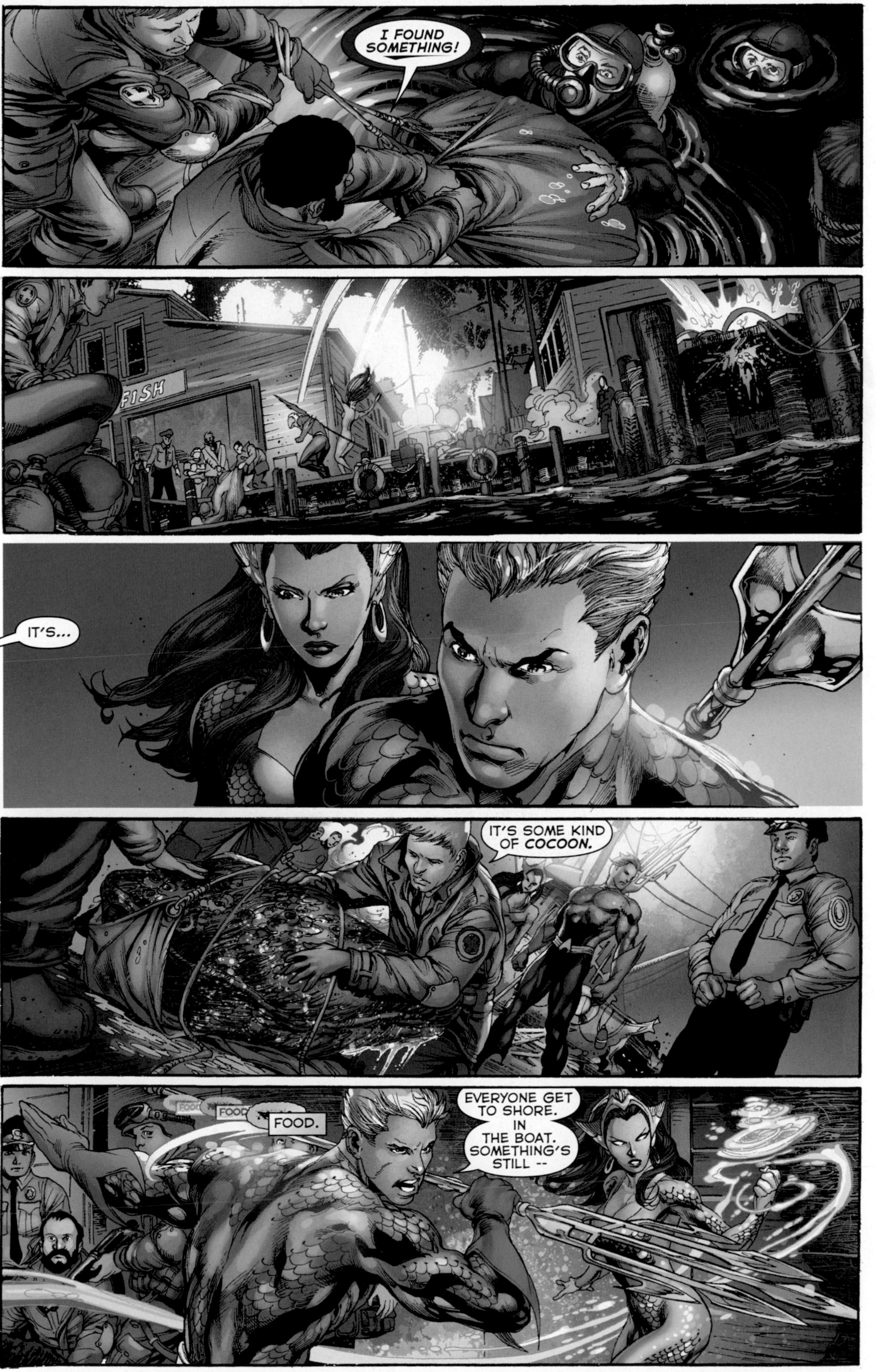
I FOUND SOMETHING!
FISH
IT'S...
IT'S SOME KIND OF COCOON.
FOOD.
FOOD
FOOD
EVERYONE GET TO SHORE. IN THE BOAT. SOMETHING'S STILL --

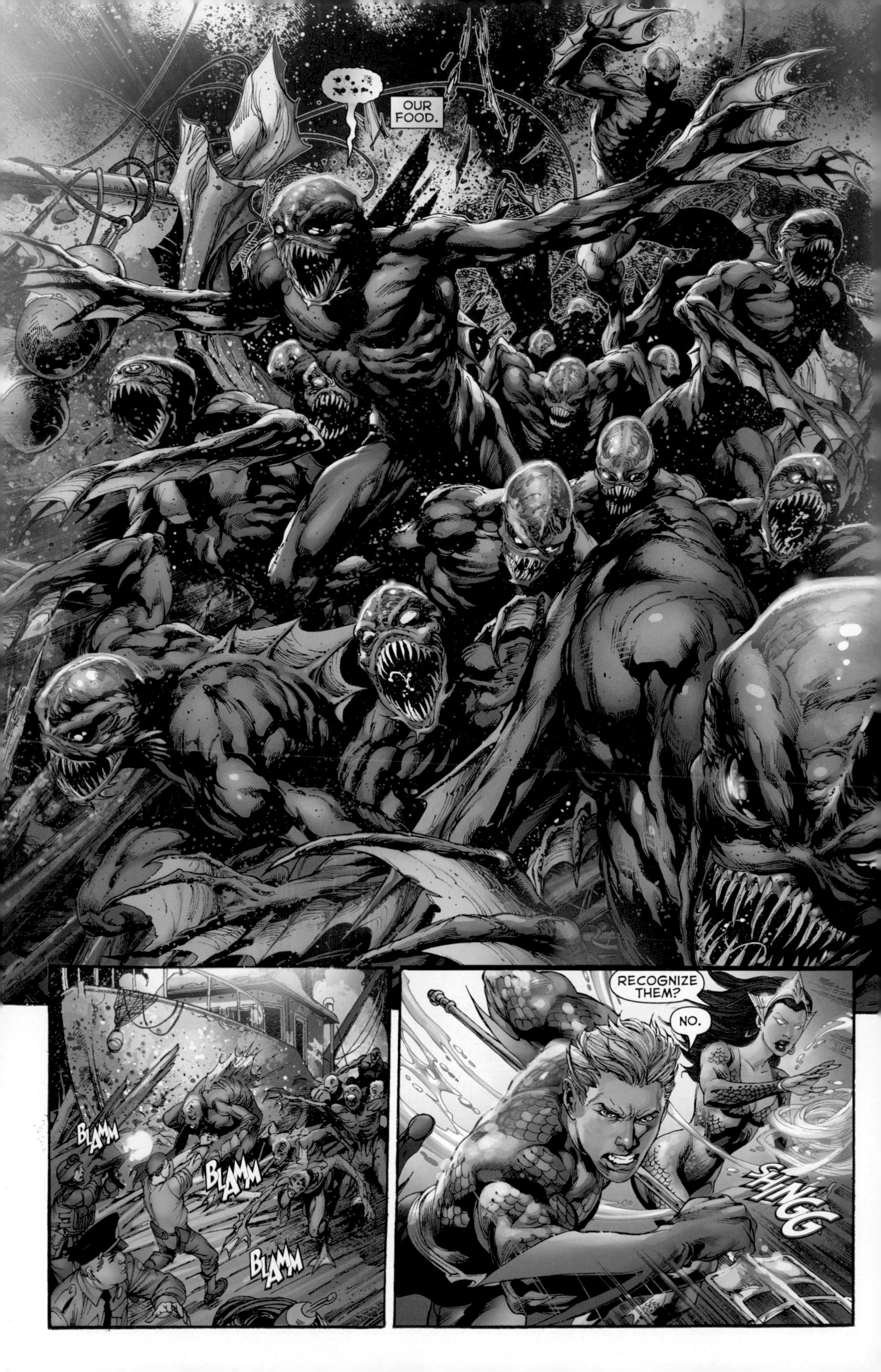
OUR FOOD.
BLAMM
BLAMM
BLAMM
RECOGNIZE THEM?
NO.
SHINGG

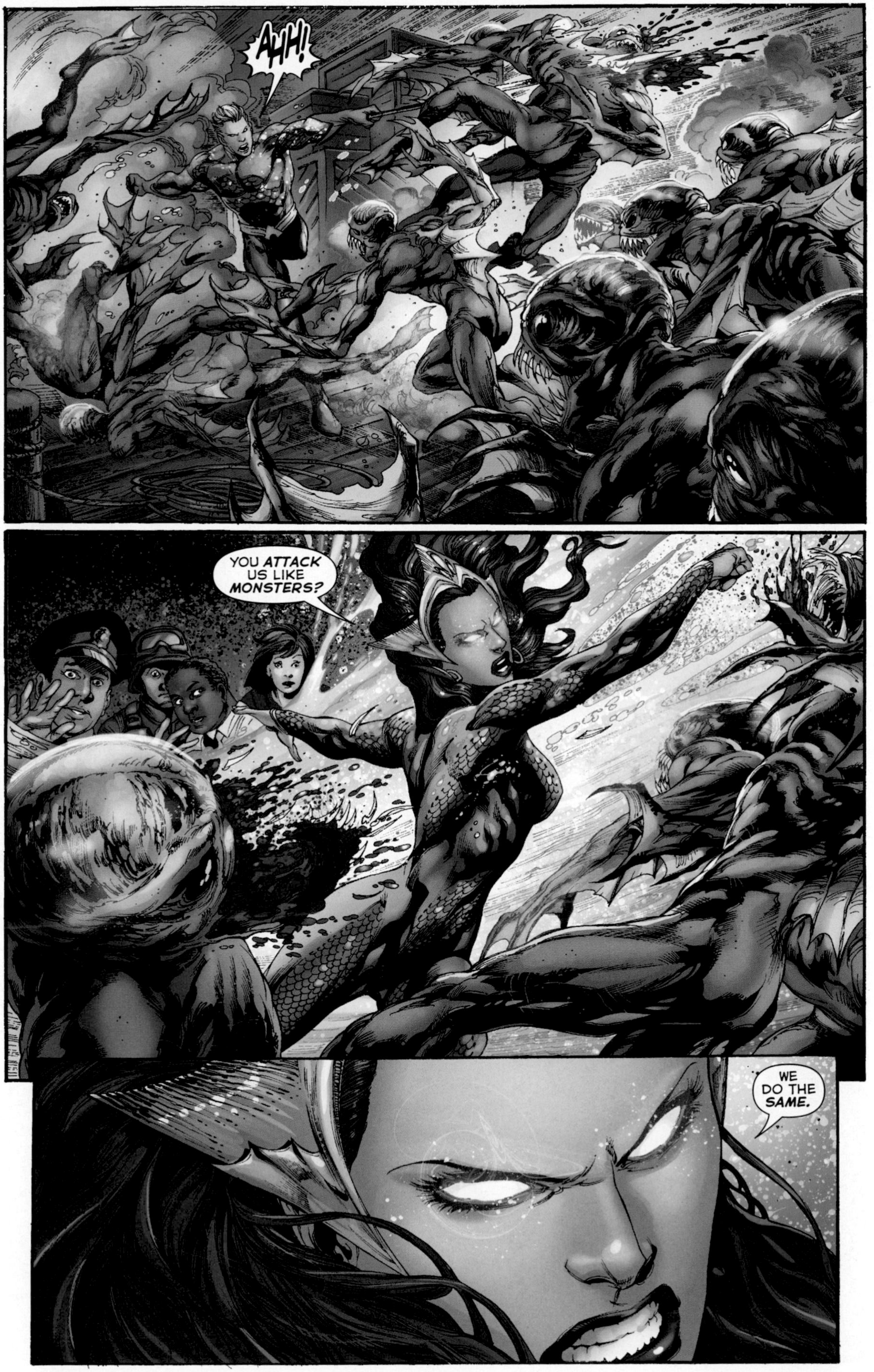
AHH!
YOU ATTACK US LIKE MONSTERS?
WE DO THE SAME.

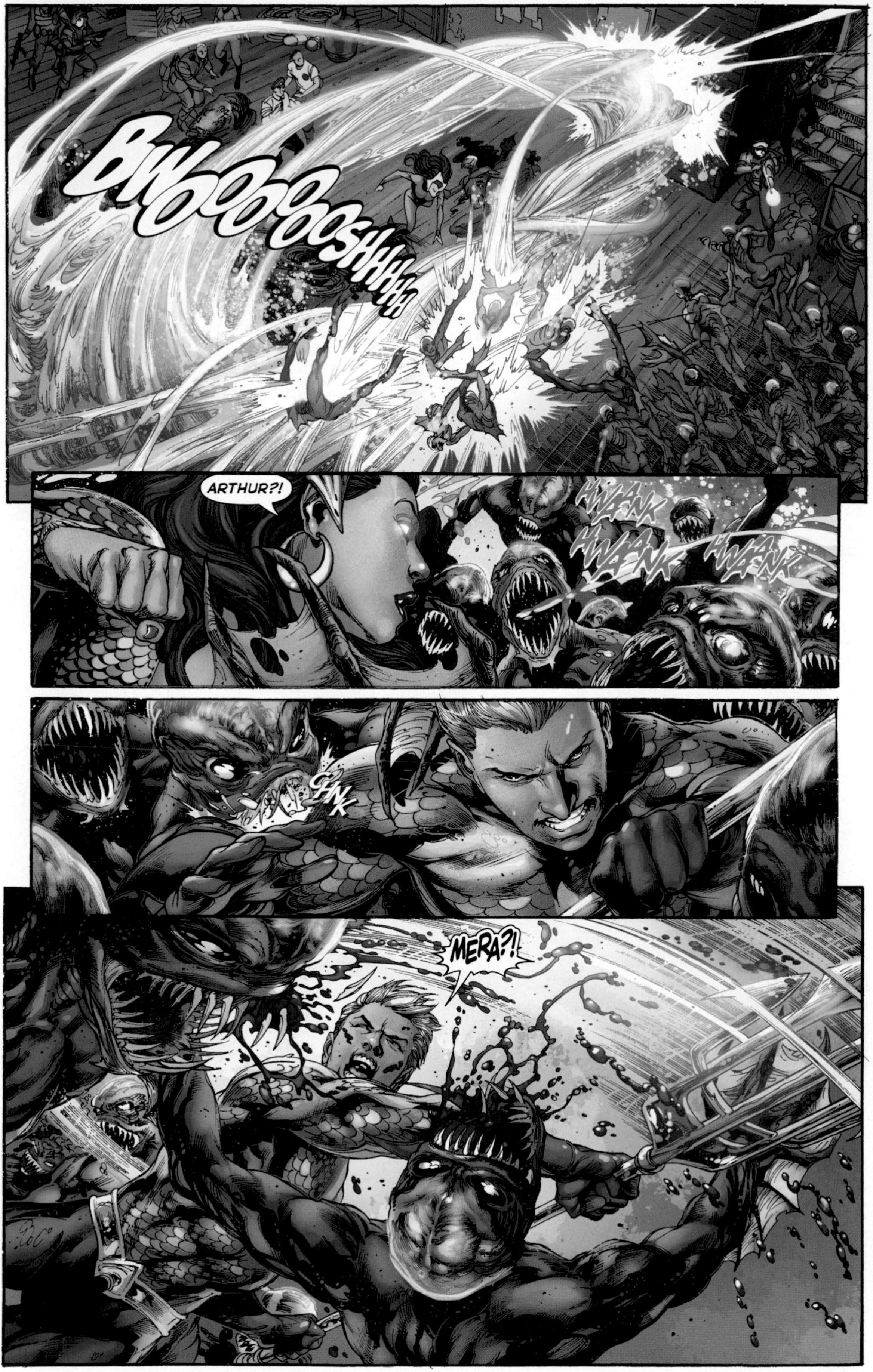
BWOOOOOOOSHHHHH
ARTHUR?!
HWAANK
HWAANK
HWAANK
CHNK
MERA?!

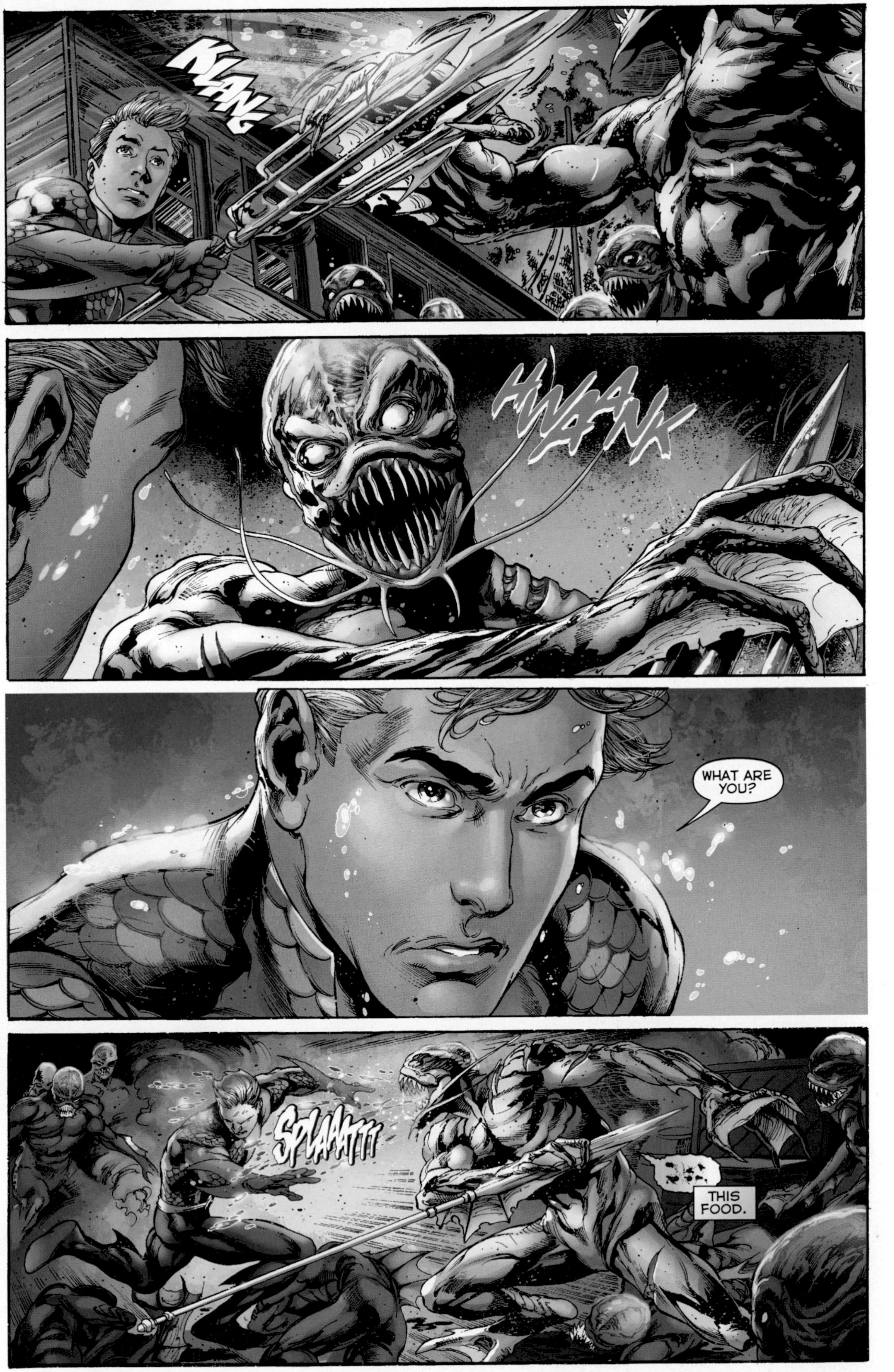
KLANG
HWAANK
WHAT ARE YOU?
SPLAAATTT
THIS FOOD.

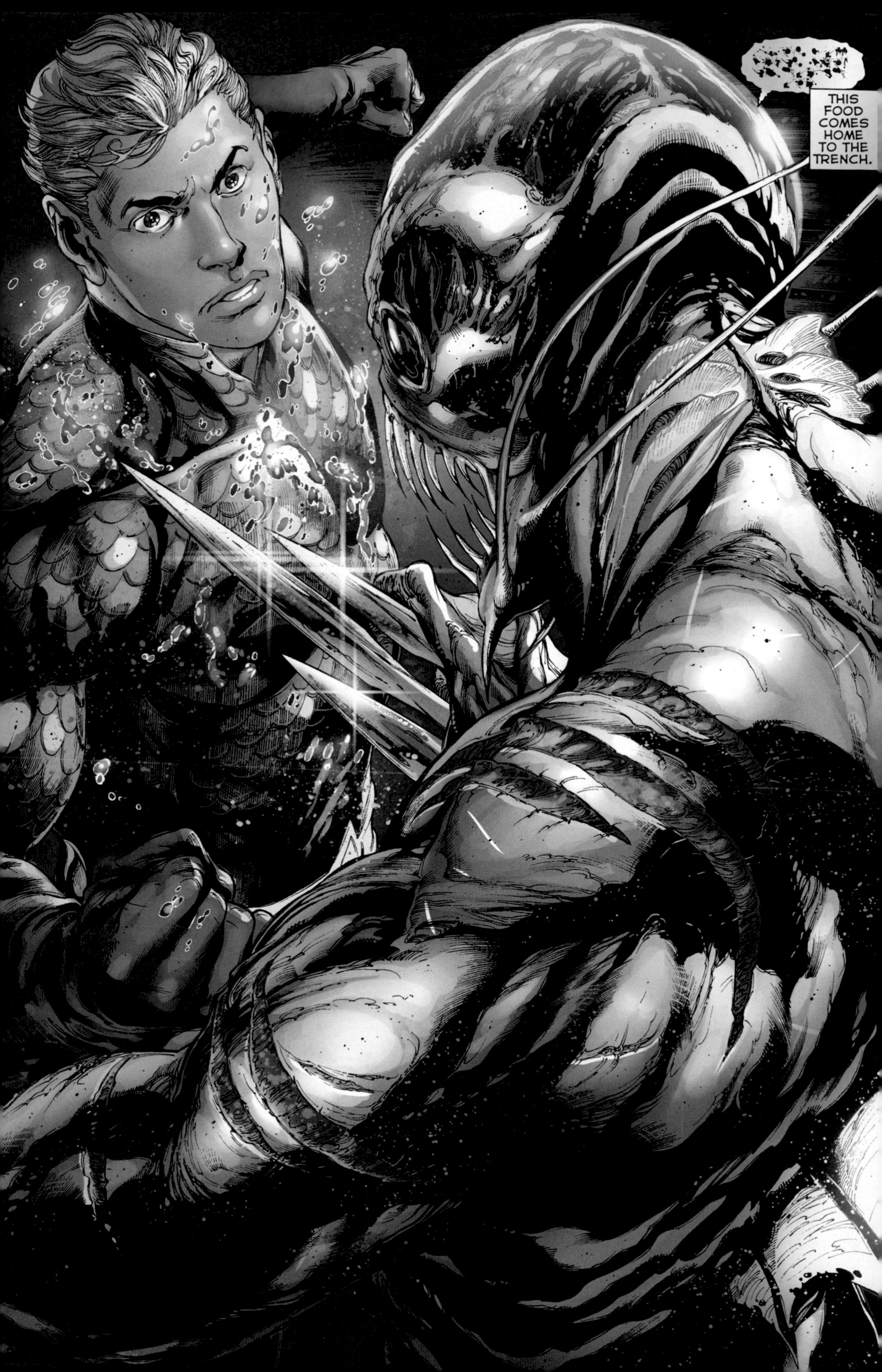
THIS FOOD COMES HOME TO THE TRENCH.

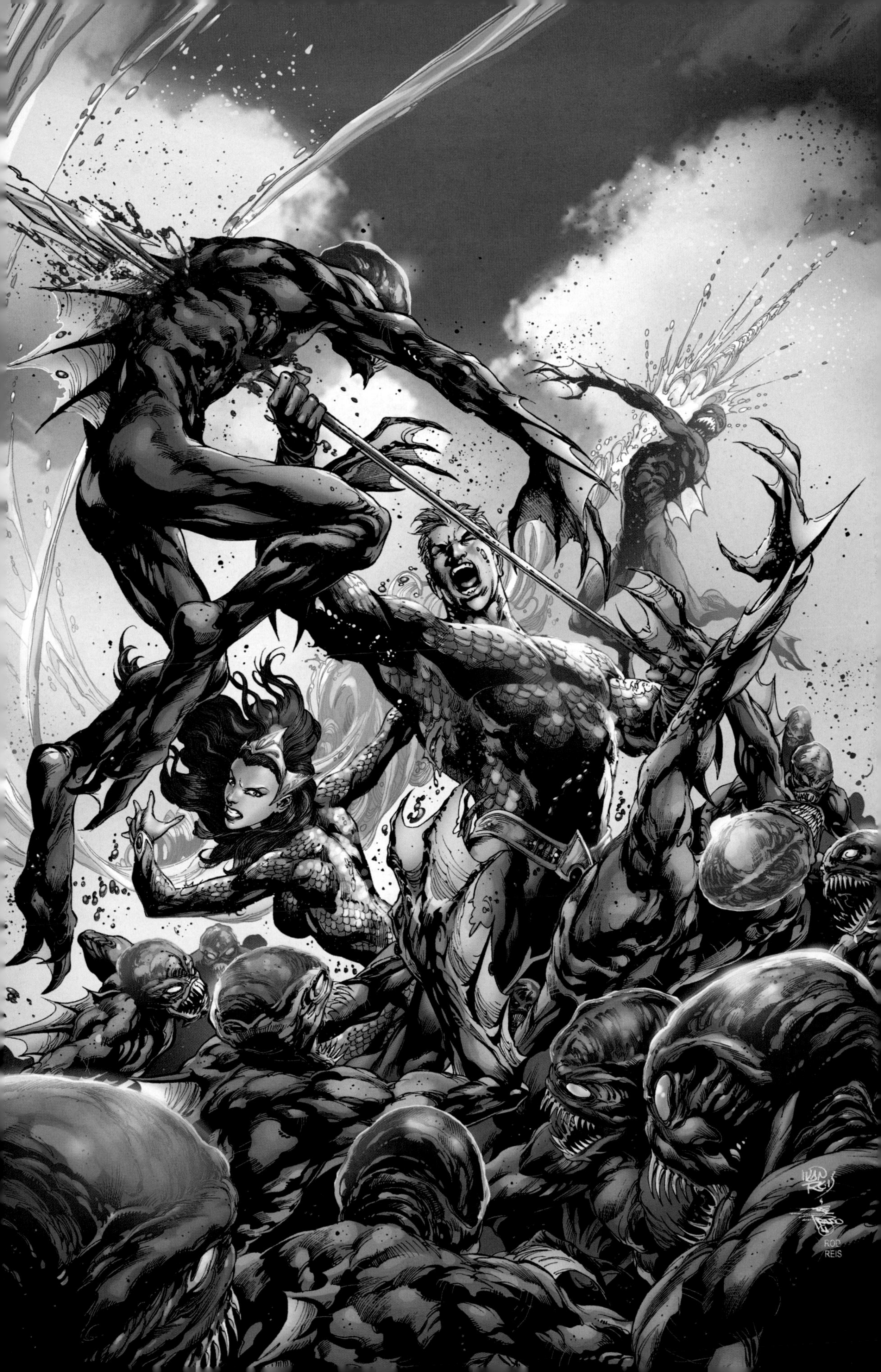
ROD
REIS

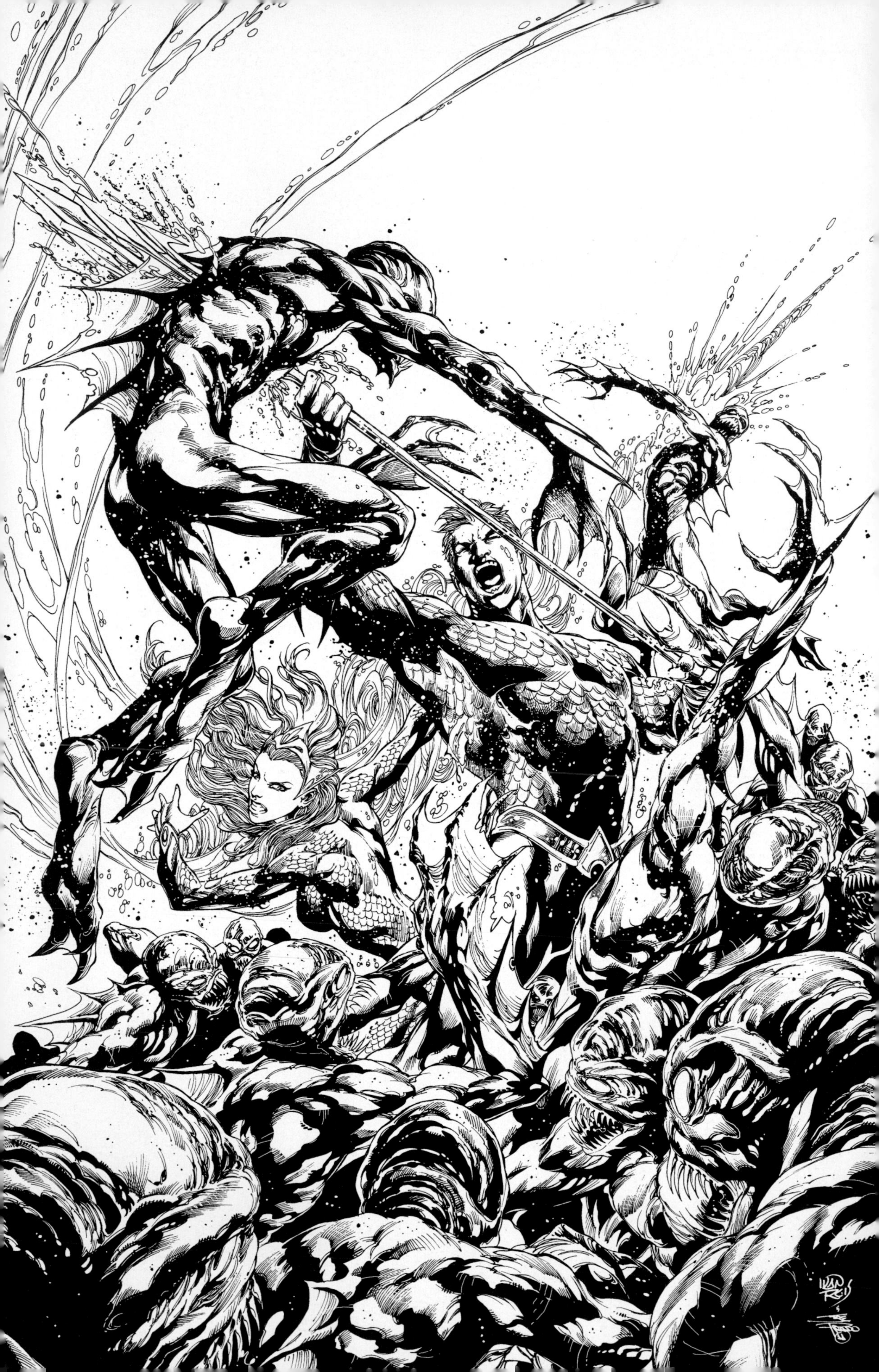

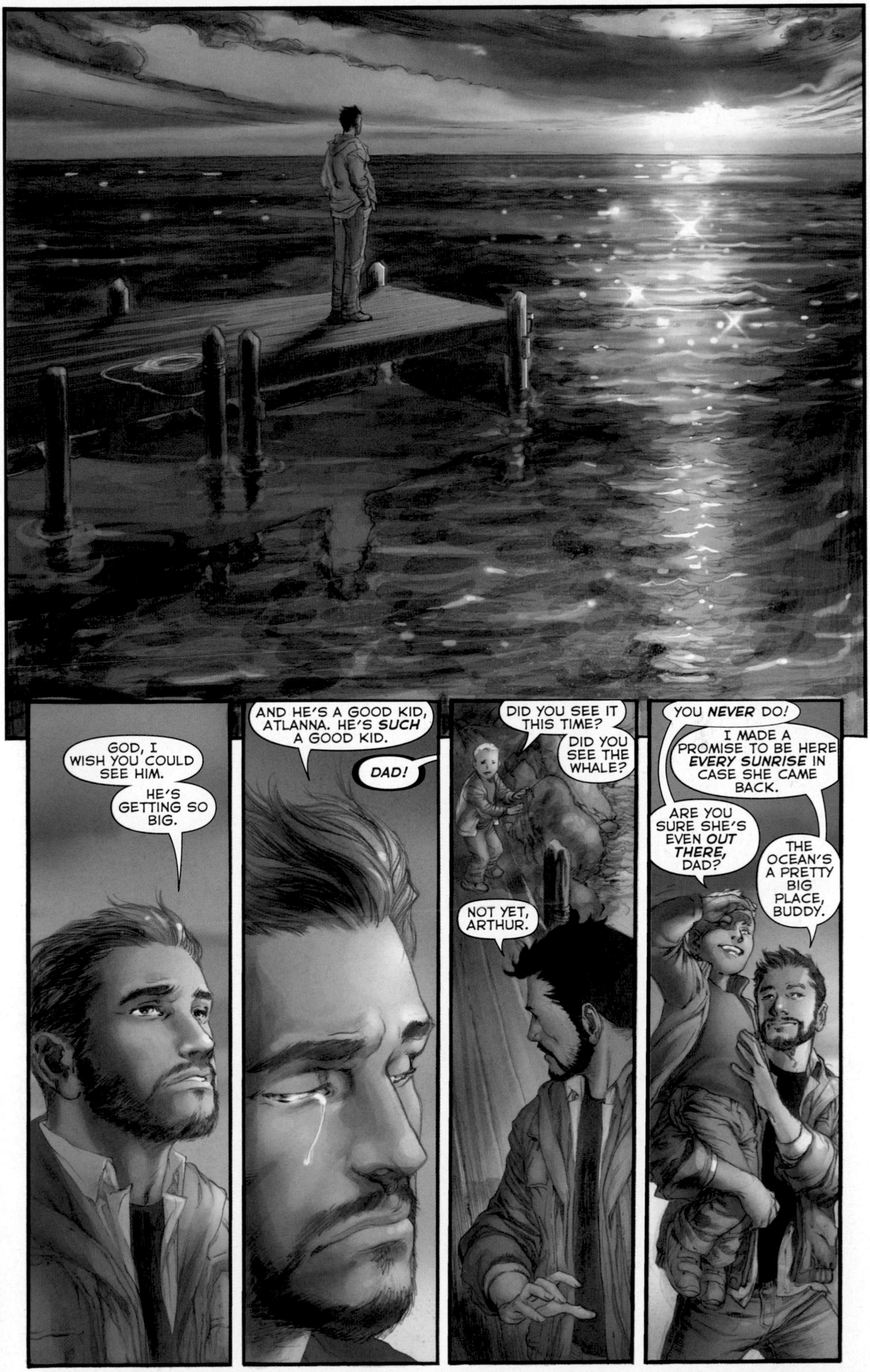
GOD, I WISH YOU COULD SEE HIM.
HE'S GETTING SO BIG.
AND HE'S A GOOD KID, ATLANNA. HE'S SUCH A GOOD KID.
DAD!
DID YOU SEE IT THIS TIME?
DID YOU SEE THE WHALE?
NOT YET, ARTHUR.
YOU NEVER DO!
I MADE A PROMISE TO BE HERE EVERY SUNRISE IN CASE SHE CAME BACK.
ARE YOU SURE SHE'S EVEN OUT THERE, DAD?
THE OCEAN'S A PRETTY BIG PLACE, BUDDY.

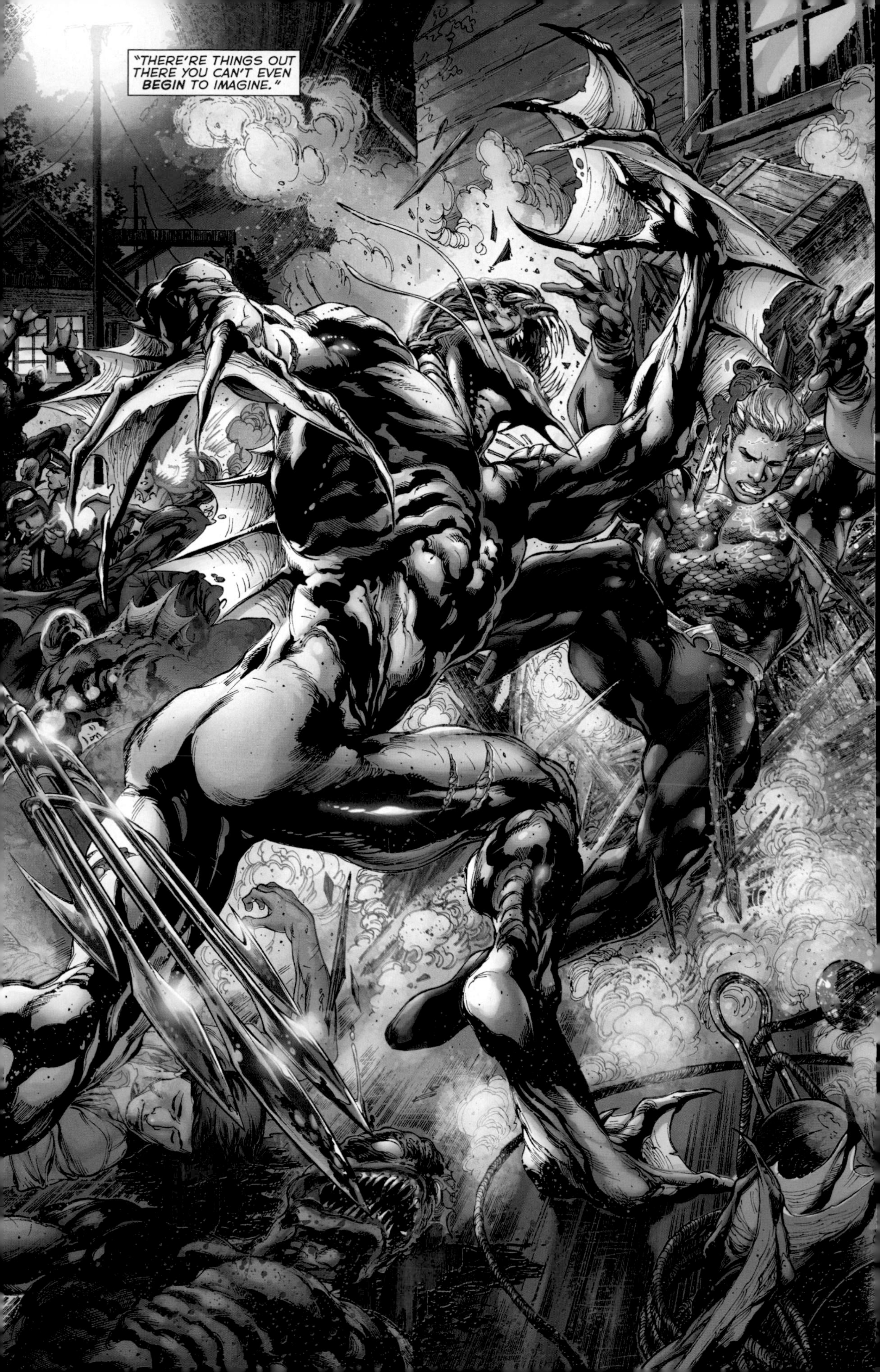
"THERE'RE THINGS OUT THERE YOU CAN'T EVEN BEGIN TO IMAGINE."

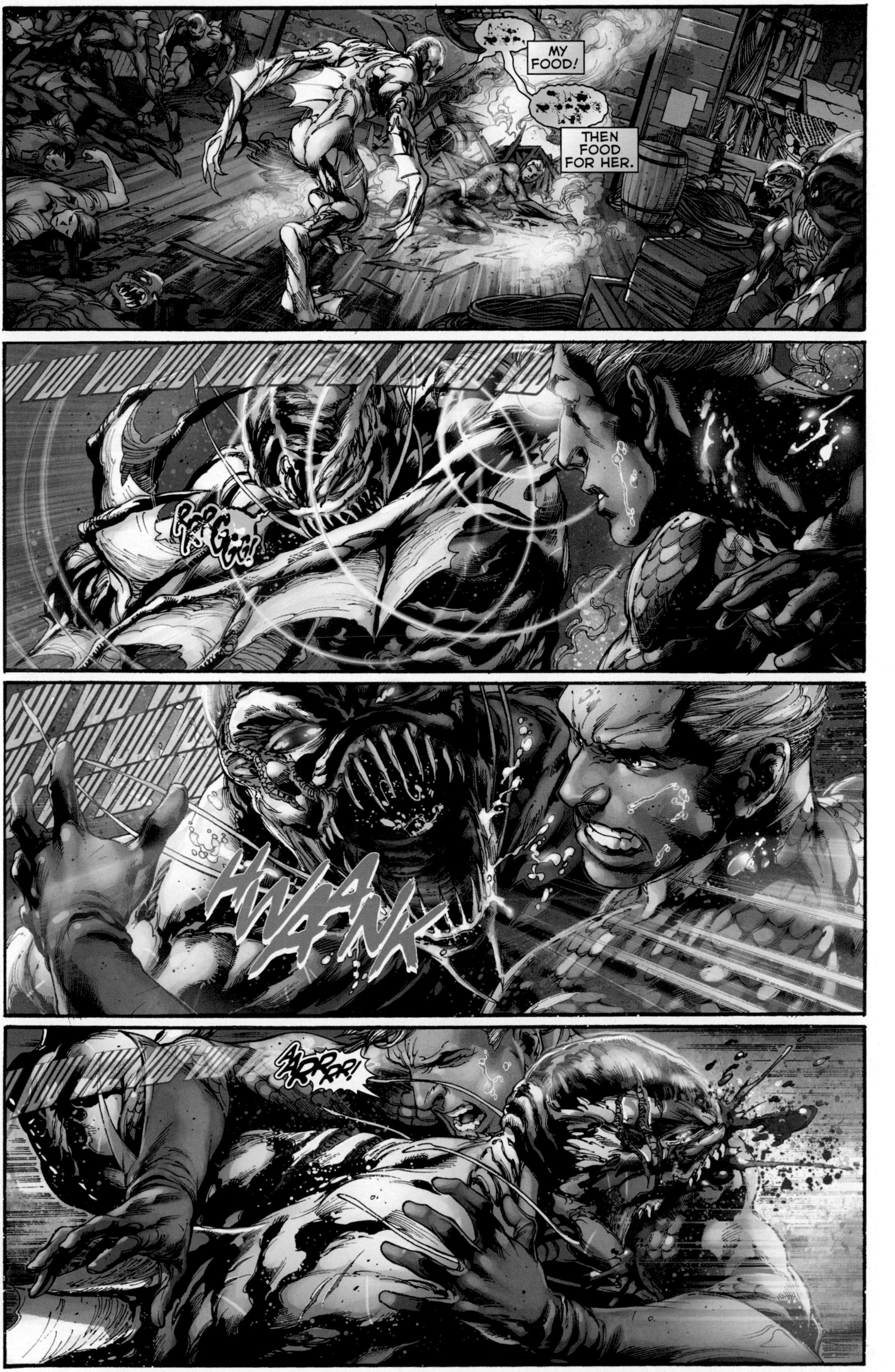
MY FOOD!
THEN FOOD FOR HER.
HWANK

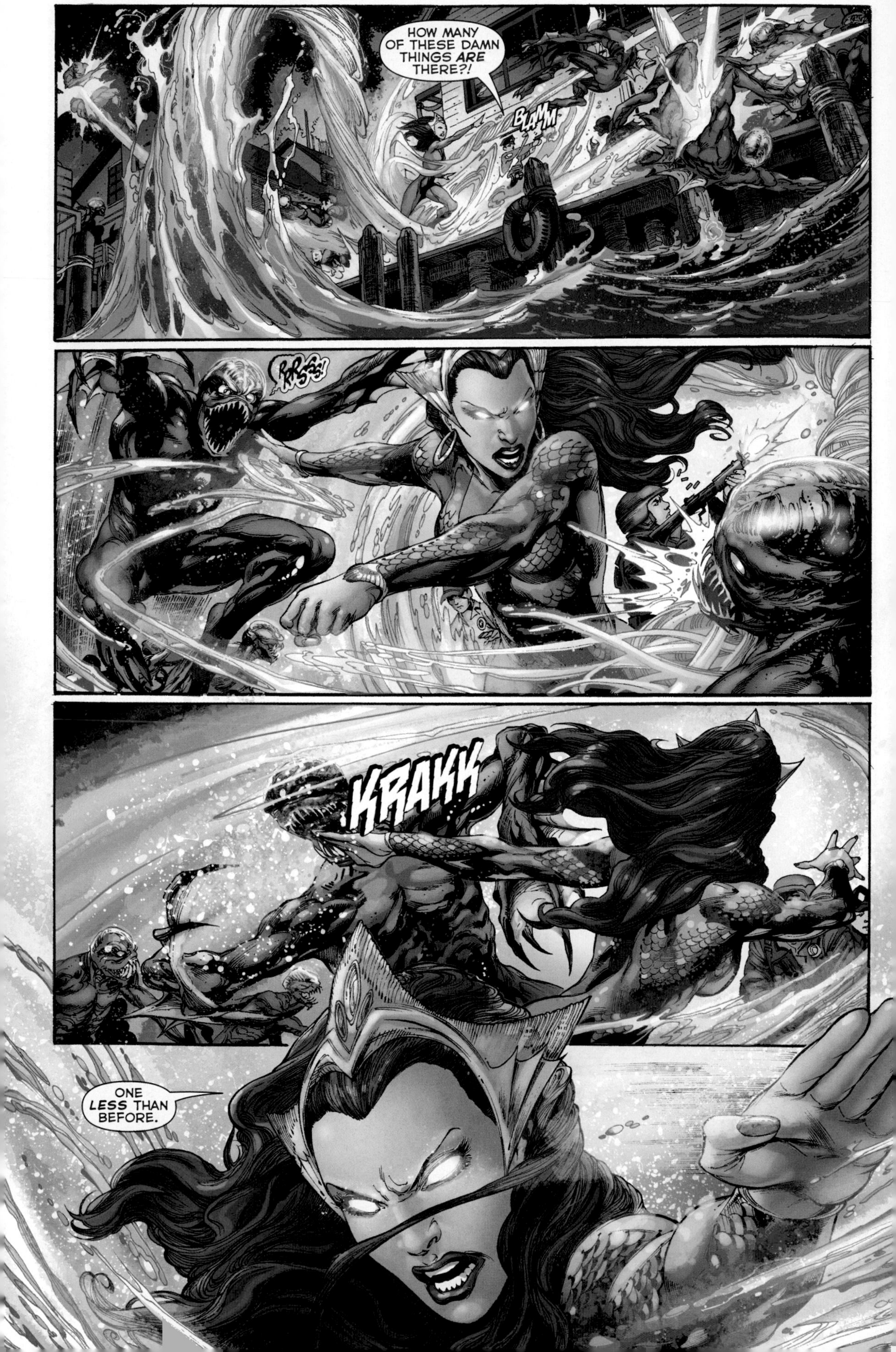
HOW MANY OF THESE DAMN THINGS ARE THERE?!
BLAMM
KRAKK
ONE LESS THAN BEFORE.

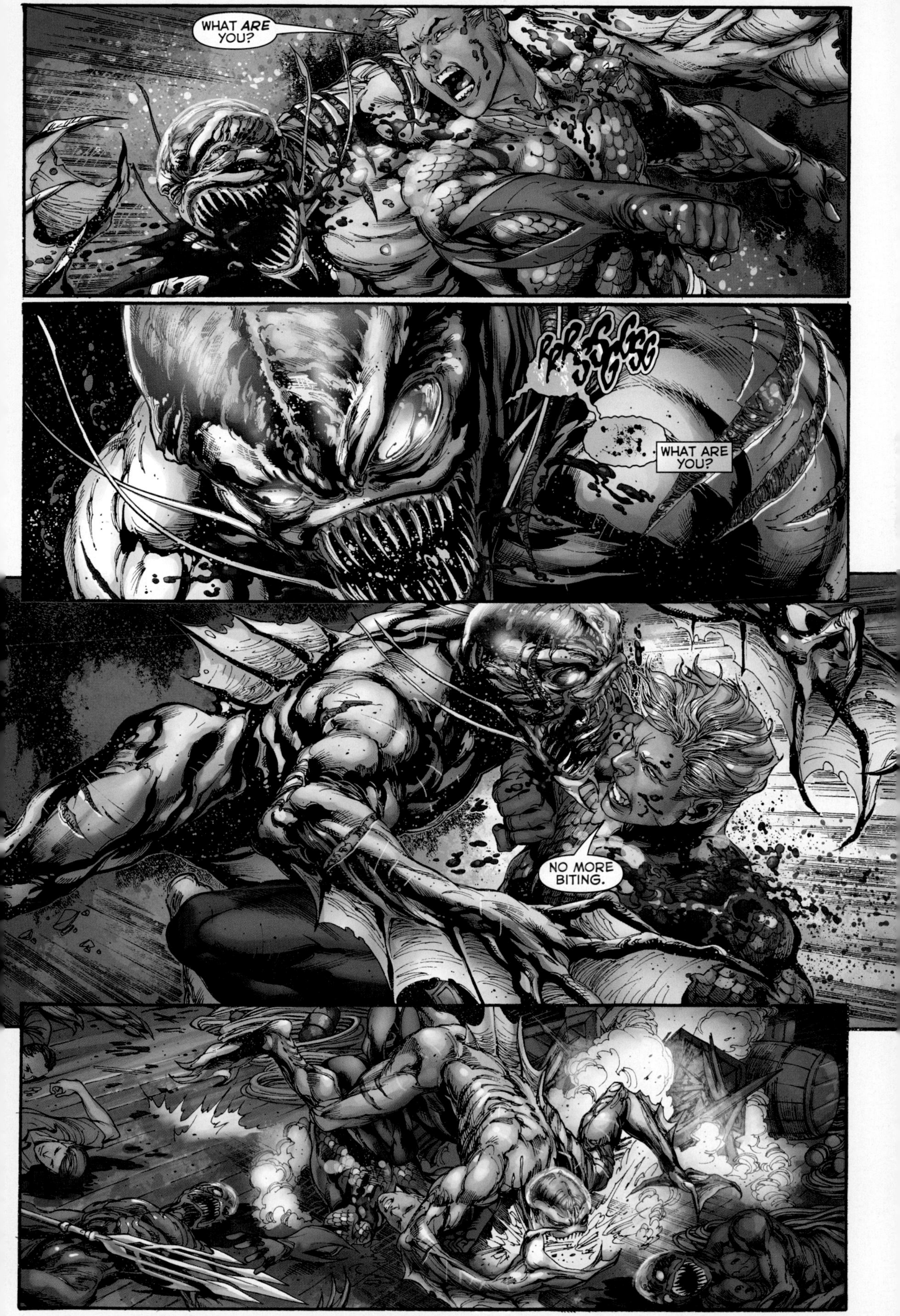
WHAT ARE YOU?
RRRSGGGG
WHAT ARE YOU?
NO MORE BITING.

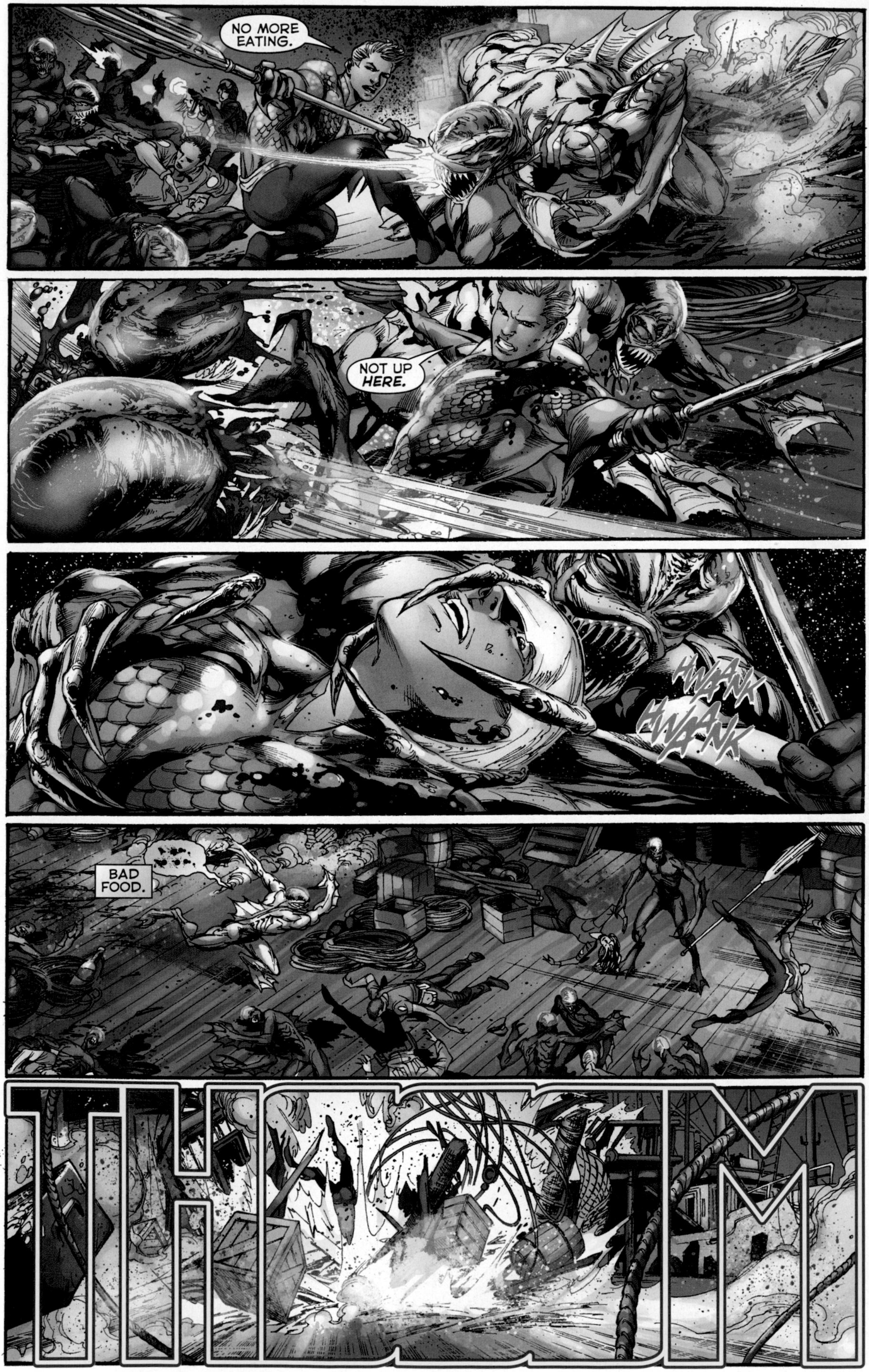
NO MORE EATING.
NOT UP HERE.
HWAANK HWAANK
BAD FOOD.
THOOM

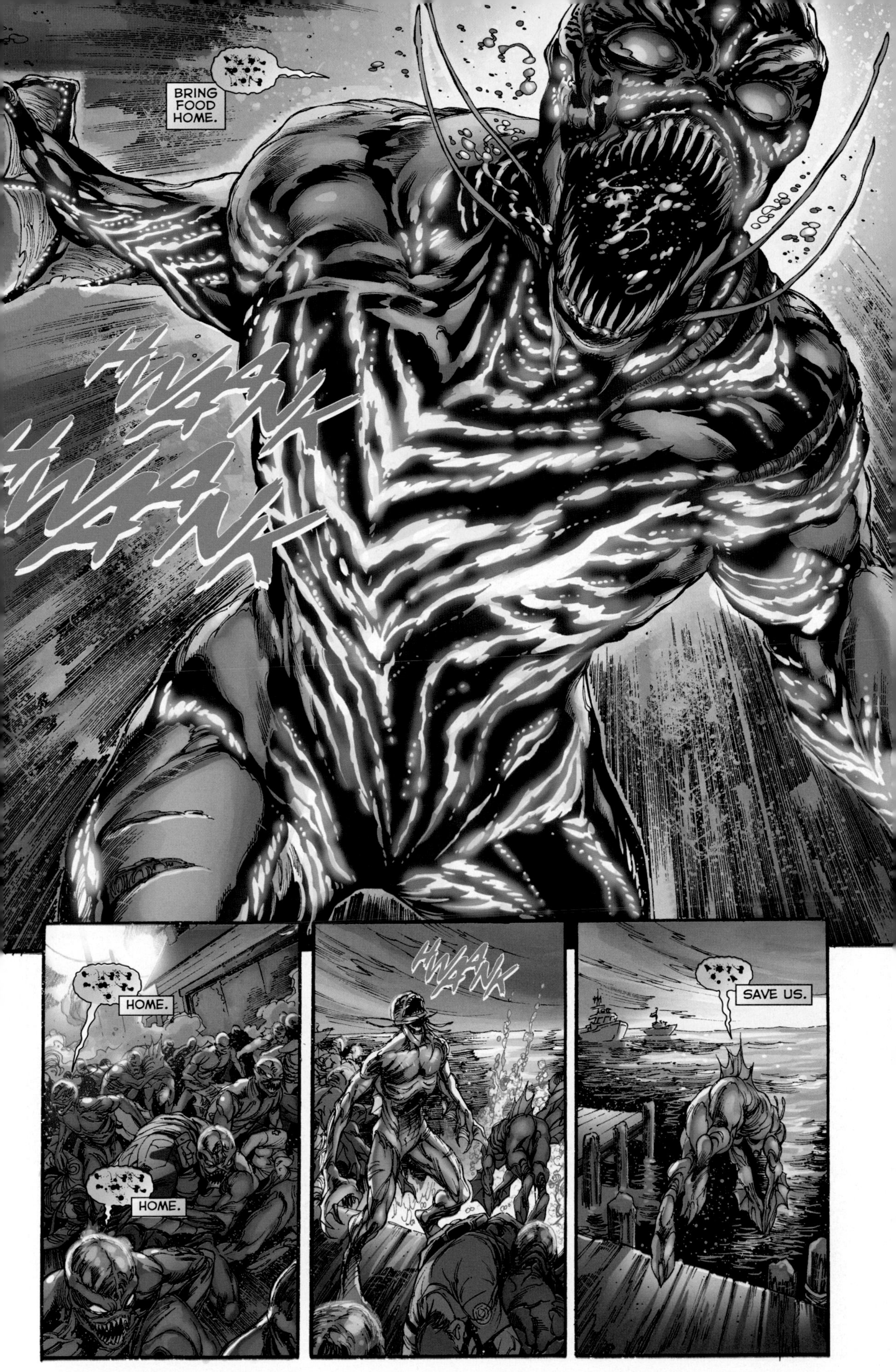
BRING FOOD HOME.
HWANK
HWANK
HOME.
HOME.
HWANK
SAVE US.

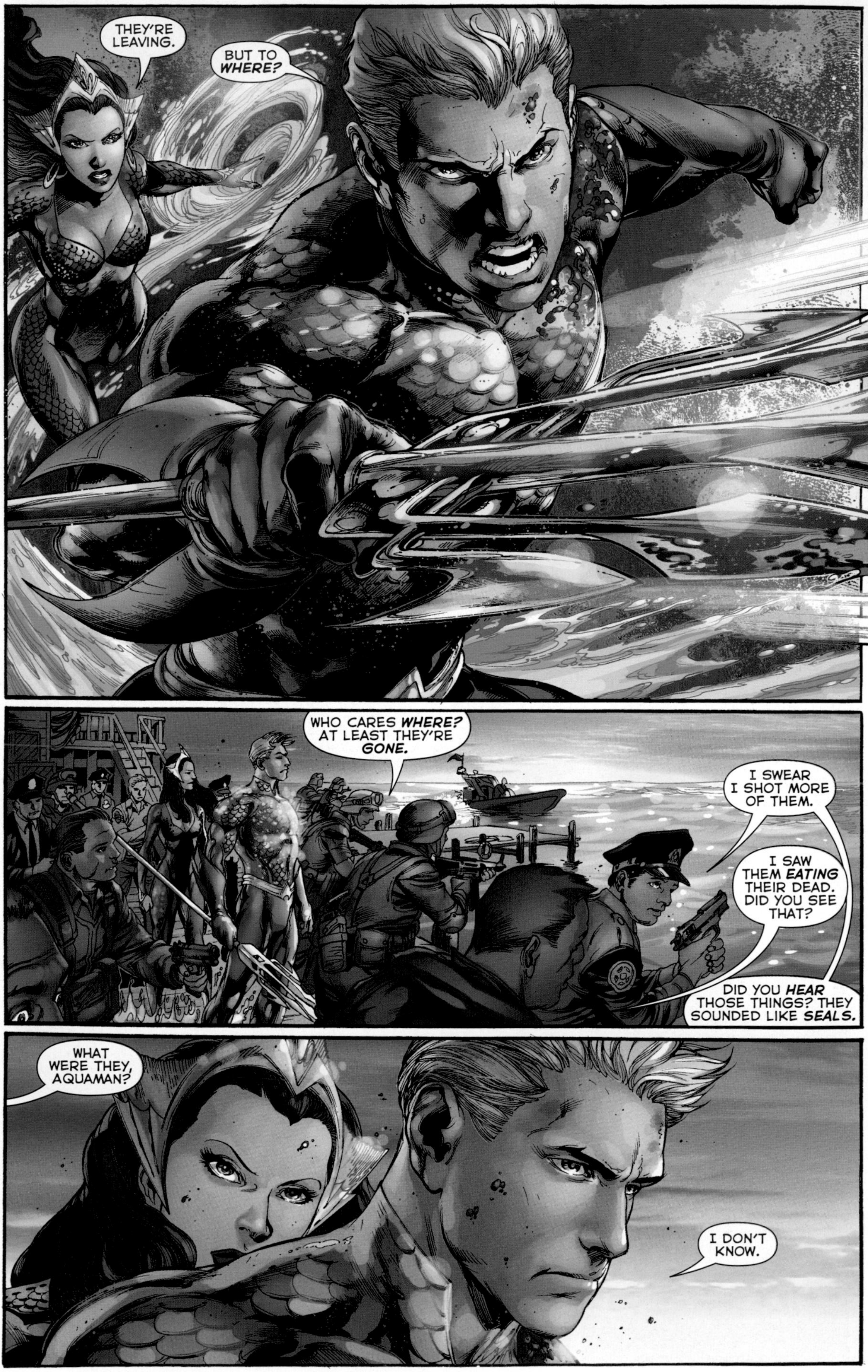
THEY'RE LEAVING.
BUT TO *WHERE?*
WHO CARES *WHERE?* AT LEAST THEY'RE *GONE.*
I SWEAR I SHOT MORE OF THEM.
I SAW THEM *EATING* THEIR DEAD. DID YOU SEE THAT?
DID YOU *HEAR* THOSE THINGS? THEY SOUNDED LIKE *SEALS.*
WHAT WERE THEY, AQUAMAN?
I DON'T KNOW.

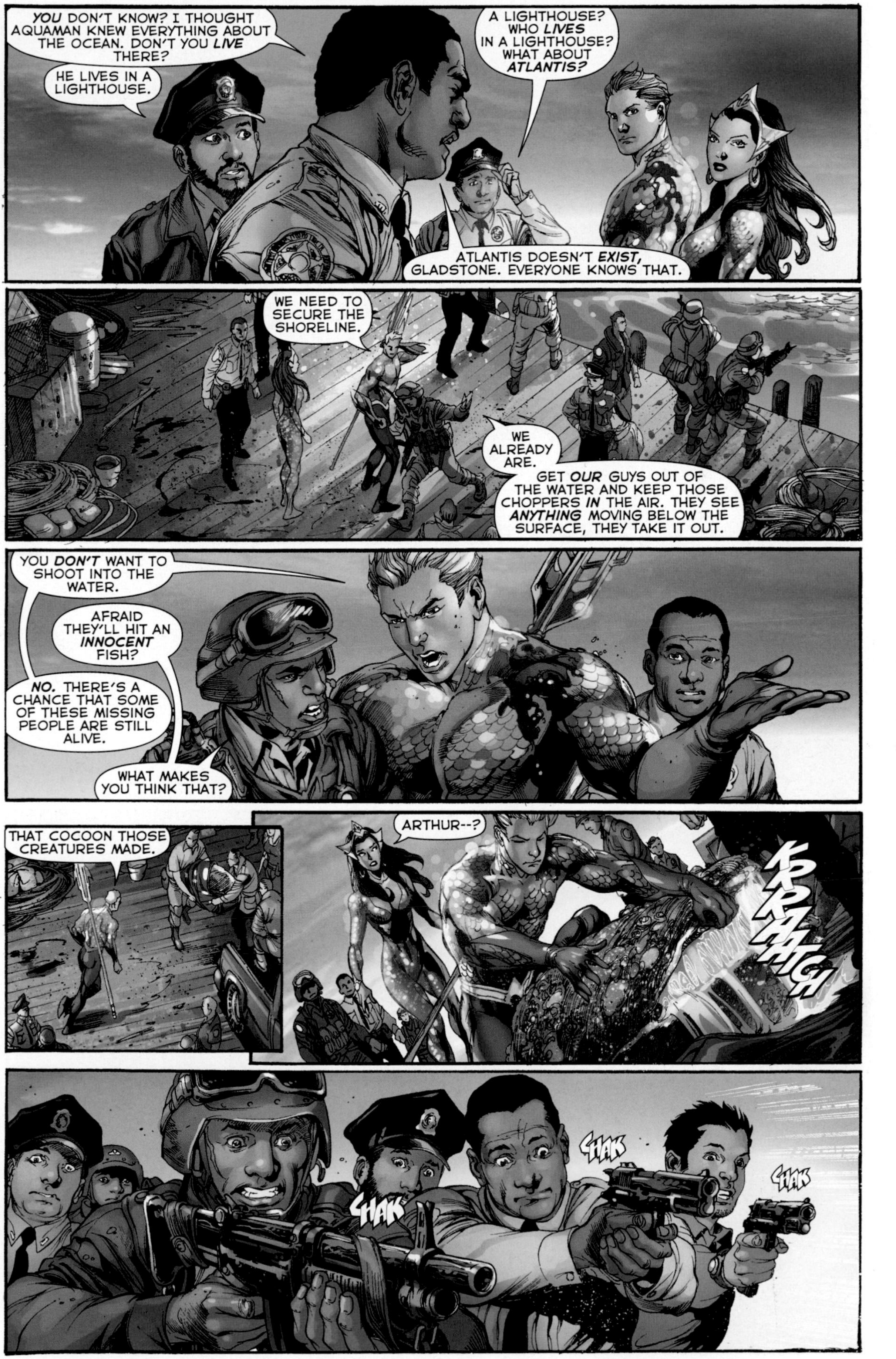

YOU DON'T KNOW? I THOUGHT AQUAMAN KNEW EVERYTHING ABOUT THE OCEAN. DON'T YOU *LIVE* THERE?
HE LIVES IN A LIGHTHOUSE.
A LIGHTHOUSE? WHO *LIVES* IN A LIGHTHOUSE? WHAT ABOUT *ATLANTIS?*
ATLANTIS DOESN'T *EXIST,* GLADSTONE. EVERYONE KNOWS THAT.
WE NEED TO SECURE THE SHORELINE.
WE ALREADY ARE.
GET *OUR* GUYS OUT OF THE WATER AND KEEP THOSE CHOPPERS *IN* THE AIR. THEY SEE *ANYTHING* MOVING BELOW THE SURFACE, THEY TAKE IT OUT.
YOU *DON'T* WANT TO SHOOT INTO THE WATER.
AFRAID THEY'LL HIT AN *INNOCENT* FISH?
NO. THERE'S A CHANCE THAT SOME OF THESE MISSING PEOPLE ARE STILL ALIVE.
WHAT MAKES YOU THINK THAT?
THAT COCOON THOSE CREATURES MADE.
ARTHUR--?
KRRAAATCH
CHAK
CHAK
CHAK

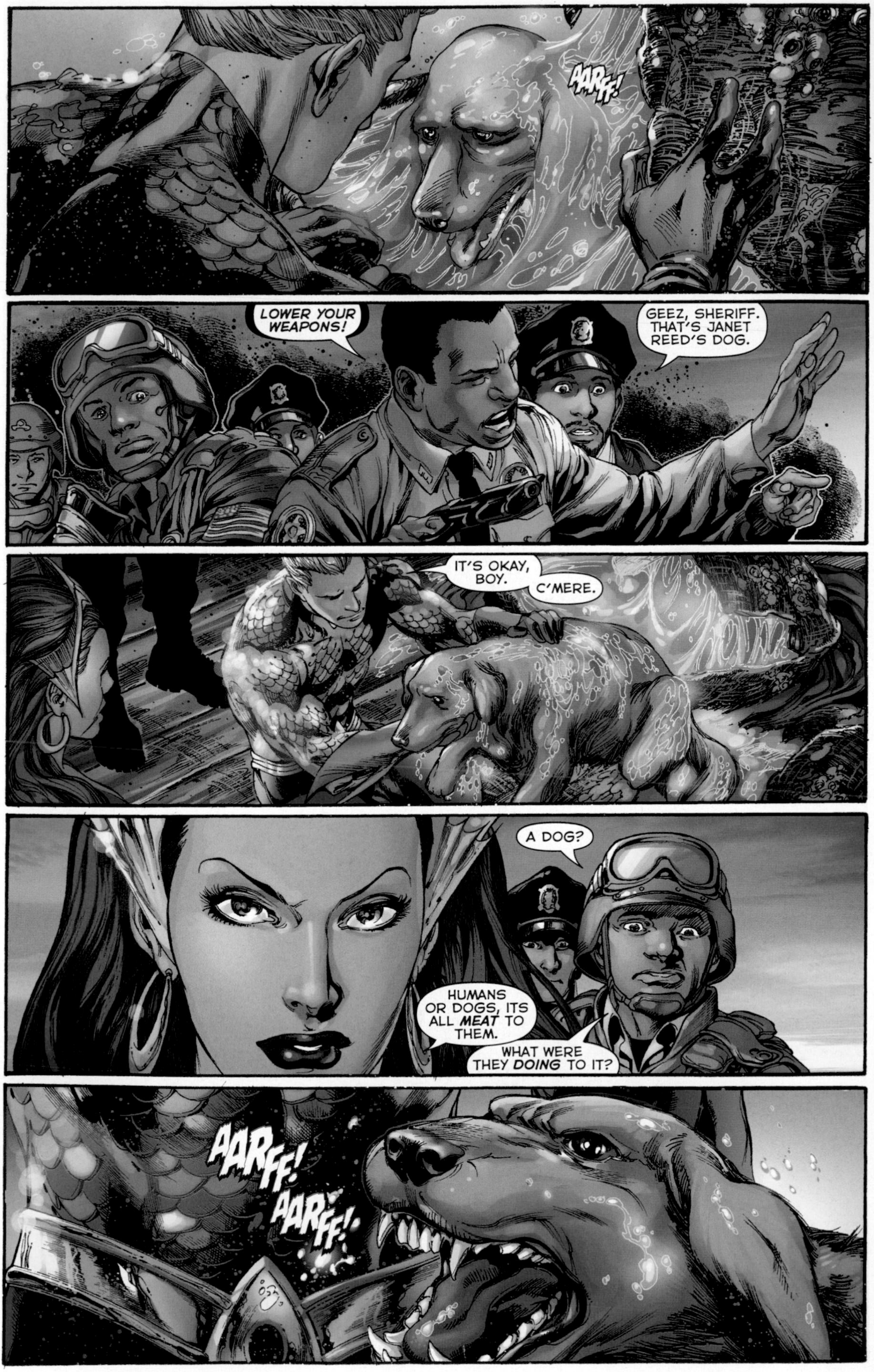
AARFF!
LOWER YOUR WEAPONS!
GEEZ, SHERIFF. THAT'S JANET REED'S DOG.
IT'S OKAY, BOY.
C'MERE.
A DOG?
HUMANS OR DOGS, ITS ALL MEAT TO THEM.
WHAT WERE THEY DOING TO IT?
AARFF!
AARFF!

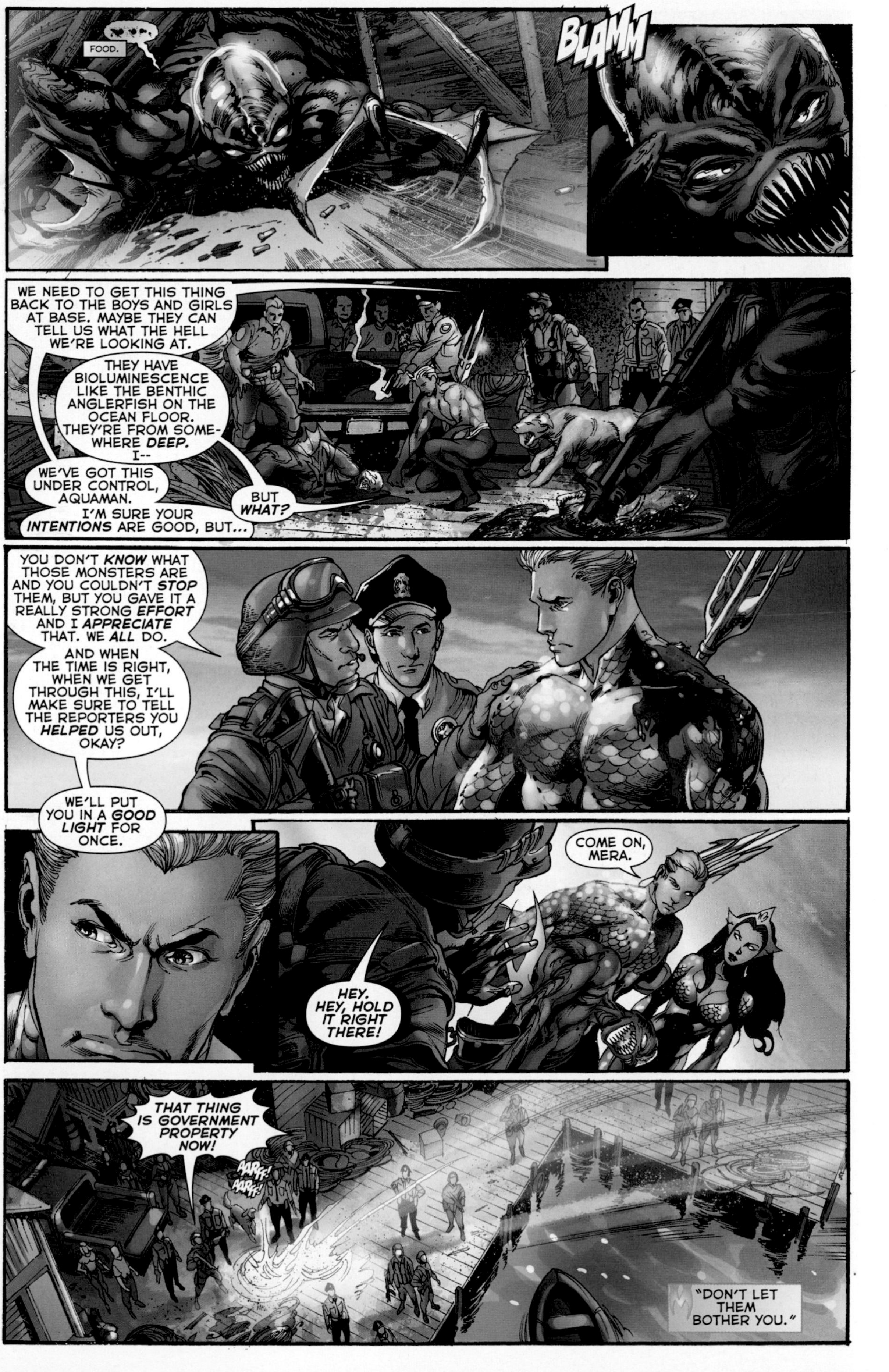
FOOD.
BLAMM
WE NEED TO GET THIS THING BACK TO THE BOYS AND GIRLS AT BASE. MAYBE THEY CAN TELL US WHAT THE HELL WE'RE LOOKING AT.
THEY HAVE BIOLUMINESCENCE LIKE THE BENTHIC ANGLERFISH ON THE OCEAN FLOOR. THEY'RE FROM SOME-WHERE DEEP. I--
WE'VE GOT THIS UNDER CONTROL, AQUAMAN.
I'M SURE YOUR INTENTIONS ARE GOOD, BUT...
BUT WHAT?
YOU DON'T KNOW WHAT THOSE MONSTERS ARE AND YOU COULDN'T STOP THEM, BUT YOU GAVE IT A REALLY STRONG EFFORT AND I APPRECIATE THAT. WE ALL DO.
AND WHEN THE TIME IS RIGHT, WHEN WE GET THROUGH THIS, I'LL MAKE SURE TO TELL THE REPORTERS YOU HELPED US OUT, OKAY?
WE'LL PUT YOU IN A GOOD LIGHT FOR ONCE.
COME ON, MERA.
HEY. HEY, HOLD IT RIGHT THERE!
THAT THING IS GOVERNMENT PROPERTY NOW!
AARFF! AARFF!
"DON'T LET THEM BOTHER YOU."

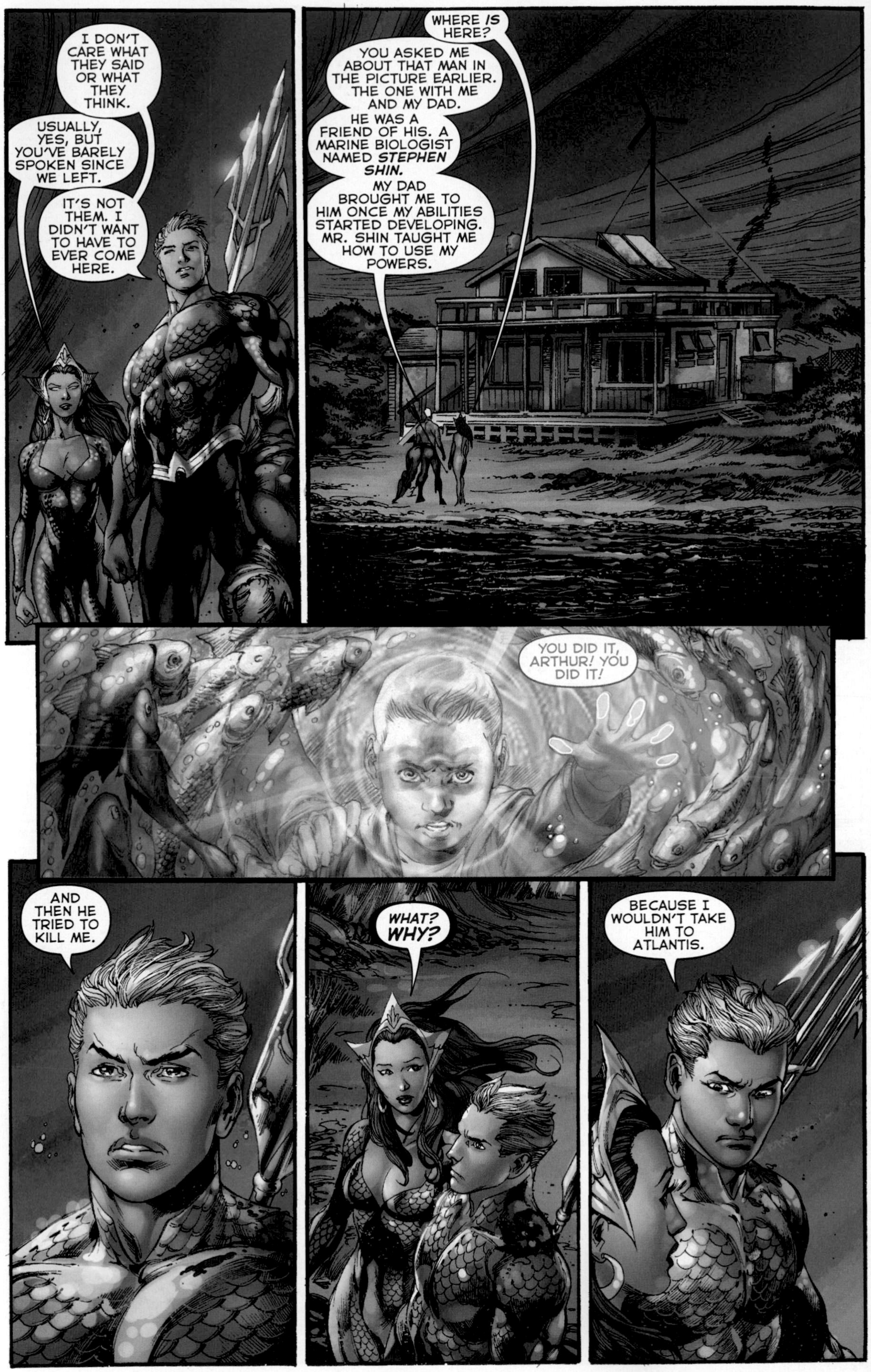

I DON'T CARE WHAT THEY SAID OR WHAT THEY THINK.
USUALLY, YES, BUT YOU'VE BARELY SPOKEN SINCE WE LEFT.
IT'S NOT THEM. I DIDN'T WANT TO HAVE TO EVER COME HERE.
WHERE *IS* HERE?
YOU ASKED ME ABOUT THAT MAN IN THE PICTURE EARLIER. THE ONE WITH ME AND MY DAD.
HE WAS A FRIEND OF HIS. A MARINE BIOLOGIST NAMED ***STEPHEN SHIN.***
MY DAD BROUGHT ME TO HIM ONCE MY ABILITIES STARTED DEVELOPING. MR. SHIN TAUGHT ME HOW TO USE MY POWERS.
YOU DID IT, ARTHUR*!* YOU DID IT*!*
AND THEN HE TRIED TO KILL ME.
WHAT? ***WHY?***
BECAUSE I WOULDN'T TAKE HIM TO ATLANTIS.

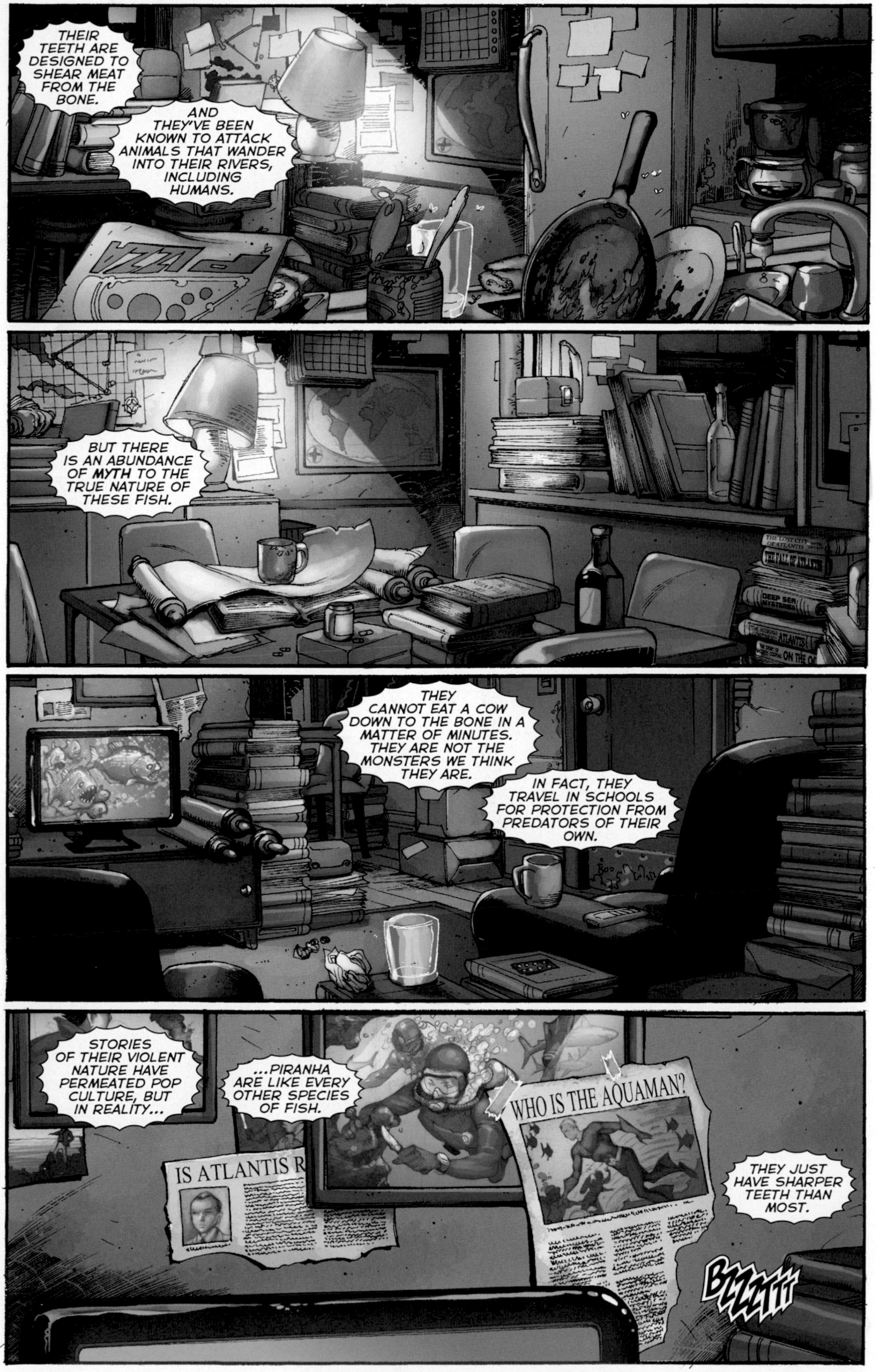
THEIR TEETH ARE DESIGNED TO SHEAR MEAT FROM THE BONE.
AND THEY'VE BEEN KNOWN TO ATTACK ANIMALS THAT WANDER INTO THEIR RIVERS, INCLUDING HUMANS.
BUT THERE IS AN ABUNDANCE OF **MYTH** TO THE TRUE NATURE OF THESE FISH.
THE FALL OF ATLANTIS
DEEP SEA MYSTERIES
THEY CANNOT EAT A COW DOWN TO THE BONE IN A MATTER OF MINUTES. THEY ARE NOT THE MONSTERS WE THINK THEY ARE.
IN FACT, THEY TRAVEL IN SCHOOLS FOR PROTECTION FROM PREDATORS OF THEIR OWN.
STORIES OF THEIR VIOLENT NATURE HAVE PERMEATED POP CULTURE, BUT IN REALITY...
...PIRANHA ARE LIKE EVERY OTHER SPECIES OF FISH.
IS ATLANTIS R
WHO IS THE AQUAMAN?
THEY JUST HAVE SHARPER TEETH THAN MOST.
BZZZTTT

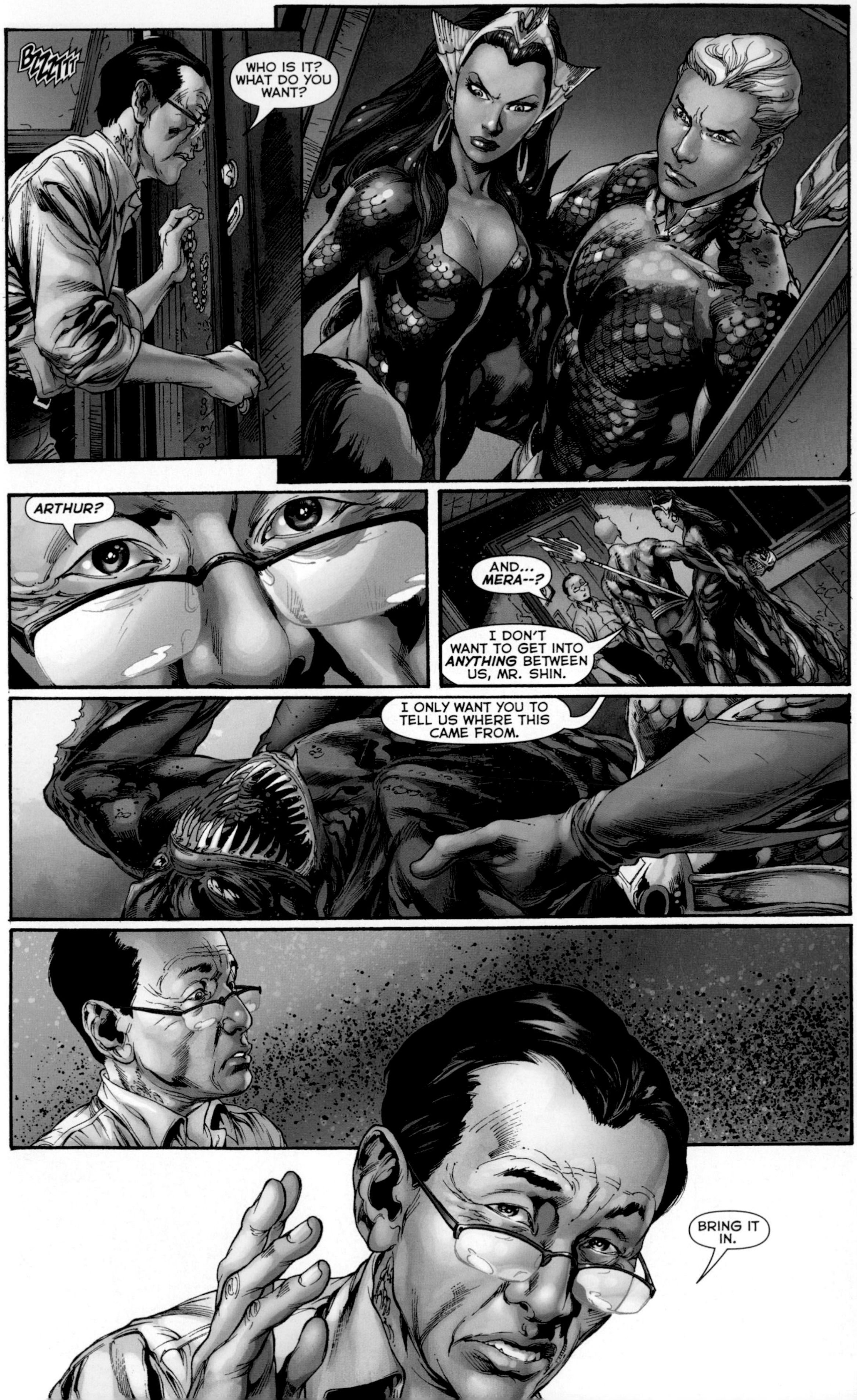
BZZZTTT
WHO IS IT? WHAT DO YOU WANT?
ARTHUR?
AND... MERA--?
I DON'T WANT TO GET INTO ANYTHING BETWEEN US, MR. SHIN.
I ONLY WANT YOU TO TELL US WHERE THIS CAME FROM.
BRING IT IN.

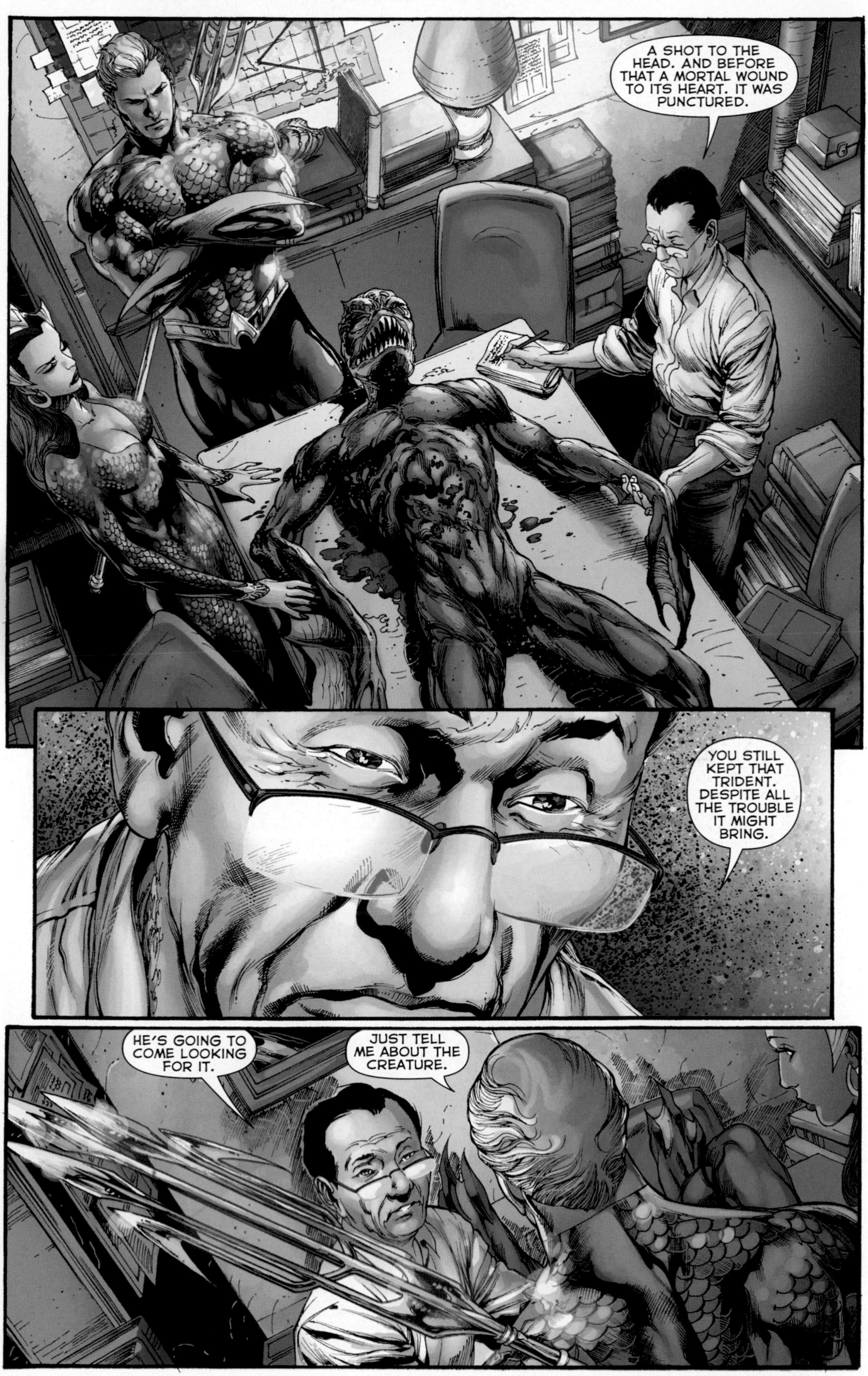
A SHOT TO THE HEAD. AND BEFORE THAT A MORTAL WOUND TO ITS HEART. IT WAS PUNCTURED.
YOU STILL KEPT THAT TRIDENT. DESPITE ALL THE TROUBLE IT MIGHT BRING.
HE'S GOING TO COME LOOKING FOR IT.
JUST TELL ME ABOUT THE CREATURE.

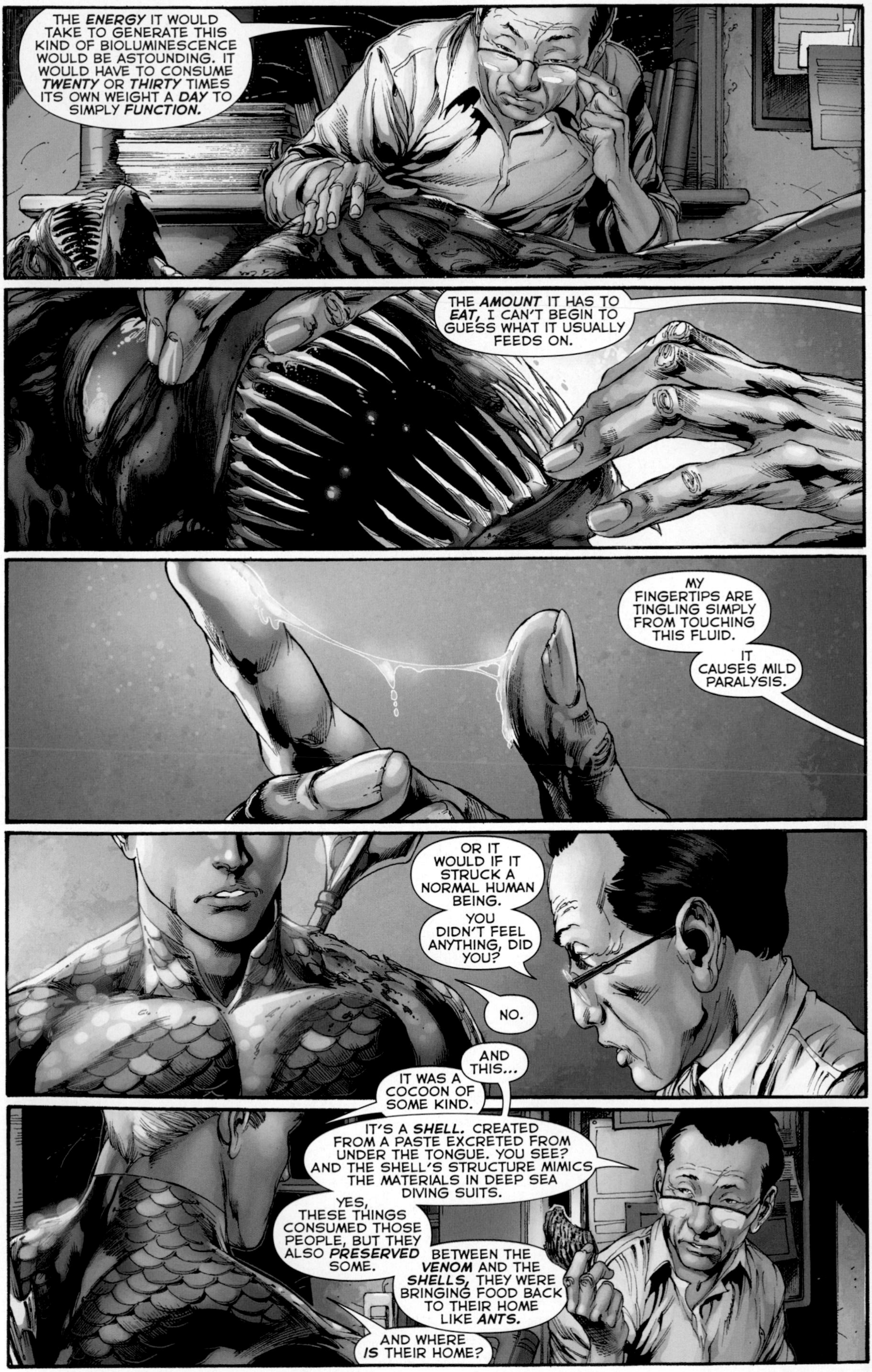
THE *ENERGY* IT WOULD TAKE TO GENERATE THIS KIND OF BIOLUMINESCENCE WOULD BE ASTOUNDING. IT WOULD HAVE TO CONSUME *TWENTY* OR *THIRTY* TIMES ITS OWN WEIGHT A *DAY* TO SIMPLY *FUNCTION.*
THE *AMOUNT* IT HAS TO *EAT,* I CAN'T BEGIN TO GUESS WHAT IT USUALLY FEEDS ON.
MY FINGERTIPS ARE TINGLING SIMPLY FROM TOUCHING THIS FLUID.
IT CAUSES MILD PARALYSIS.
OR IT WOULD IF IT STRUCK A NORMAL HUMAN BEING.
YOU DIDN'T FEEL ANYTHING, DID YOU?
NO.
AND THIS...
IT WAS A COCOON OF SOME KIND.
IT'S A *SHELL.* CREATED FROM A PASTE EXCRETED FROM UNDER THE TONGUE. YOU SEE? AND THE SHELL'S STRUCTURE MIMICS THE MATERIALS IN DEEP SEA DIVING SUITS.
YES, THESE THINGS CONSUMED THOSE PEOPLE, BUT THEY ALSO *PRESERVED* SOME.
BETWEEN THE *VENOM* AND THE *SHELLS,* THEY WERE BRINGING FOOD BACK TO THEIR HOME LIKE *ANTS.*
AND WHERE *IS* THEIR HOME?

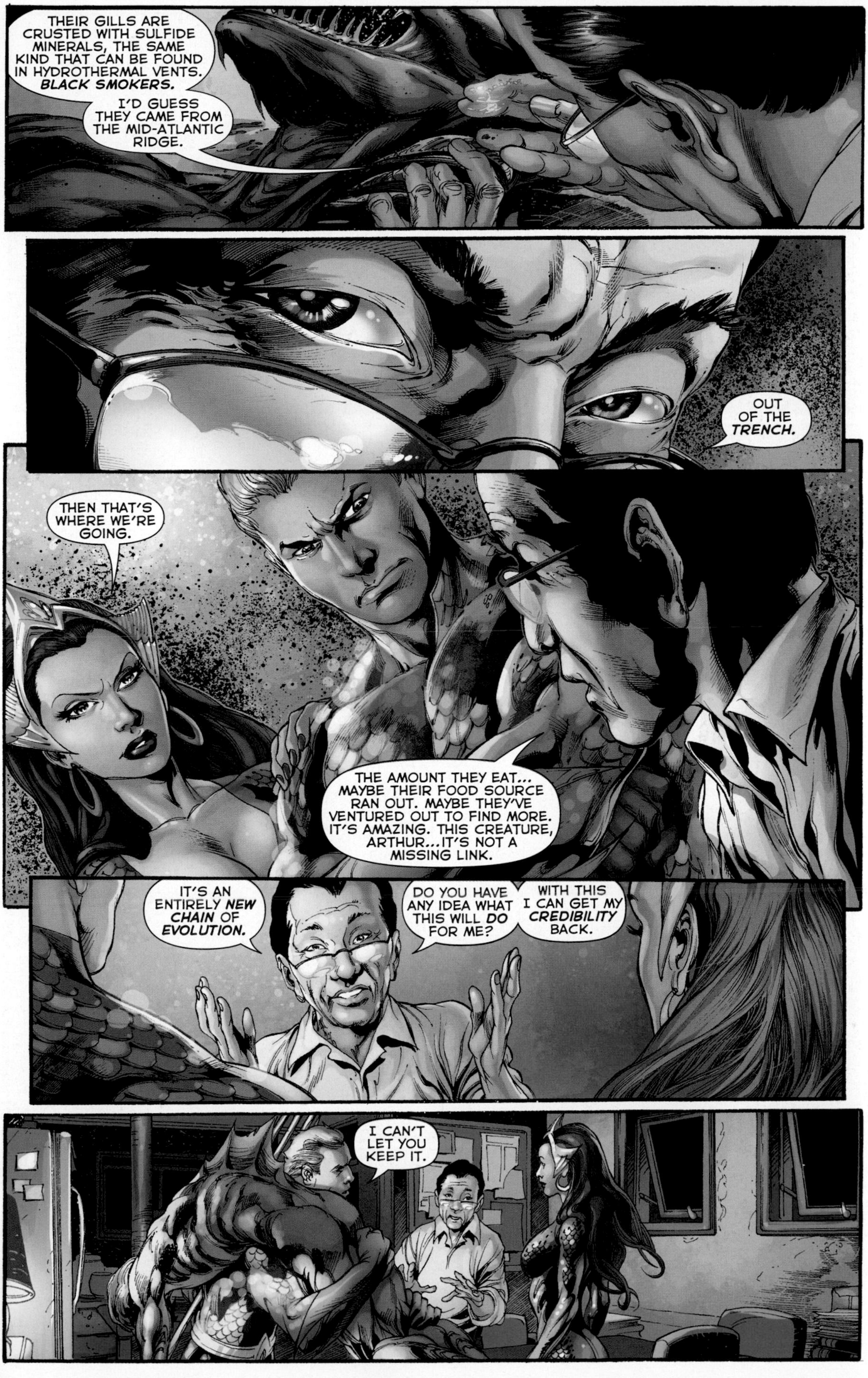
THEIR GILLS ARE CRUSTED WITH SULFIDE MINERALS, THE SAME KIND THAT CAN BE FOUND IN HYDROTHERMAL VENTS. ***BLACK SMOKERS.***
I'D GUESS THEY CAME FROM THE MID-ATLANTIC RIDGE.
OUT OF THE ***TRENCH.***
THEN THAT'S WHERE WE'RE GOING.
THE AMOUNT THEY EAT... MAYBE THEIR FOOD SOURCE RAN OUT. MAYBE THEY'VE VENTURED OUT TO FIND MORE. IT'S AMAZING. THIS CREATURE, ARTHUR...IT'S NOT A MISSING LINK.
IT'S AN ENTIRELY ***NEW CHAIN*** OF ***EVOLUTION.***
DO YOU HAVE ANY IDEA WHAT THIS WILL ***DO*** FOR ME?
WITH THIS I CAN GET MY ***CREDIBILITY*** BACK.
I CAN'T LET YOU KEEP IT.

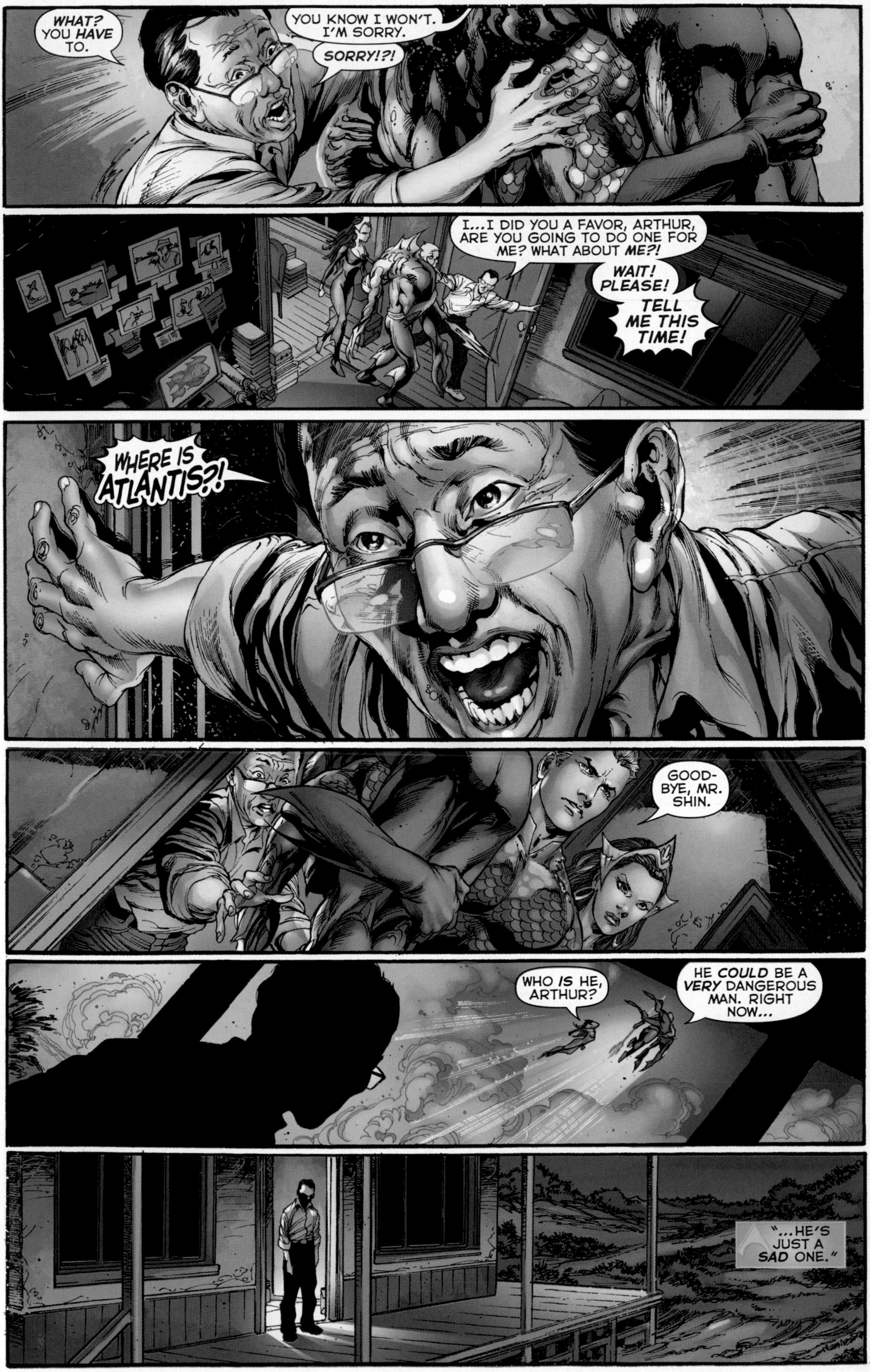
WHAT? YOU HAVE TO.
YOU KNOW I WON'T. I'M SORRY.
SORRY!?!
I...I DID YOU A FAVOR, ARTHUR, ARE YOU GOING TO DO ONE FOR ME? WHAT ABOUT ME?!
WAIT! PLEASE!
TELL ME THIS TIME!
WHERE IS ATLANTIS?!
GOOD-BYE, MR. SHIN.
WHO IS HE, ARTHUR?
HE COULD BE A VERY DANGEROUS MAN. RIGHT NOW...
"...HE'S JUST A SAD ONE."

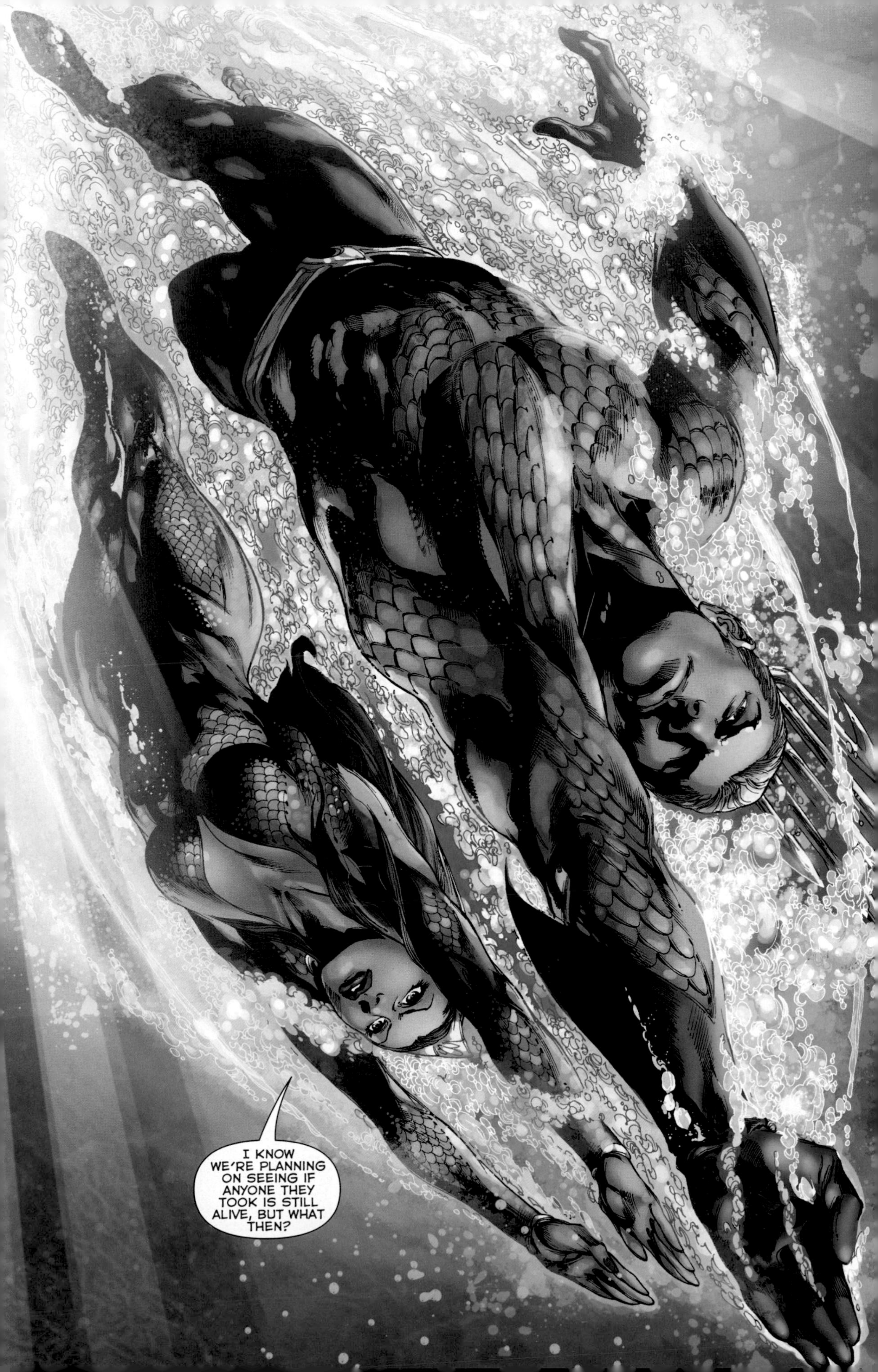
I KNOW WE'RE PLANNING ON SEEING IF ANYONE THEY TOOK IS STILL ALIVE, BUT WHAT THEN?

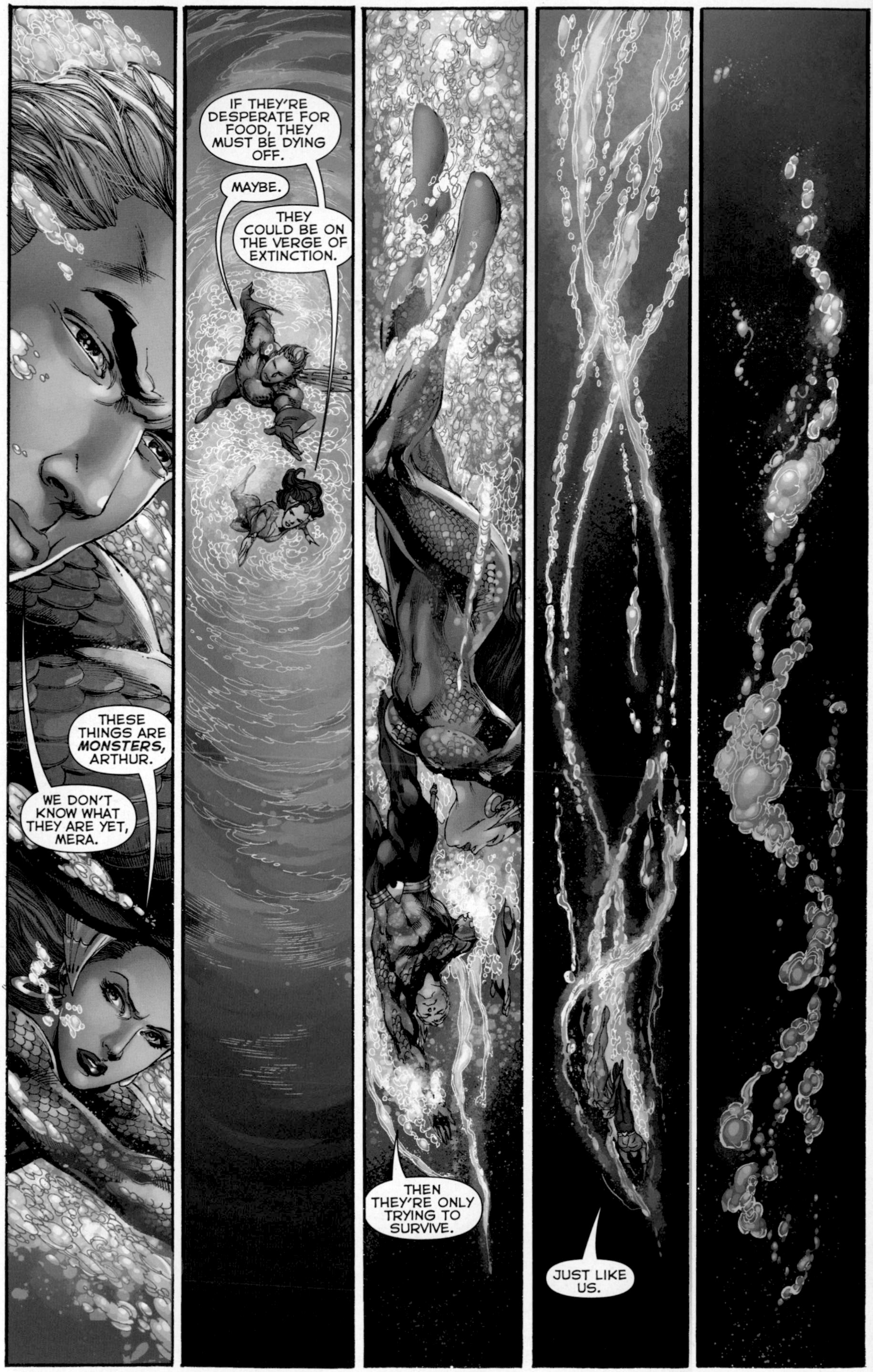
THESE THINGS ARE *MONSTERS*, ARTHUR.
WE DON'T KNOW WHAT THEY ARE YET, MERA.
IF THEY'RE DESPERATE FOR FOOD, THEY MUST BE DYING OFF.
MAYBE.
THEY COULD BE ON THE VERGE OF EXTINCTION.
THEN THEY'RE ONLY TRYING TO SURVIVE.
JUST LIKE US.

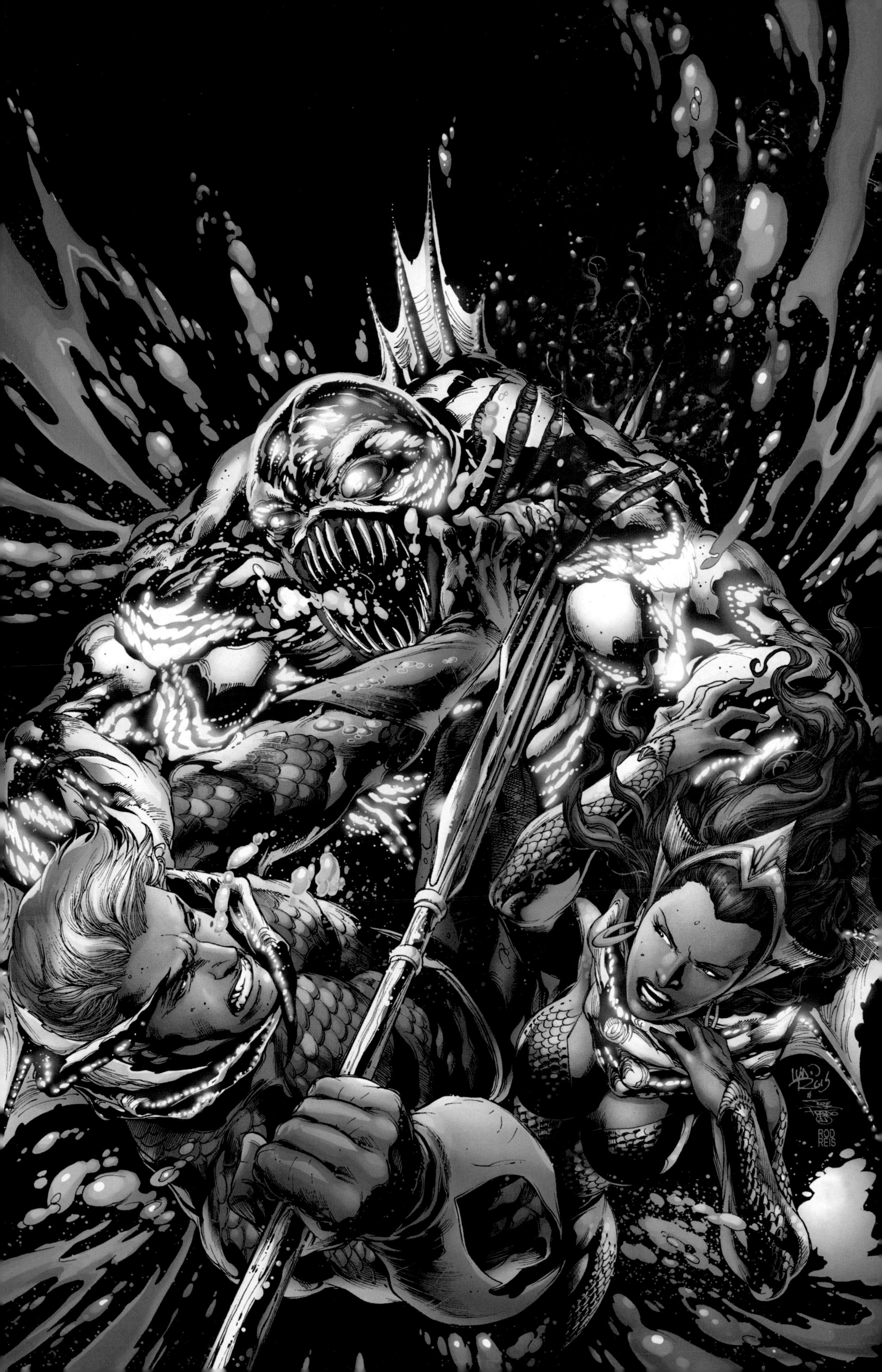
ROD REIS

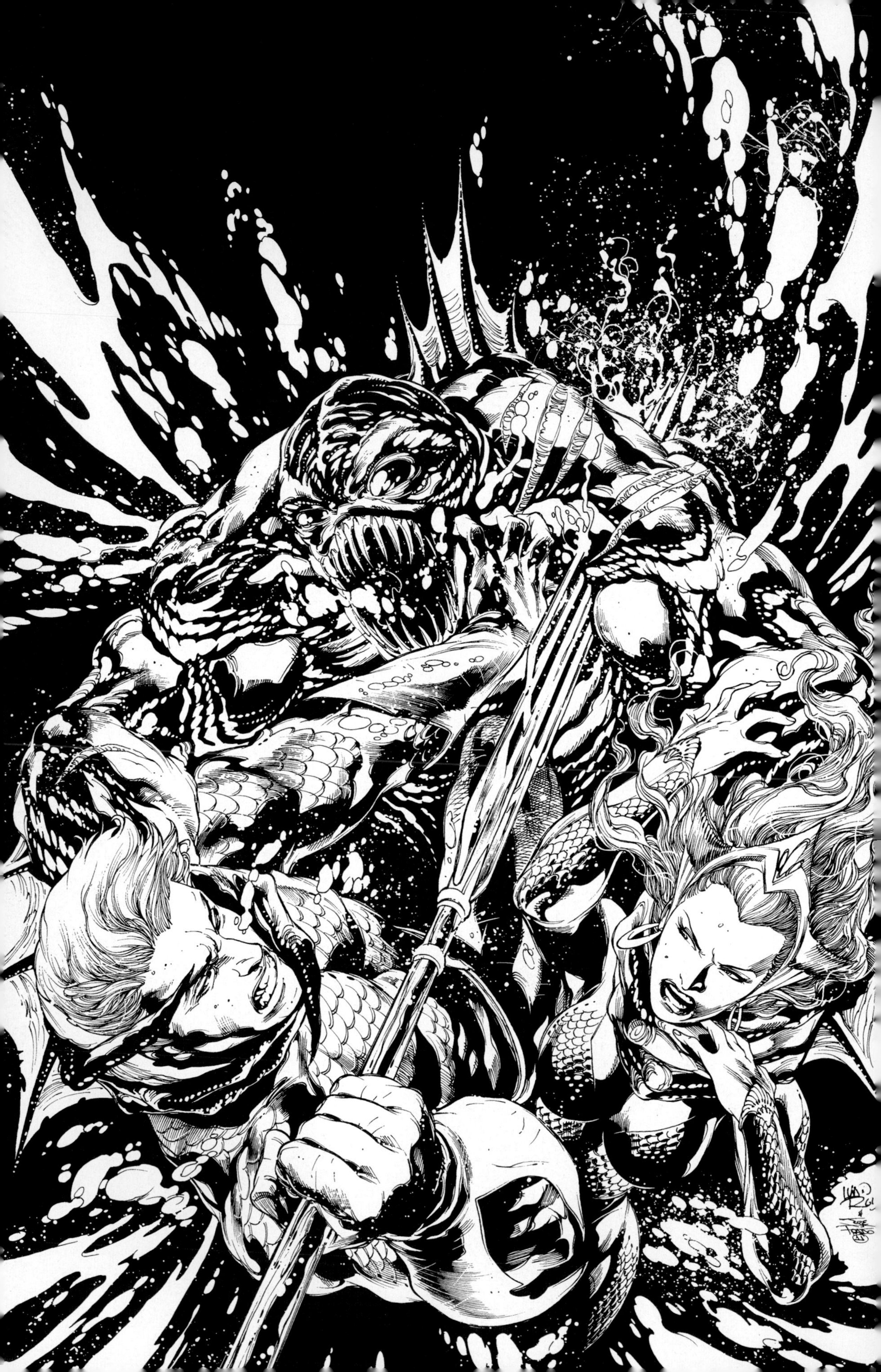

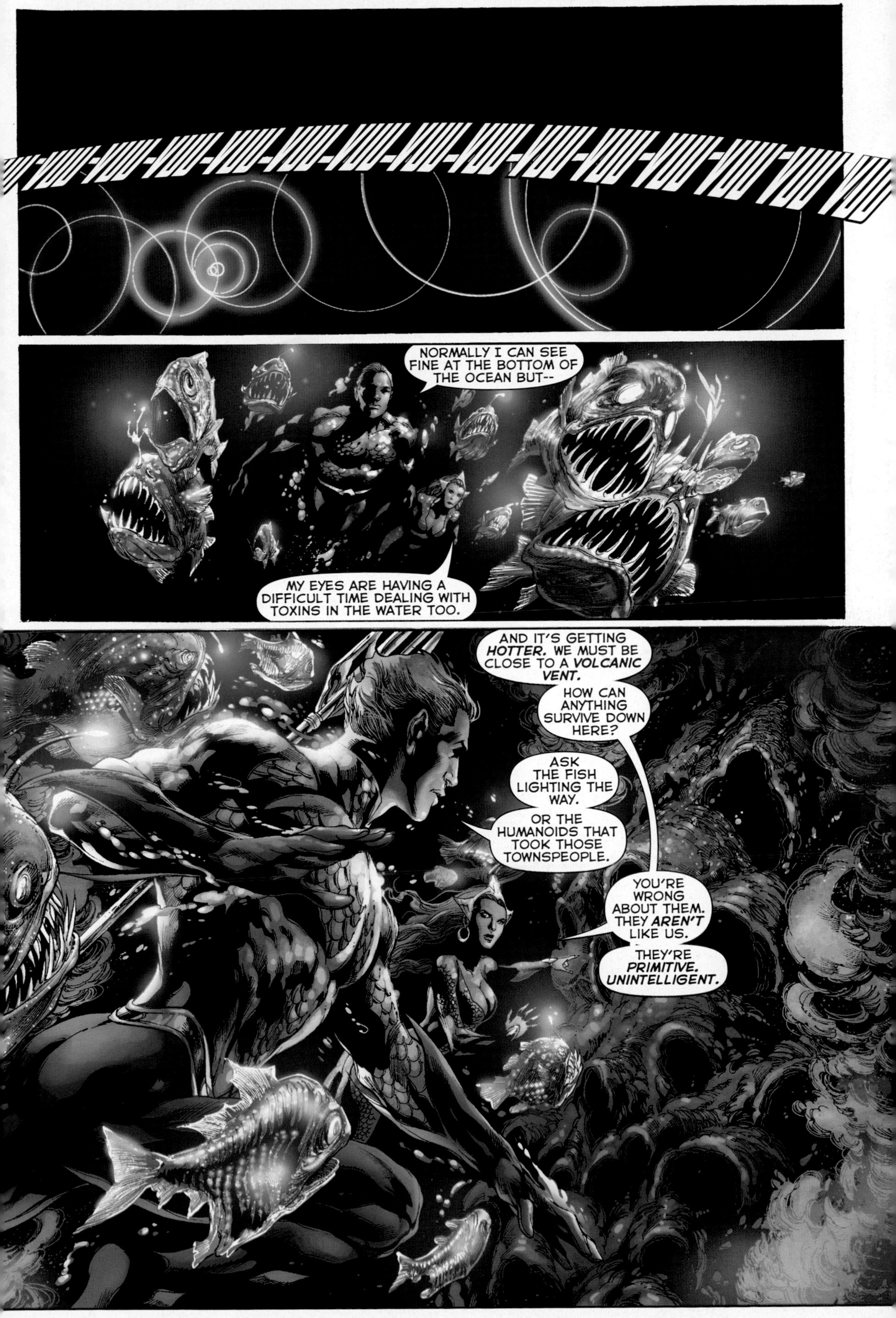

VOO-VOO-VOO-VOO-VOO-VOO-VOO-VOO-VOO-VOO-VOO-VOO-VOO-VOO-VOO-VOO-VOO-VOO-VOO-VOO
NORMALLY I CAN SEE FINE AT THE BOTTOM OF THE OCEAN BUT--
MY EYES ARE HAVING A DIFFICULT TIME DEALING WITH TOXINS IN THE WATER TOO.
AND IT'S GETTING *HOTTER.* WE MUST BE CLOSE TO A *VOLCANIC VENT.*
HOW CAN ANYTHING SURVIVE DOWN HERE?
ASK THE FISH LIGHTING THE WAY.
OR THE HUMANOIDS THAT TOOK THOSE TOWNSPEOPLE.
YOU'RE WRONG ABOUT THEM. THEY *AREN'T* LIKE US.
THEY'RE *PRIMITIVE. UNINTELLIGENT.*

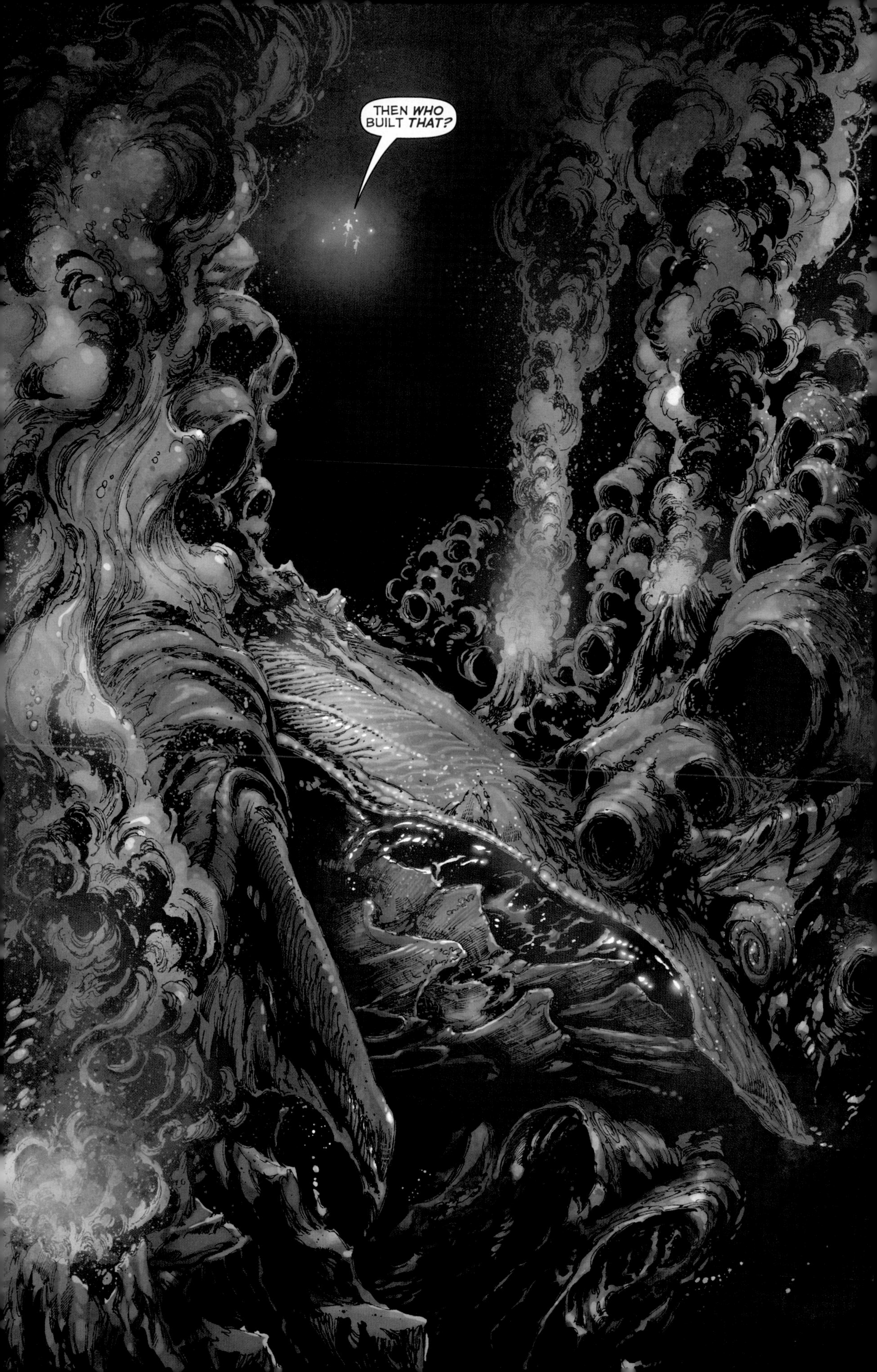
THEN *WHO* BUILT *THAT?*

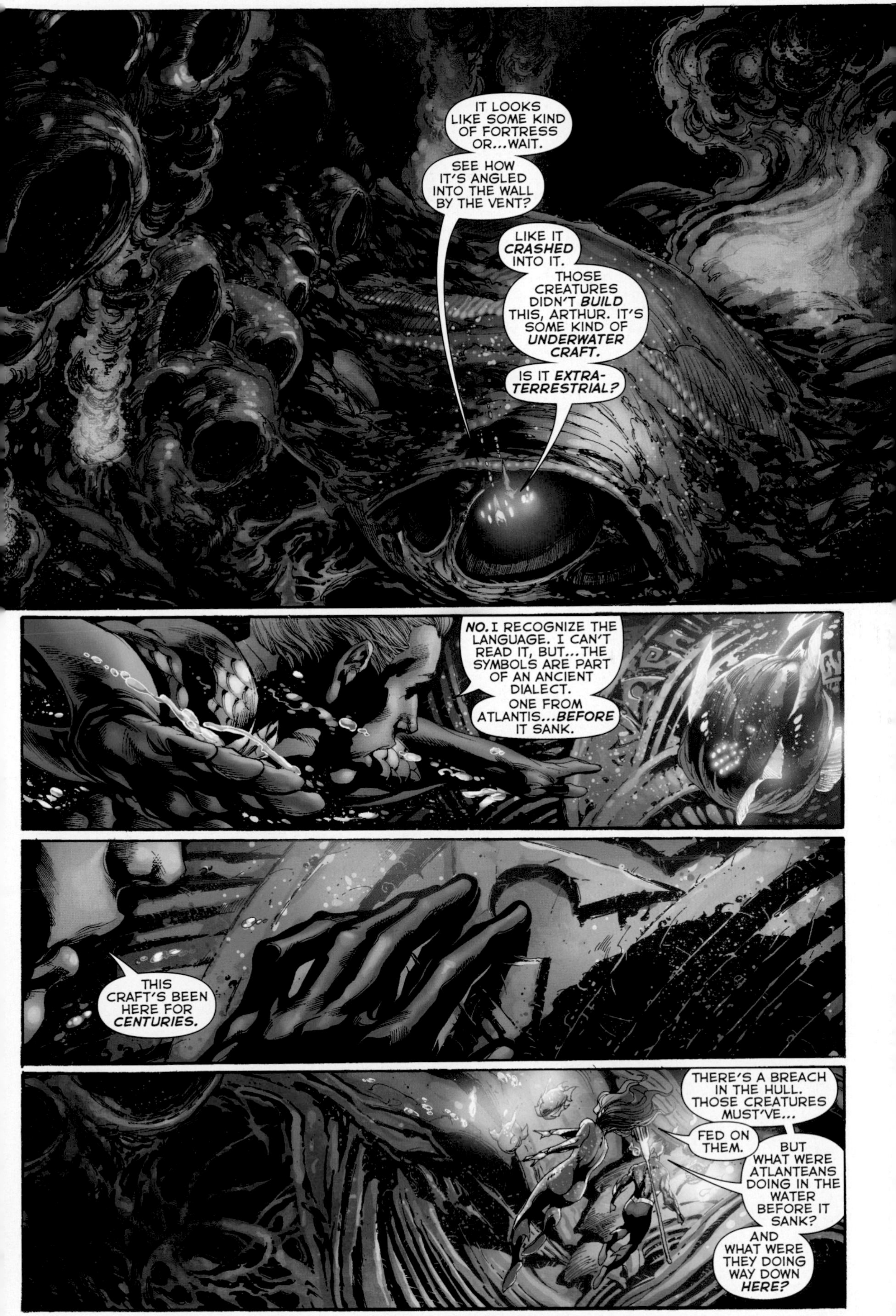
IT LOOKS LIKE SOME KIND OF FORTRESS OR...WAIT.
SEE HOW IT'S ANGLED INTO THE WALL BY THE VENT?
LIKE IT CRASHED INTO IT.
THOSE CREATURES DIDN'T BUILD THIS, ARTHUR. IT'S SOME KIND OF UNDERWATER CRAFT.
IS IT EXTRA-TERRESTRIAL?
NO. I RECOGNIZE THE LANGUAGE. I CAN'T READ IT, BUT...THE SYMBOLS ARE PART OF AN ANCIENT DIALECT.
ONE FROM ATLANTIS...BEFORE IT SANK.
THIS CRAFT'S BEEN HERE FOR CENTURIES.
THERE'S A BREACH IN THE HULL. THOSE CREATURES MUST'VE...
FED ON THEM.
BUT WHAT WERE ATLANTEANS DOING IN THE WATER BEFORE IT SANK?
AND WHAT WERE THEY DOING WAY DOWN HERE?

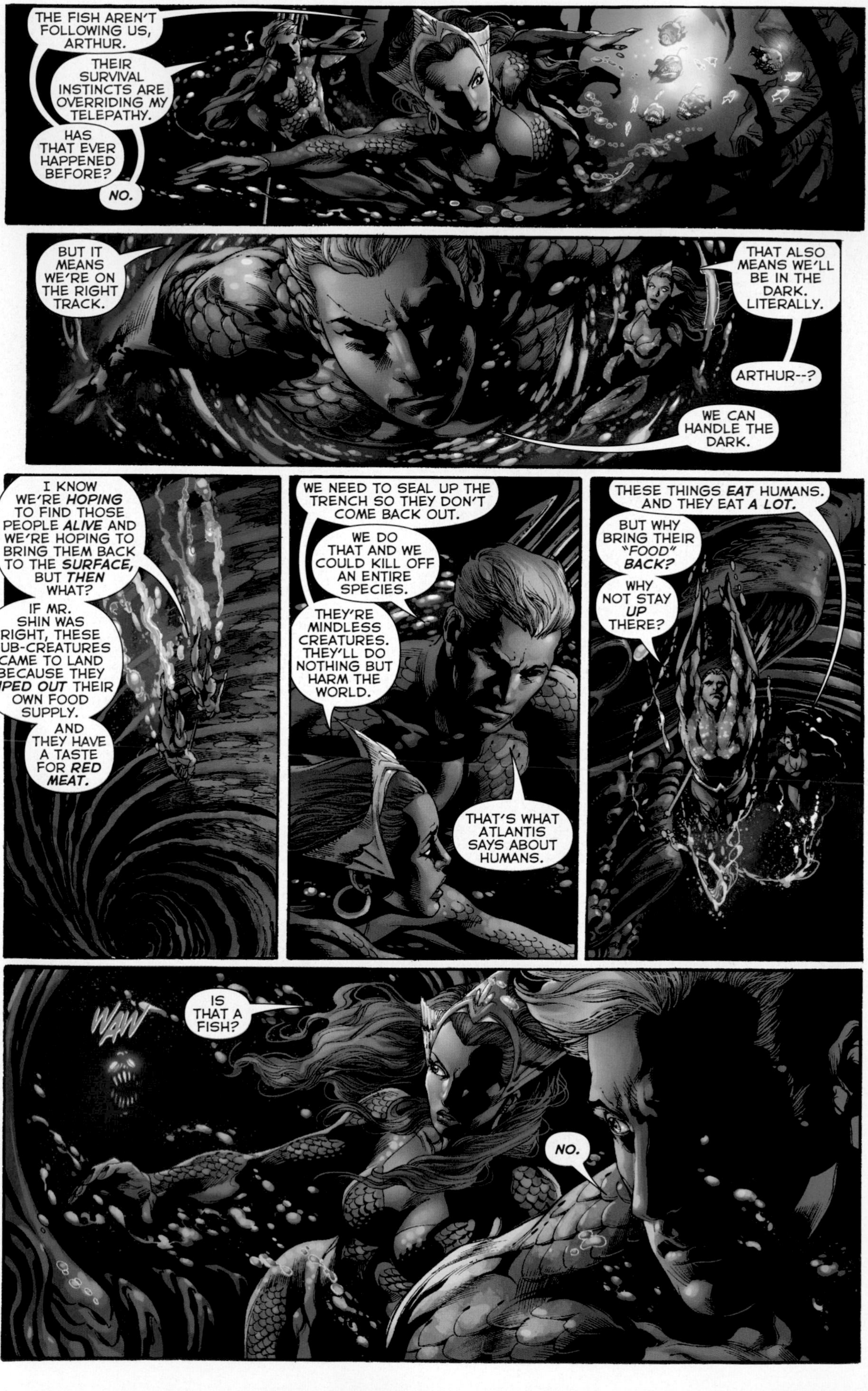
THE FISH AREN'T FOLLOWING US, ARTHUR.
THEIR SURVIVAL INSTINCTS ARE OVERRIDING MY TELEPATHY.
HAS THAT EVER HAPPENED BEFORE?
NO.
BUT IT MEANS WE'RE ON THE RIGHT TRACK.
THAT ALSO MEANS WE'LL BE IN THE DARK. LITERALLY.
ARTHUR--?
WE CAN HANDLE THE DARK.
I KNOW WE'RE HOPING TO FIND THOSE PEOPLE ALIVE AND WE'RE HOPING TO BRING THEM BACK TO THE SURFACE, BUT THEN WHAT?
IF MR. SHIN WAS RIGHT, THESE SUB-CREATURES CAME TO LAND BECAUSE THEY WIPED OUT THEIR OWN FOOD SUPPLY.
AND THEY HAVE A TASTE FOR RED MEAT.
WE NEED TO SEAL UP THE TRENCH SO THEY DON'T COME BACK OUT.
WE DO THAT AND WE COULD KILL OFF AN ENTIRE SPECIES.
THEY'RE MINDLESS CREATURES. THEY'LL DO NOTHING BUT HARM THE WORLD.
THAT'S WHAT ATLANTIS SAYS ABOUT HUMANS.
THESE THINGS EAT HUMANS. AND THEY EAT A LOT.
BUT WHY BRING THEIR "FOOD" BACK?
WHY NOT STAY UP THERE?
WAW
IS THAT A FISH?
NO.

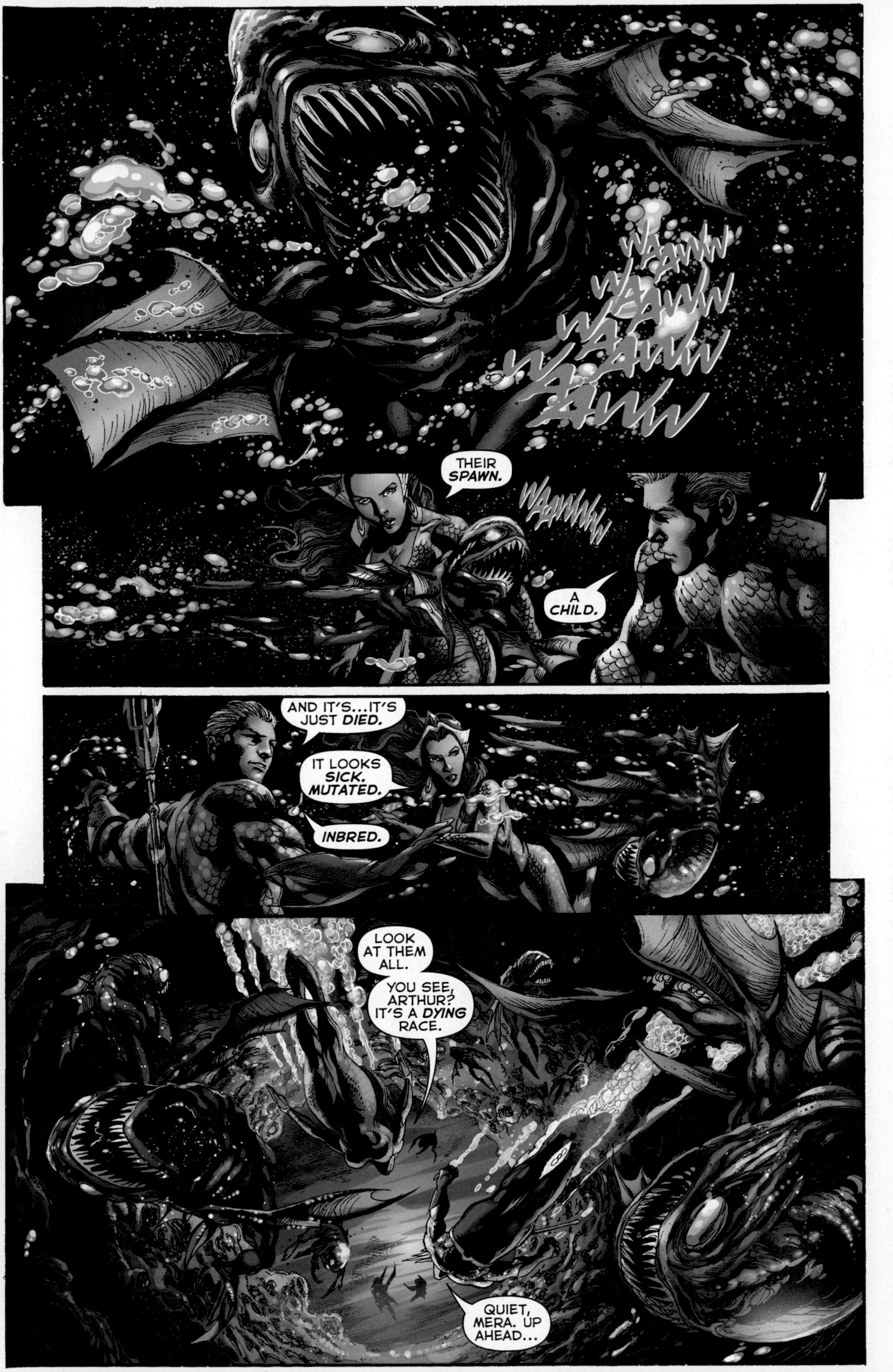
WAAWW WAAWW WAAWW WAAWW AWW
THEIR SPAWN.
WAAWWW
A CHILD.
AND IT'S...IT'S JUST DIED.
IT LOOKS SICK. MUTATED.
INBRED.
LOOK AT THEM ALL.
YOU SEE, ARTHUR? IT'S A DYING RACE.
QUIET, MERA. UP AHEAD...

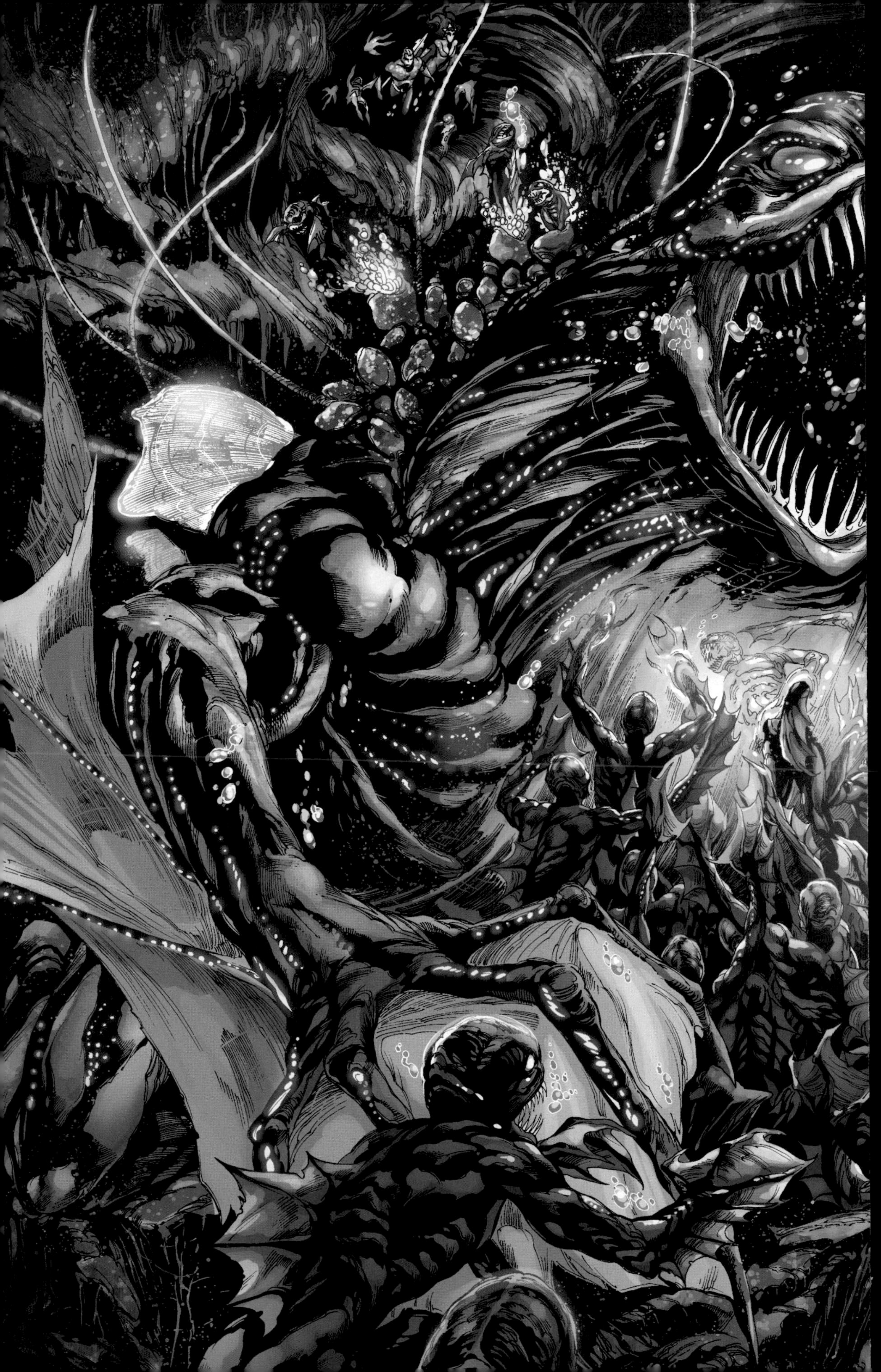

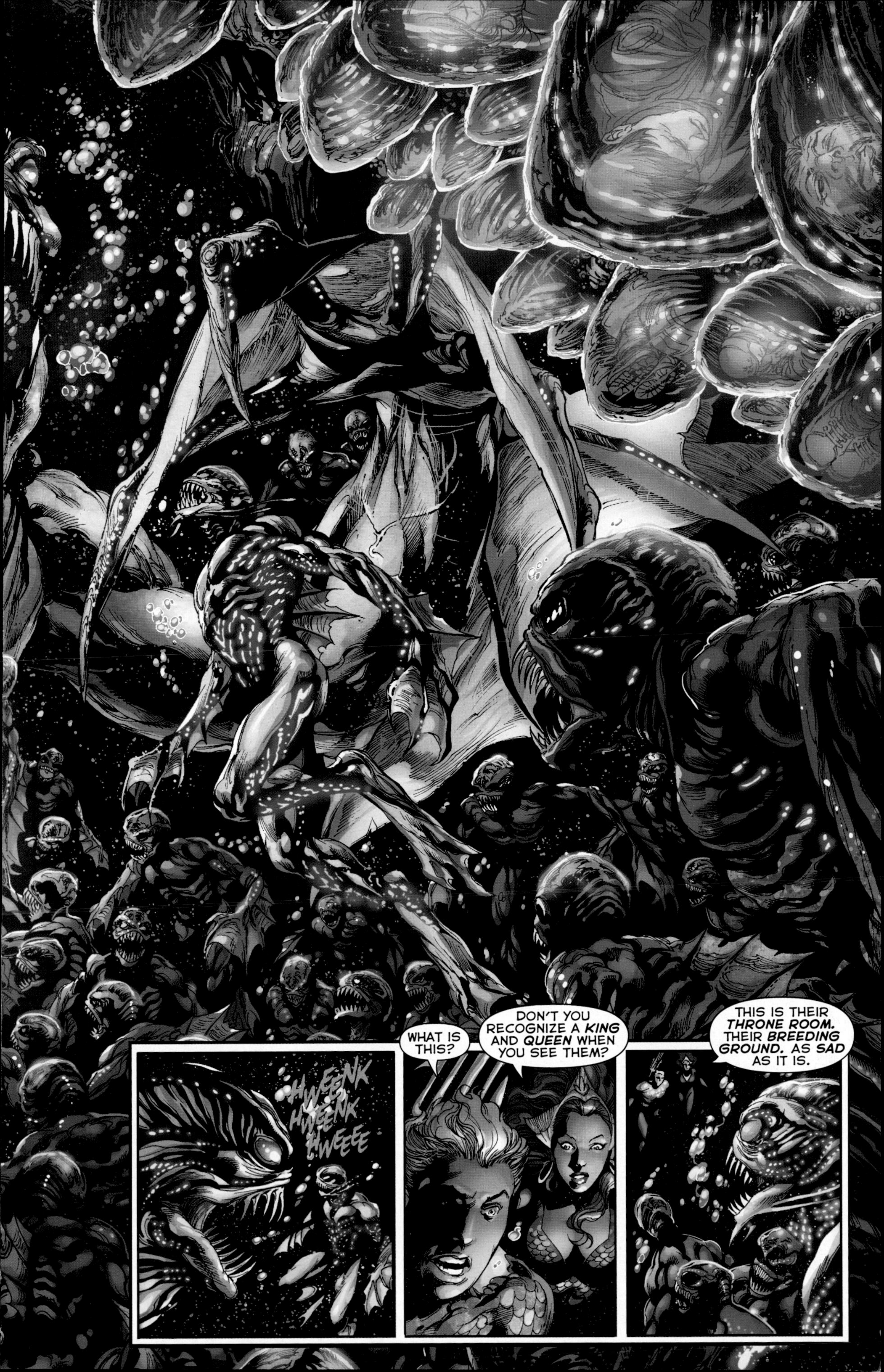
HWEENK
HWEENK
HWEEE
WHAT IS THIS?
DON'T YOU RECOGNIZE A KING AND QUEEN WHEN YOU SEE THEM?
THIS IS THEIR THRONE ROOM. THEIR BREEDING GROUND. AS SAD AS IT IS.

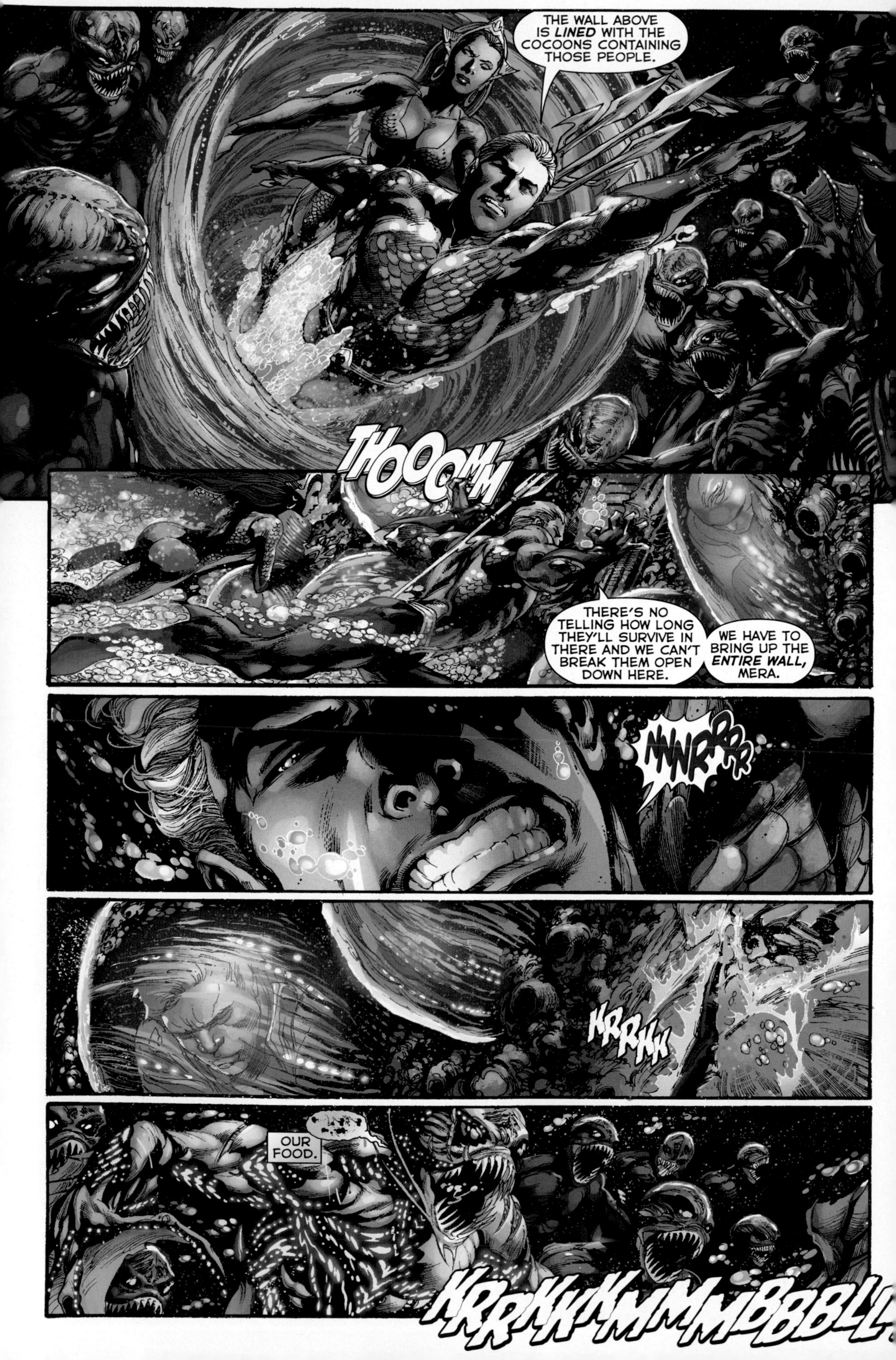
THE WALL ABOVE IS *LINED* WITH THE COCOONS CONTAINING THOSE PEOPLE.
THOOOMM
THERE'S NO TELLING HOW LONG THEY'LL SURVIVE IN THERE AND WE CAN'T BREAK THEM OPEN DOWN HERE.
WE HAVE TO BRING UP THE *ENTIRE WALL,* MERA.
NNNRRRR
KRRKK
OUR FOOD.
KRRKKMMMBBBLL

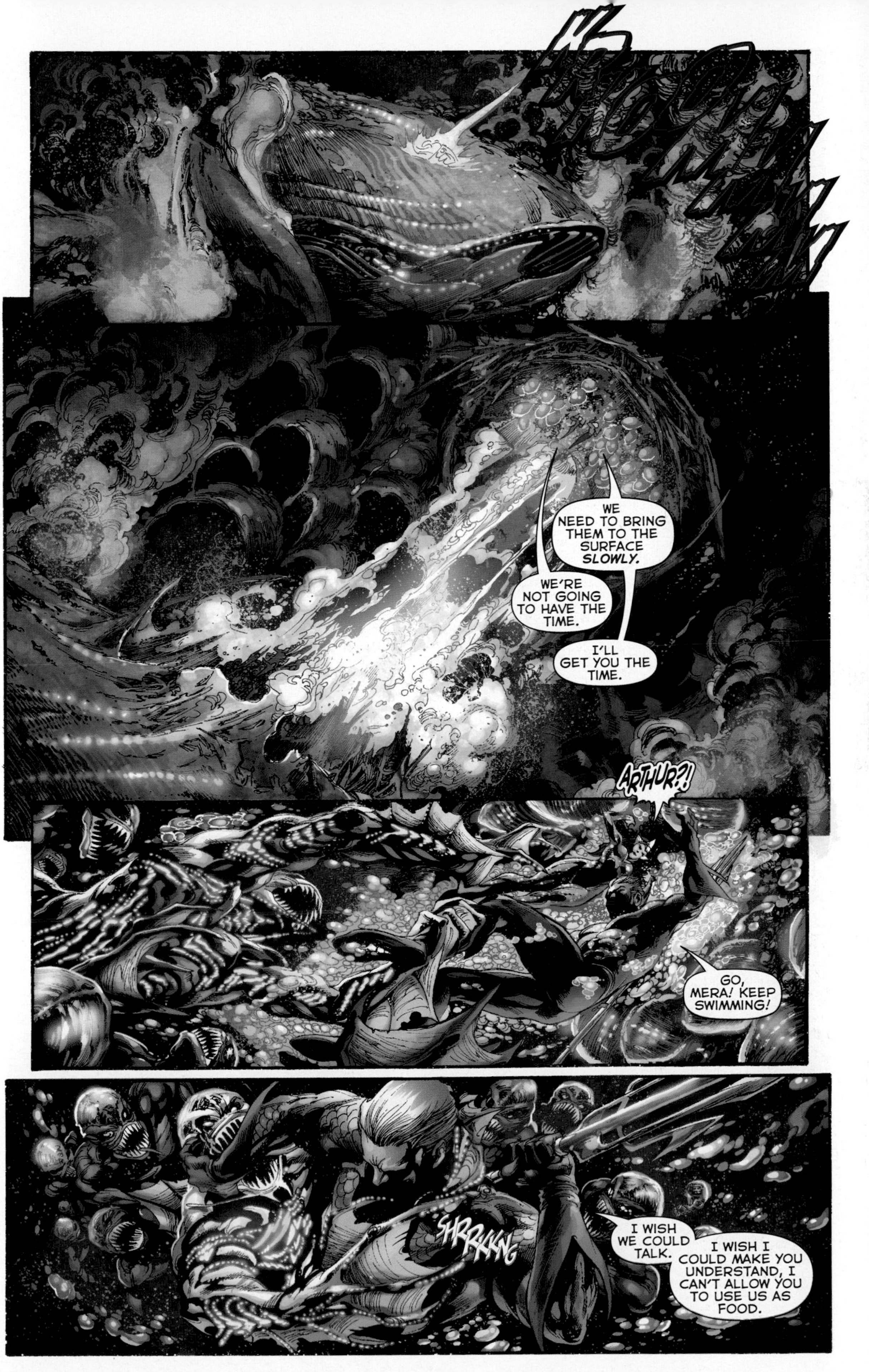
WE NEED TO BRING THEM TO THE SURFACE SLOWLY.
WE'RE NOT GOING TO HAVE THE TIME.
I'LL GET YOU THE TIME.
ARTHUR?!
GO, MERA! KEEP SWIMMING!
SHRAKKNG
I WISH WE COULD TALK.
I WISH I COULD MAKE YOU UNDERSTAND, I CAN'T ALLOW YOU TO USE US AS FOOD.

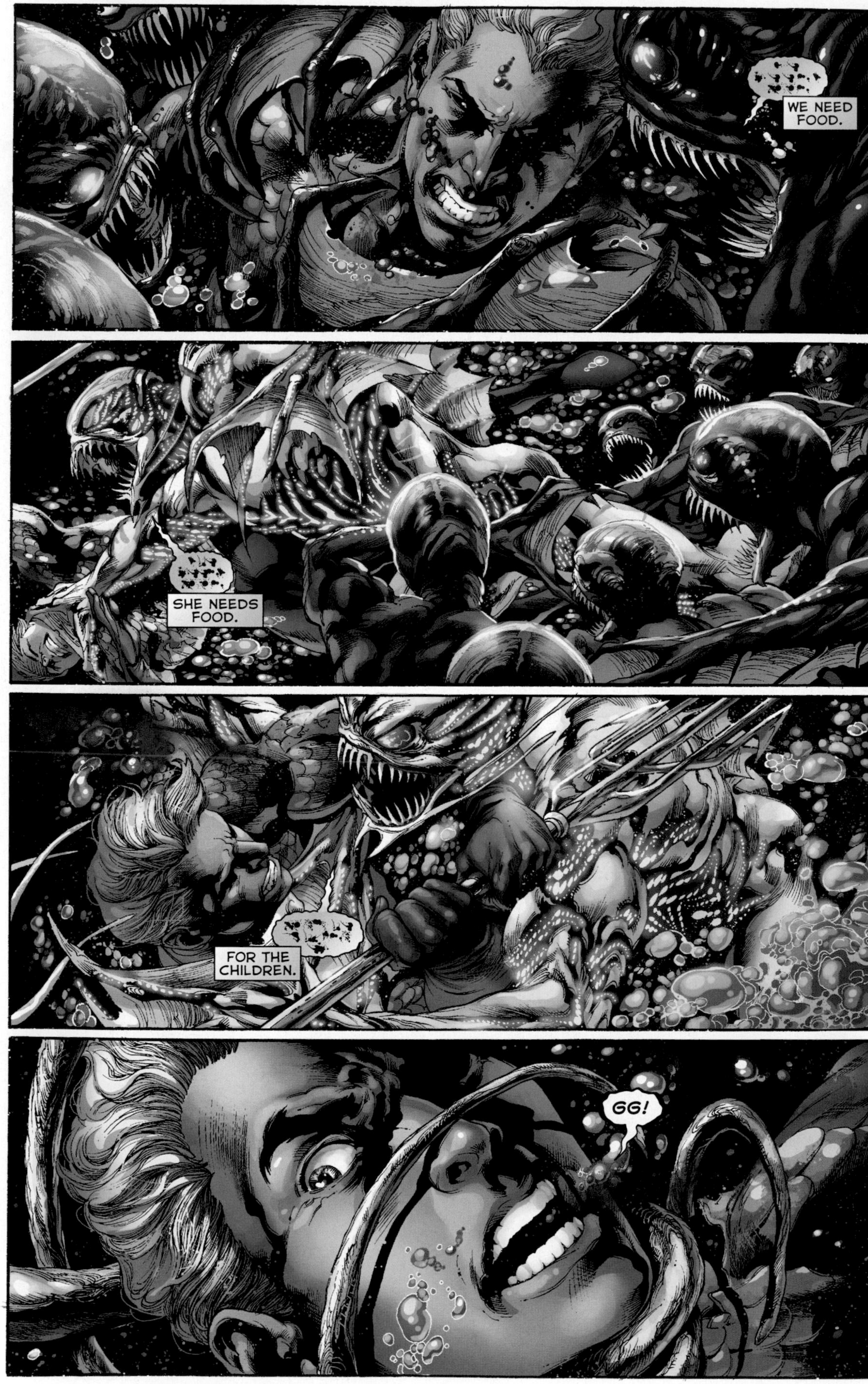
WE NEED FOOD.
SHE NEEDS FOOD.
FOR THE CHILDREN.
GG!

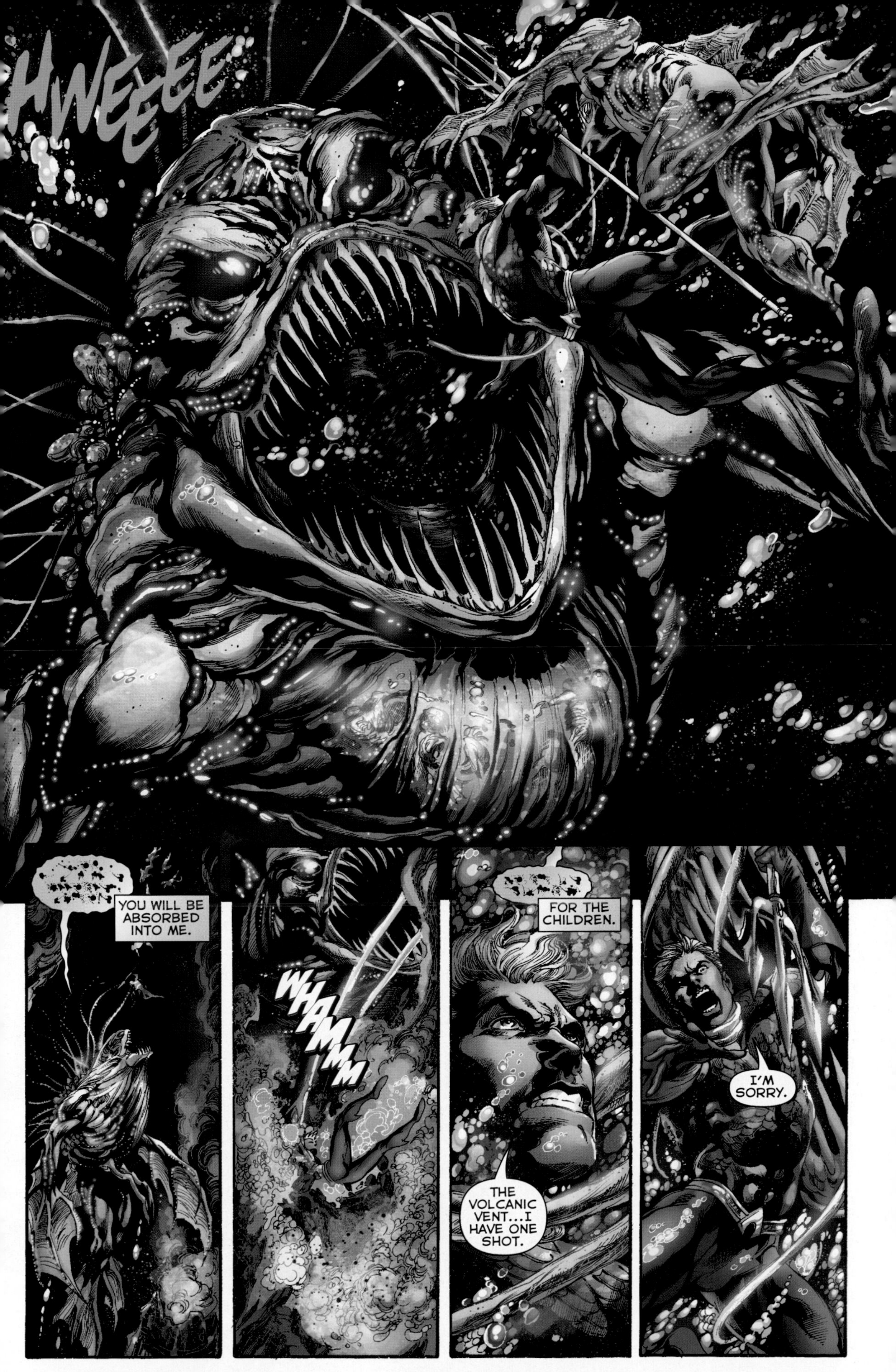
HWEEEE
YOU WILL BE ABSORBED INTO ME.
WHAMMM
FOR THE CHILDREN.
THE VOLCANIC VENT...I HAVE ONE SHOT.
I'M SORRY.

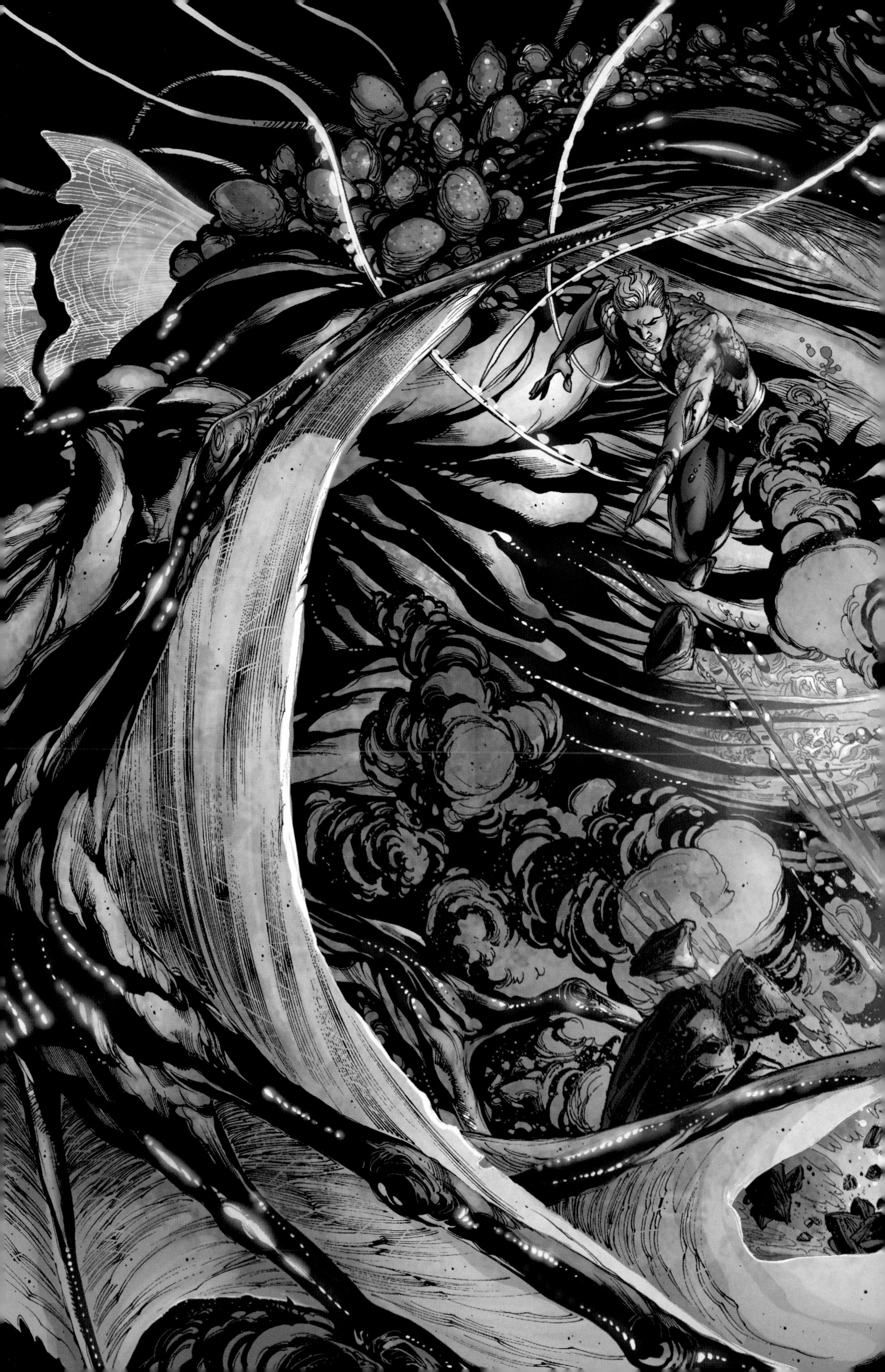

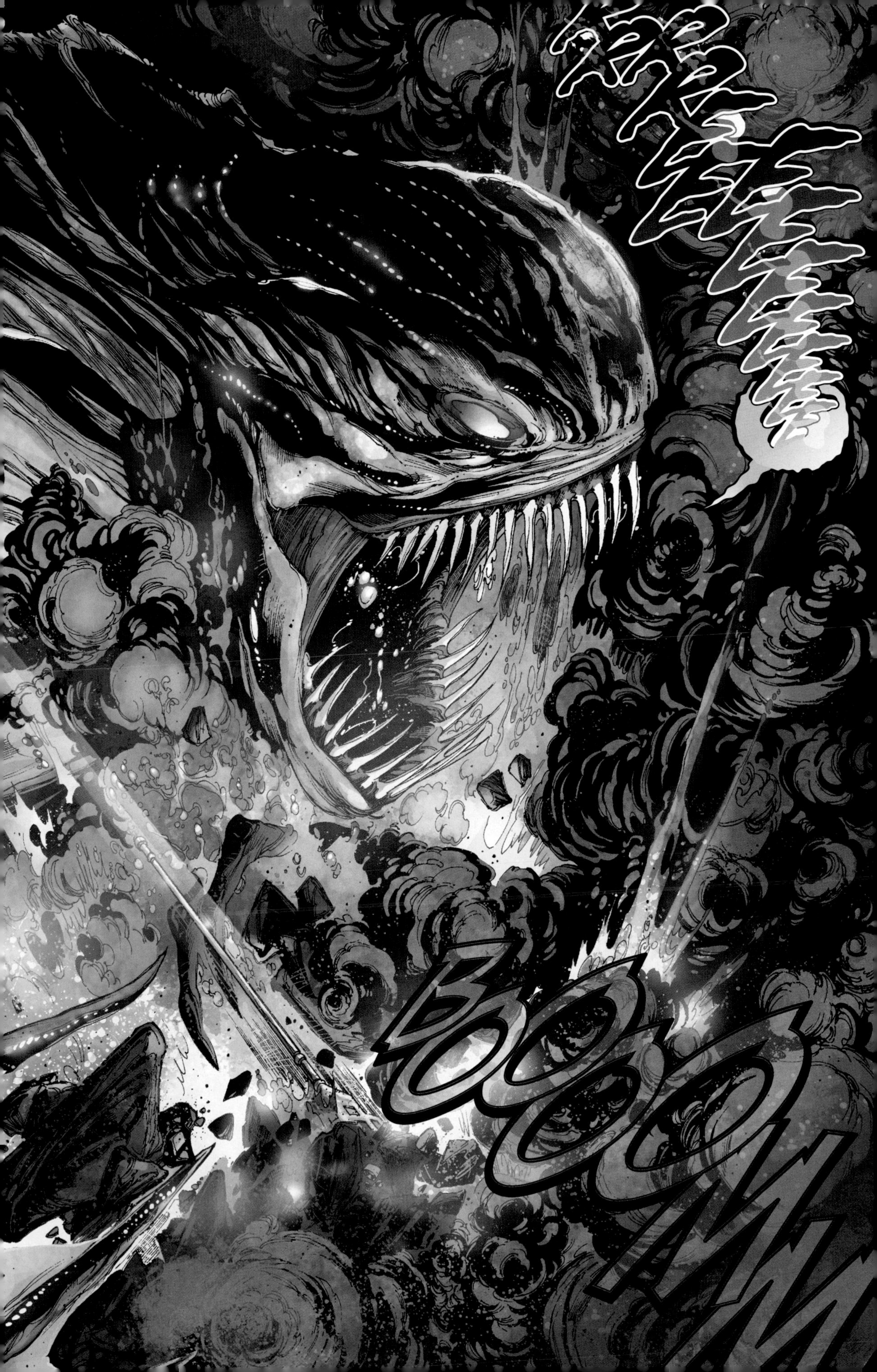
BOOOOMM

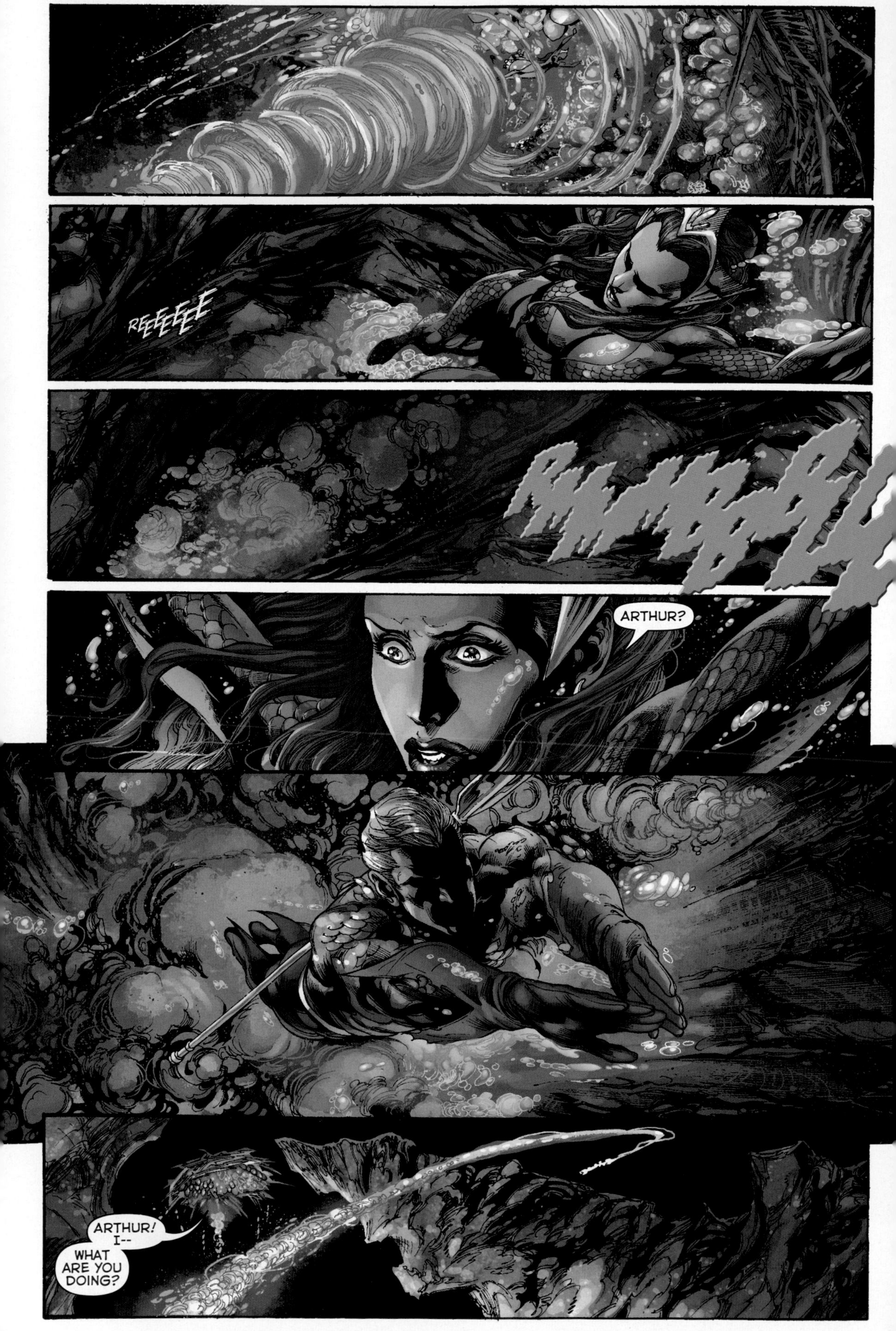
REEEEEEE
ARTHUR?
ARTHUR! I--
WHAT ARE YOU DOING?

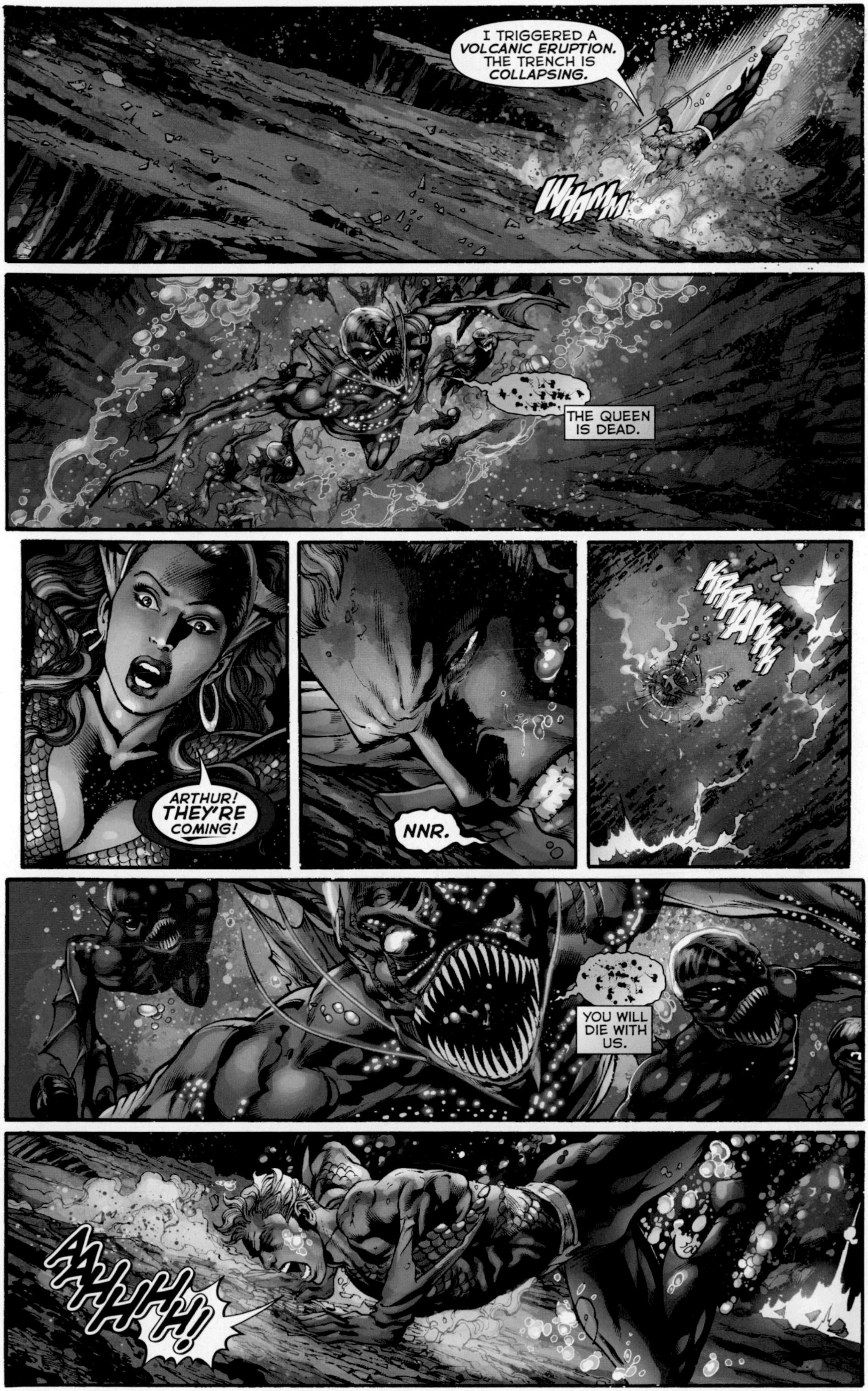
I TRIGGERED A VOLCANIC ERUPTION. THE TRENCH IS COLLAPSING.
WHAMM
THE QUEEN IS DEAD.
ARTHUR! THEY'RE COMING!
NNR.
KRRAKKK
YOU WILL DIE WITH US.
AAHHHH!

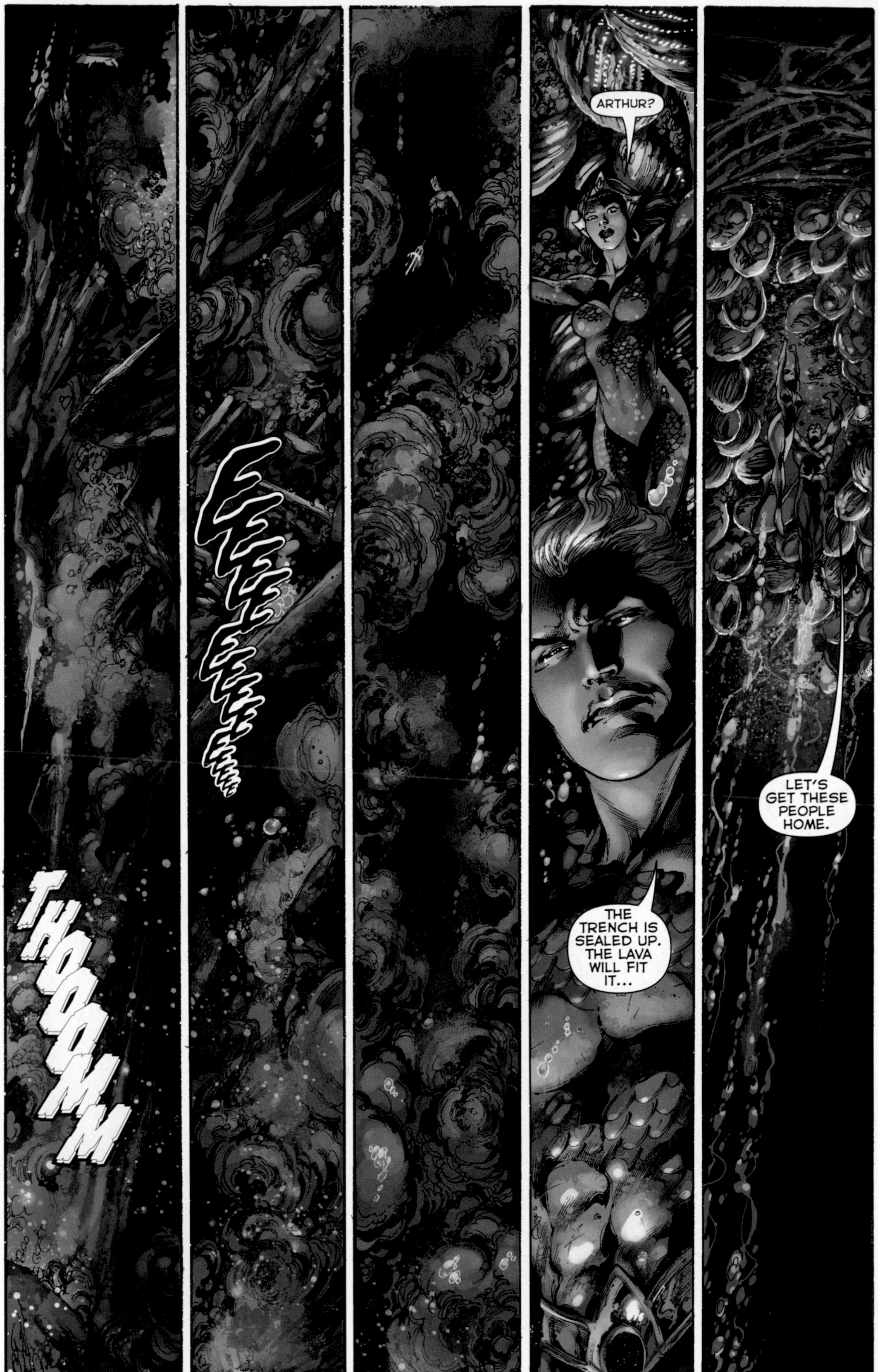
THOOOMM
EEEEEEEEE
ARTHUR?
THE TRENCH IS SEALED UP. THE LAVA WILL FIT IT...
LET'S GET THESE PEOPLE HOME.

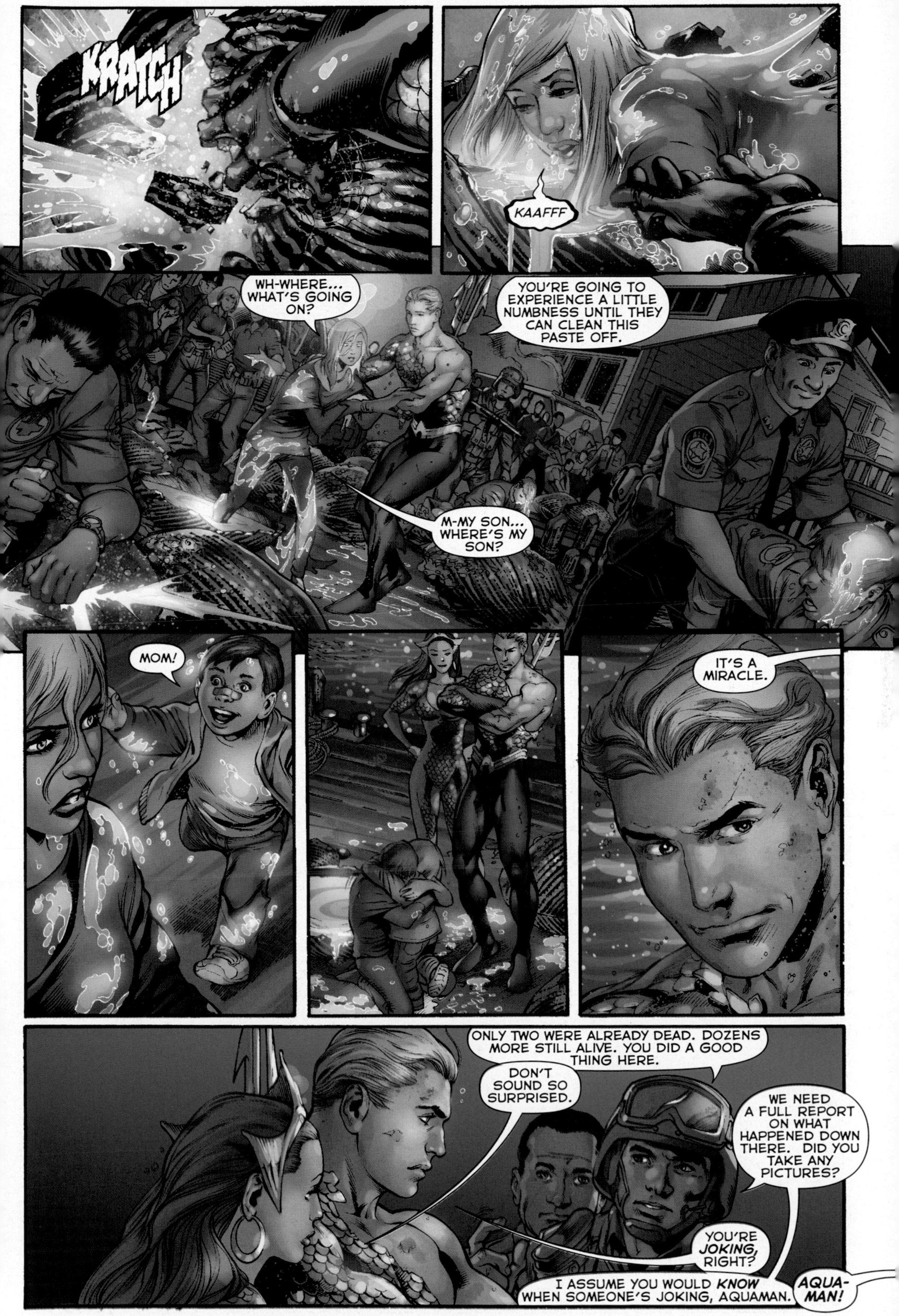
KRATCH
KAAFFF
WH-WHERE... WHAT'S GOING ON?
YOU'RE GOING TO EXPERIENCE A LITTLE NUMBNESS UNTIL THEY CAN CLEAN THIS PASTE OFF.
M-MY SON... WHERE'S MY SON?
MOM!
IT'S A MIRACLE.
ONLY TWO WERE ALREADY DEAD. DOZENS MORE STILL ALIVE. YOU DID A GOOD THING HERE.
DON'T SOUND SO SURPRISED.
WE NEED A FULL REPORT ON WHAT HAPPENED DOWN THERE. DID YOU TAKE ANY PICTURES?
YOU'RE *JOKING*, RIGHT?
I ASSUME YOU WOULD *KNOW* WHEN SOMEONE'S JOKING, AQUAMAN.
AQUA-MAN!

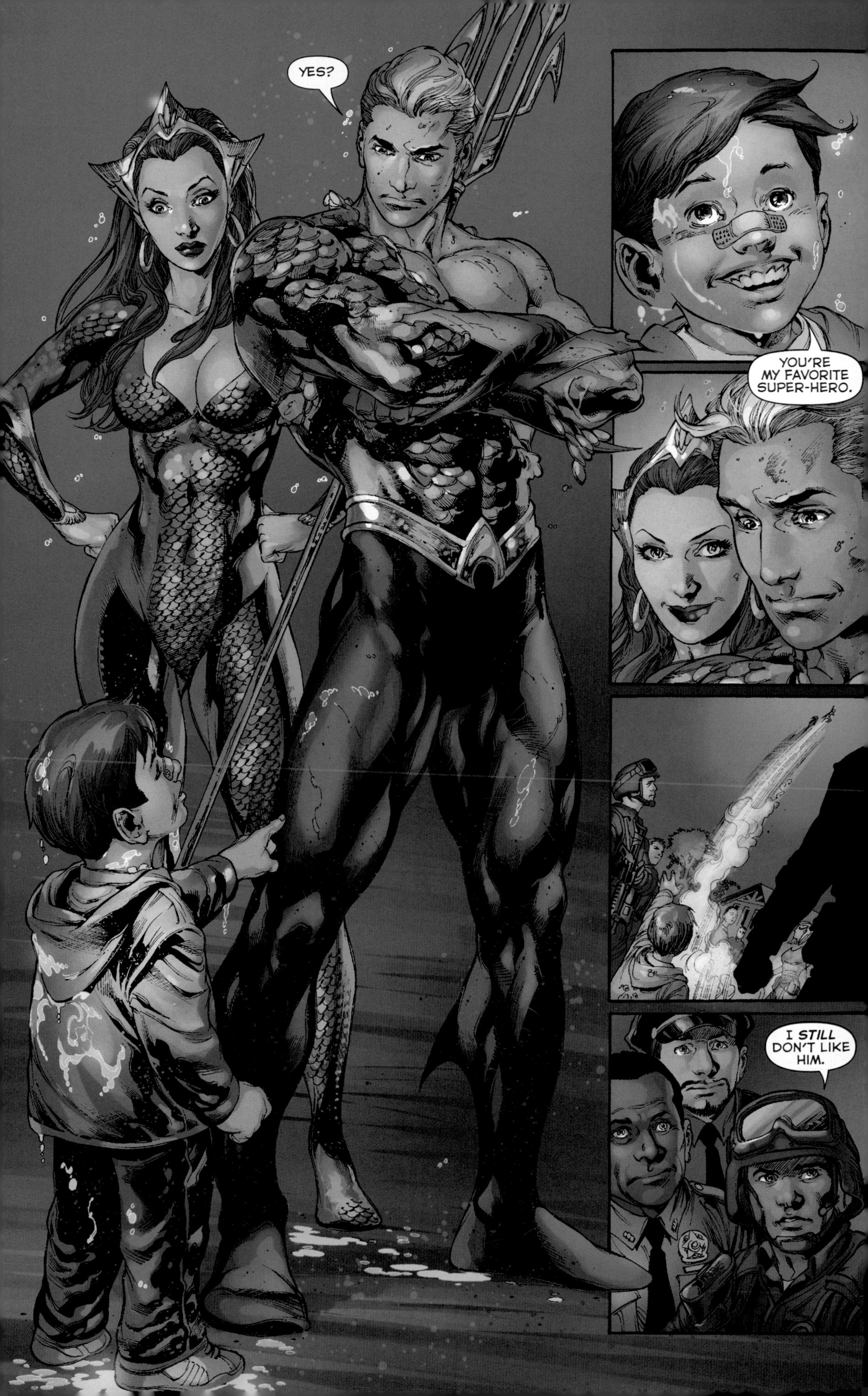
YES?
YOU'RE MY FAVORITE SUPER-HERO.
I *STILL* DON'T LIKE HIM.

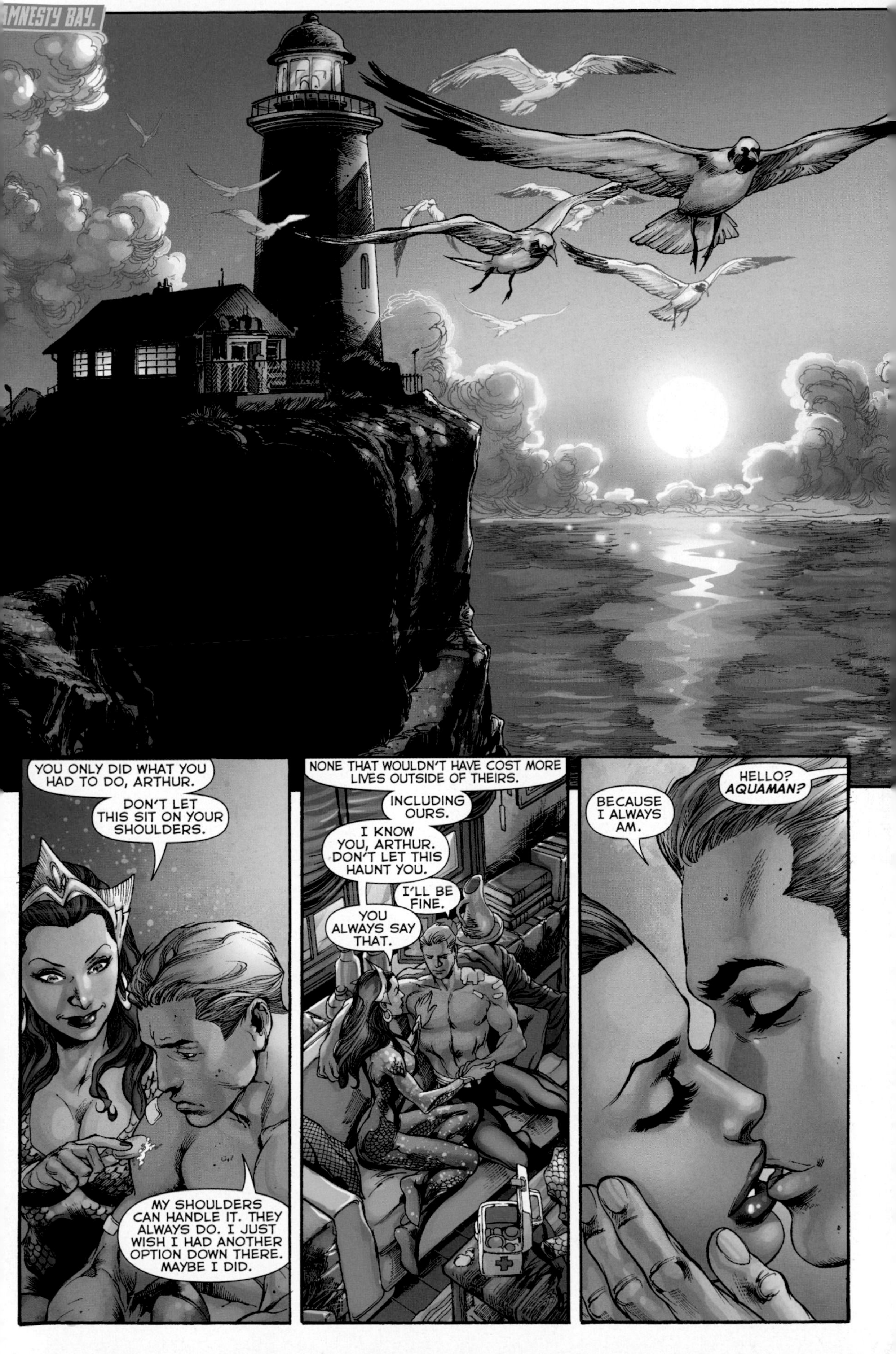
AMNESTY BAY.
YOU ONLY DID WHAT YOU HAD TO DO, ARTHUR.
DON'T LET THIS SIT ON YOUR SHOULDERS.
MY SHOULDERS CAN HANDLE IT. THEY ALWAYS DO. I JUST WISH I HAD ANOTHER OPTION DOWN THERE. MAYBE I DID.
NONE THAT WOULDN'T HAVE COST MORE LIVES OUTSIDE OF THEIRS.
INCLUDING OURS.
I KNOW YOU, ARTHUR. DON'T LET THIS HAUNT YOU.
I'LL BE FINE.
YOU ALWAYS SAY THAT.
BECAUSE I ALWAYS AM.
HELLO? AQUAMAN?

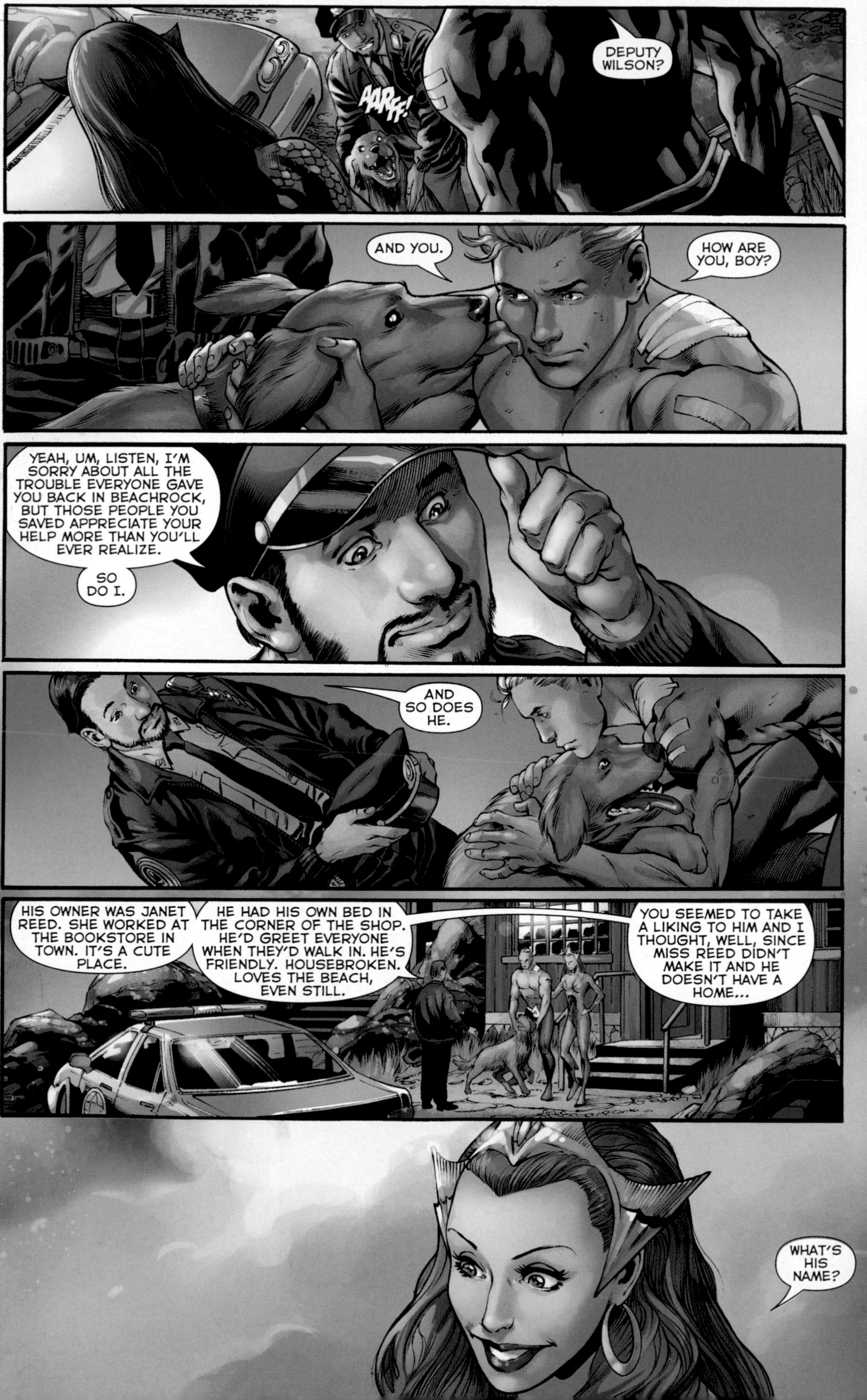
AARFF!
DEPUTY WILSON?
AND YOU.
HOW ARE YOU, BOY?
YEAH, UM, LISTEN, I'M SORRY ABOUT ALL THE TROUBLE EVERYONE GAVE YOU BACK IN BEACHROCK, BUT THOSE PEOPLE YOU SAVED APPRECIATE YOUR HELP MORE THAN YOU'LL EVER REALIZE.
SO DO I.
AND SO DOES HE.
HIS OWNER WAS JANET REED. SHE WORKED AT THE BOOKSTORE IN TOWN. IT'S A CUTE PLACE.
HE HAD HIS OWN BED IN THE CORNER OF THE SHOP. HE'D GREET EVERYONE WHEN THEY'D WALK IN. HE'S FRIENDLY. HOUSEBROKEN. LOVES THE BEACH, EVEN STILL.
YOU SEEMED TO TAKE A LIKING TO HIM AND I THOUGHT, WELL, SINCE MISS REED DIDN'T MAKE IT AND HE DOESN'T HAVE A HOME...
WHAT'S HIS NAME?

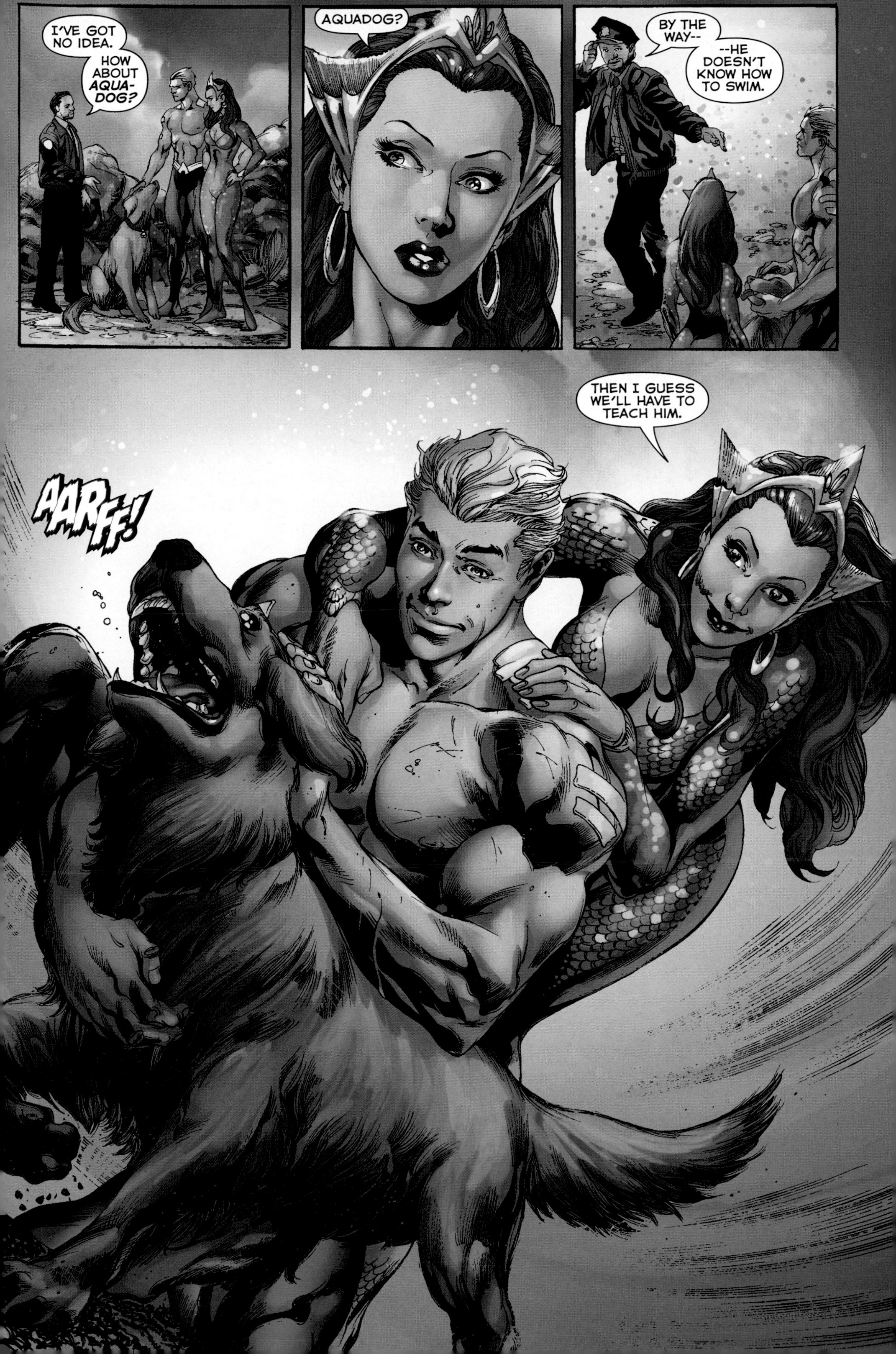
I'VE GOT NO IDEA.
HOW ABOUT AQUA-DOG?
AQUADOG?
BY THE WAY--
--HE DOESN'T KNOW HOW TO SWIM.
THEN I GUESS WE'LL HAVE TO TEACH HIM.
AARFF!

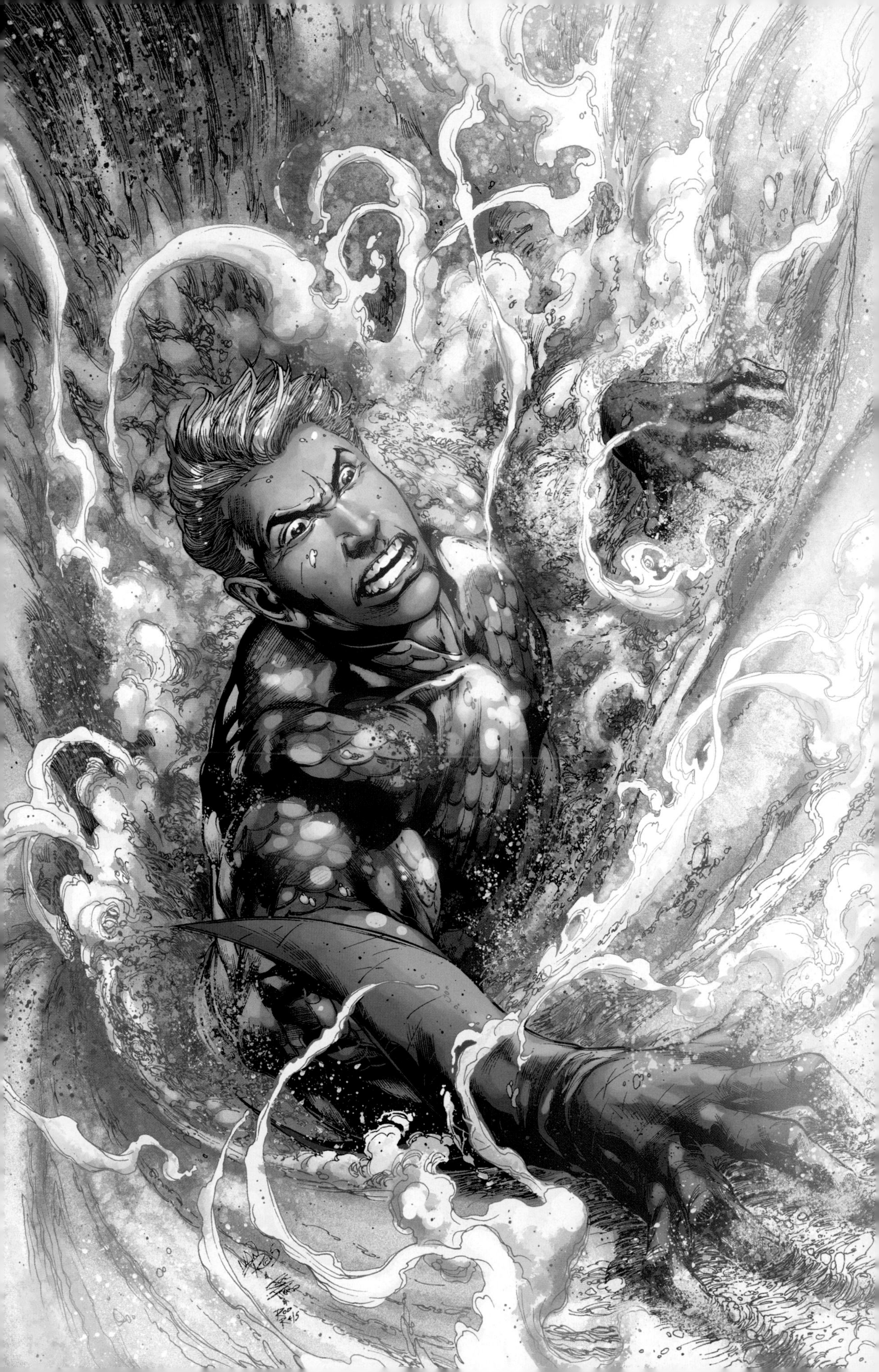

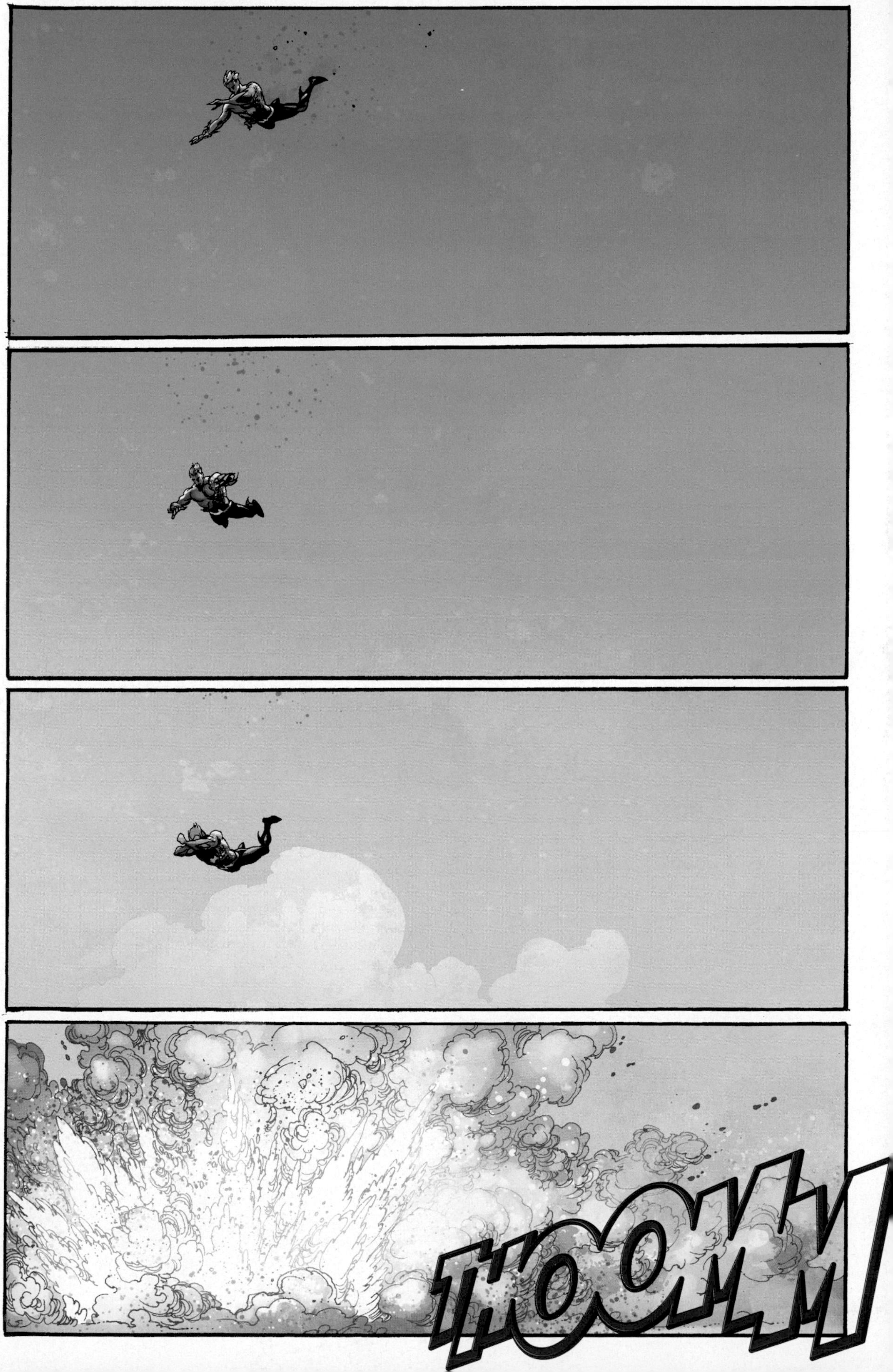
THOOMM

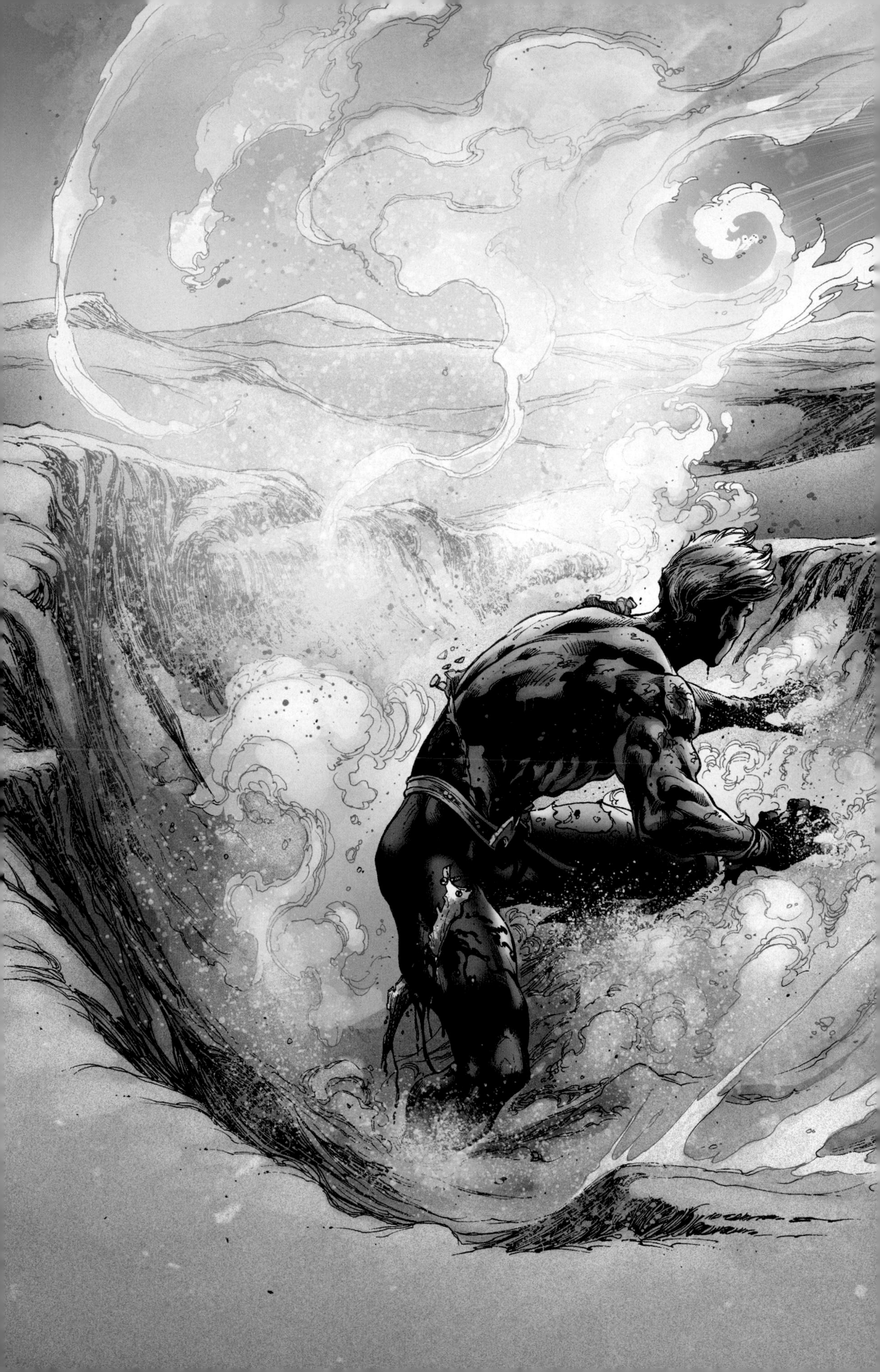

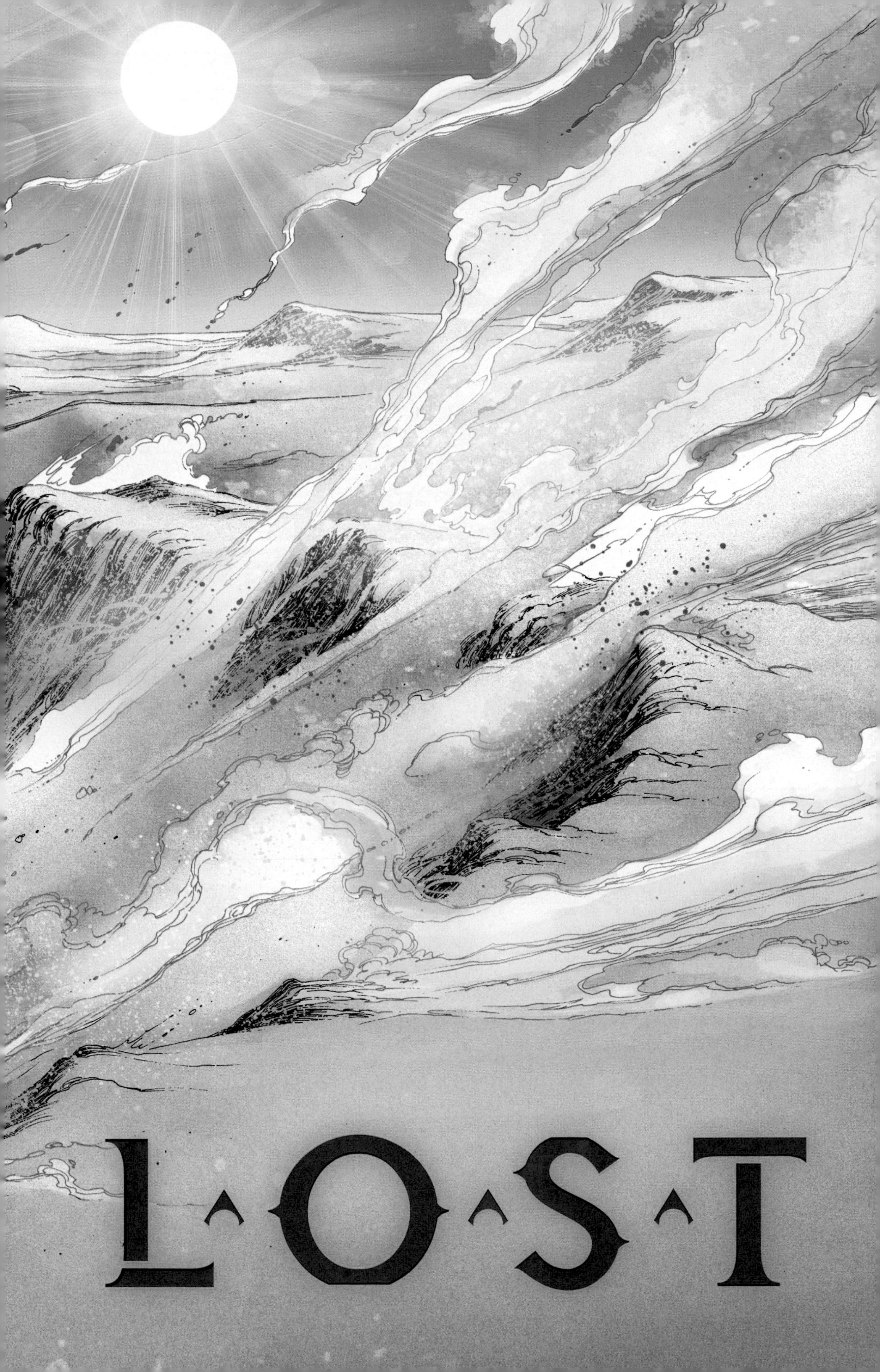
LOST

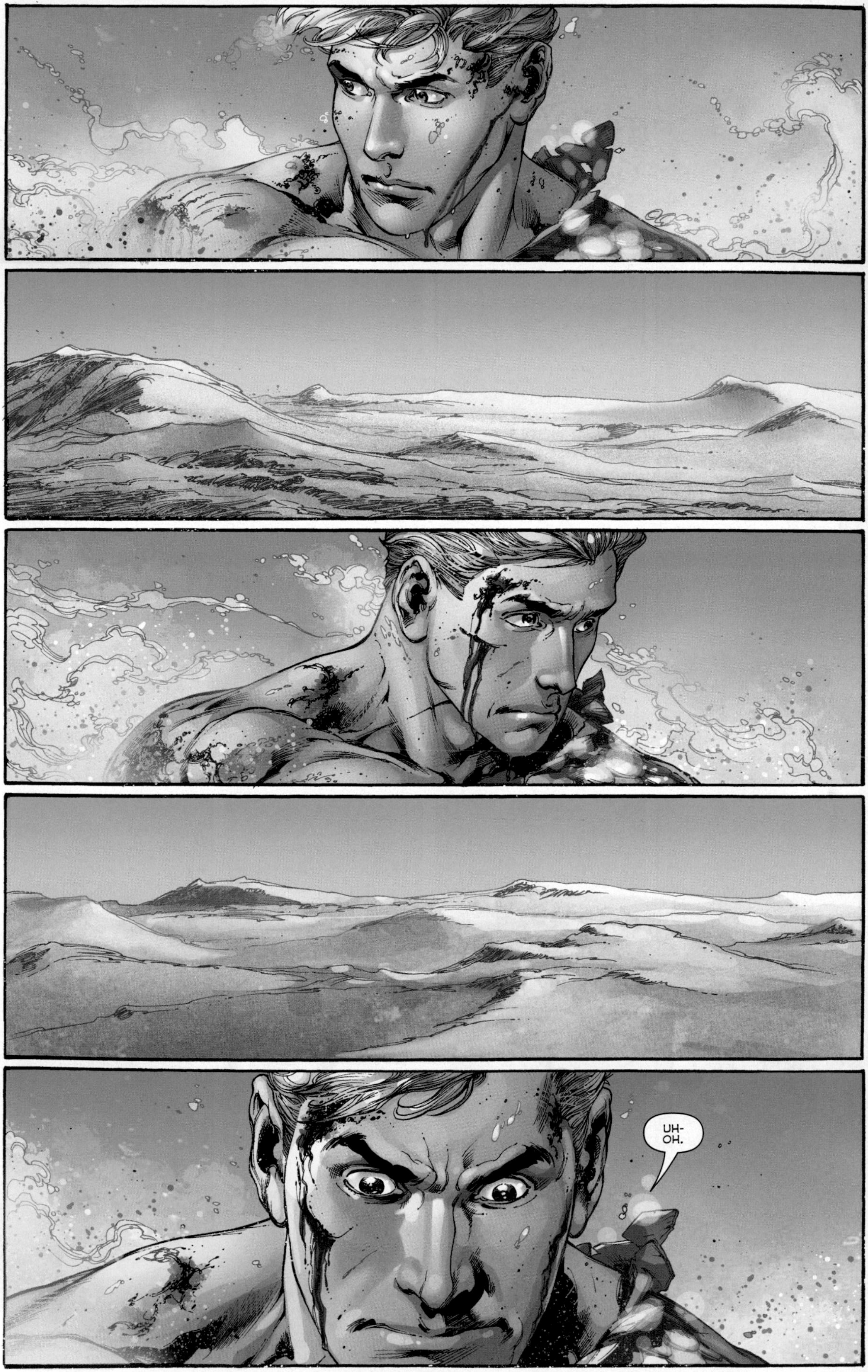
UH-
OH.

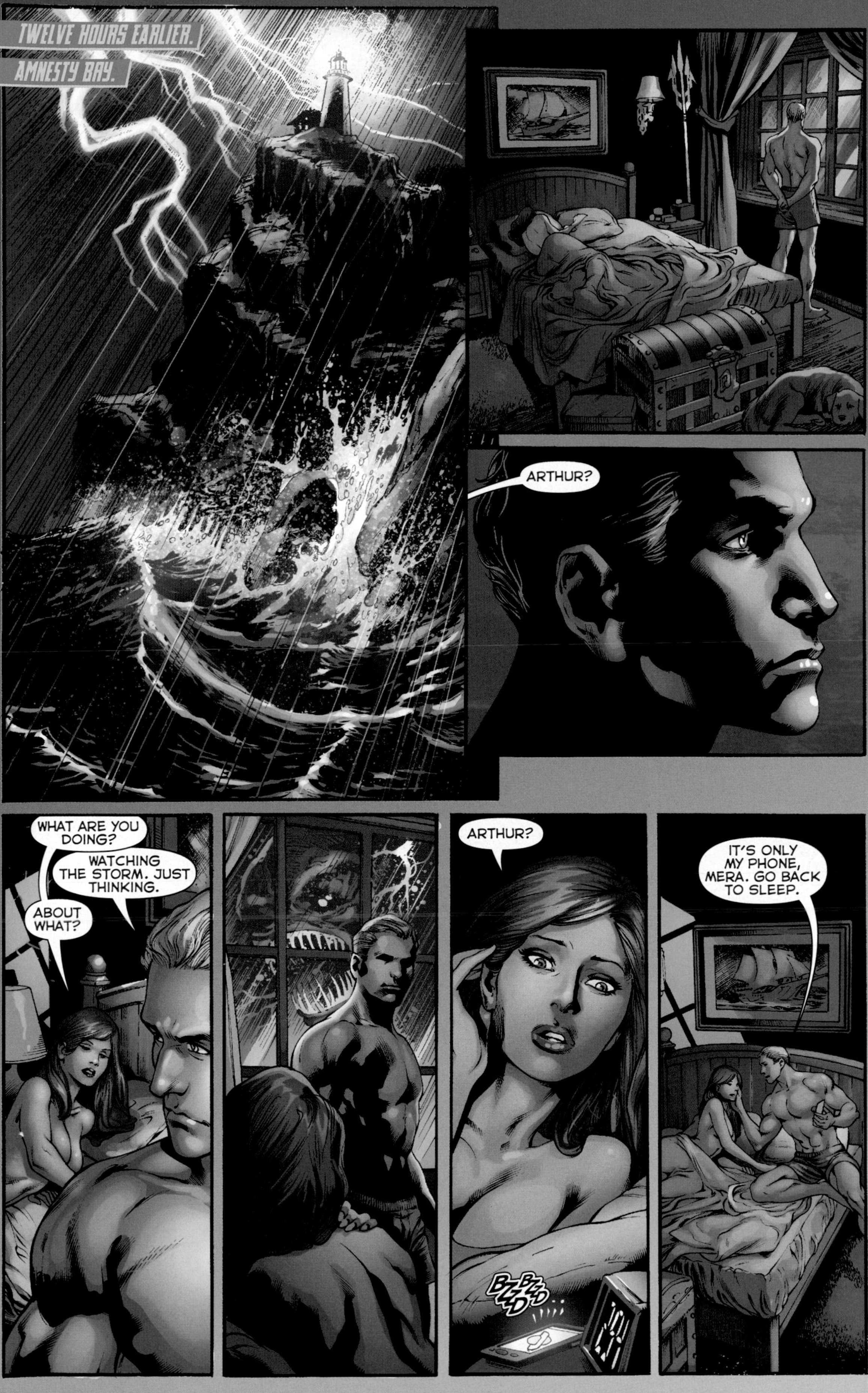
TWELVE HOURS EARLIER.
AMNESTY BAY.
ARTHUR?
WHAT ARE YOU DOING?
WATCHING THE STORM. JUST THINKING.
ABOUT WHAT?
ARTHUR?
BZZD BZZD
IT'S ONLY MY PHONE, MERA. GO BACK TO SLEEP.

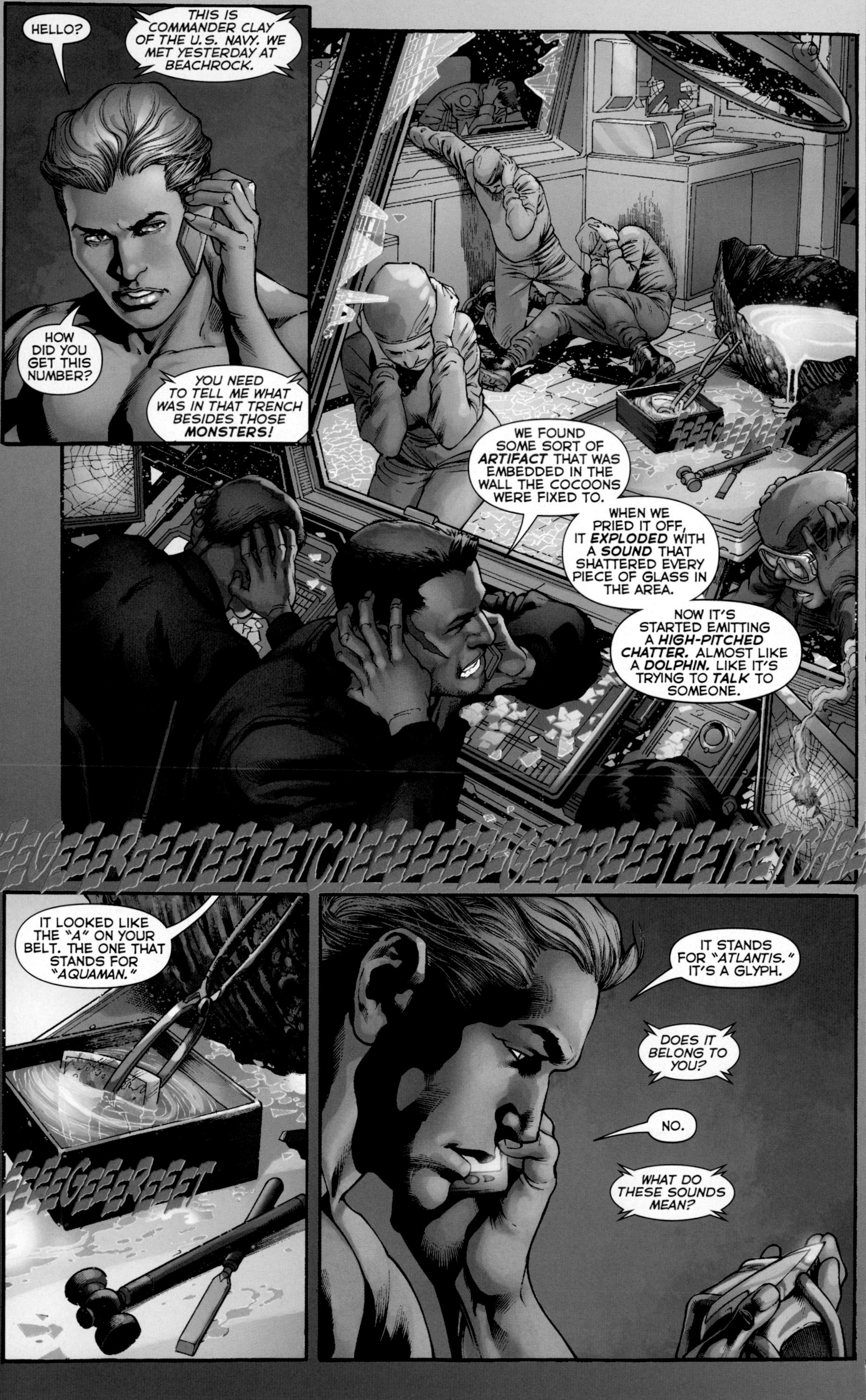
HELLO?
THIS IS COMMANDER CLAY OF THE U.S. NAVY. WE MET YESTERDAY AT BEACHROCK.
HOW DID YOU GET THIS NUMBER?
YOU NEED TO TELL ME WHAT WAS IN THAT TRENCH BESIDES THOSE MONSTERS!
WE FOUND SOME SORT OF ARTIFACT THAT WAS EMBEDDED IN THE WALL THE COCOONS WERE FIXED TO.
WHEN WE PRIED IT OFF, IT EXPLODED WITH A SOUND THAT SHATTERED EVERY PIECE OF GLASS IN THE AREA.
NOW IT'S STARTED EMITTING A HIGH-PITCHED CHATTER. ALMOST LIKE A DOLPHIN. LIKE IT'S TRYING TO TALK TO SOMEONE.
EEEGEEEREEET
EEEGEEEREEETEEETEEETCHEEEEEEEEEGEEEREEETEEETEEETCHEE
IT LOOKED LIKE THE "A" ON YOUR BELT. THE ONE THAT STANDS FOR "AQUAMAN."
EEEGEEEREEET
IT STANDS FOR "ATLANTIS." IT'S A GLYPH.
DOES IT BELONG TO YOU?
NO.
WHAT DO THESE SOUNDS MEAN?

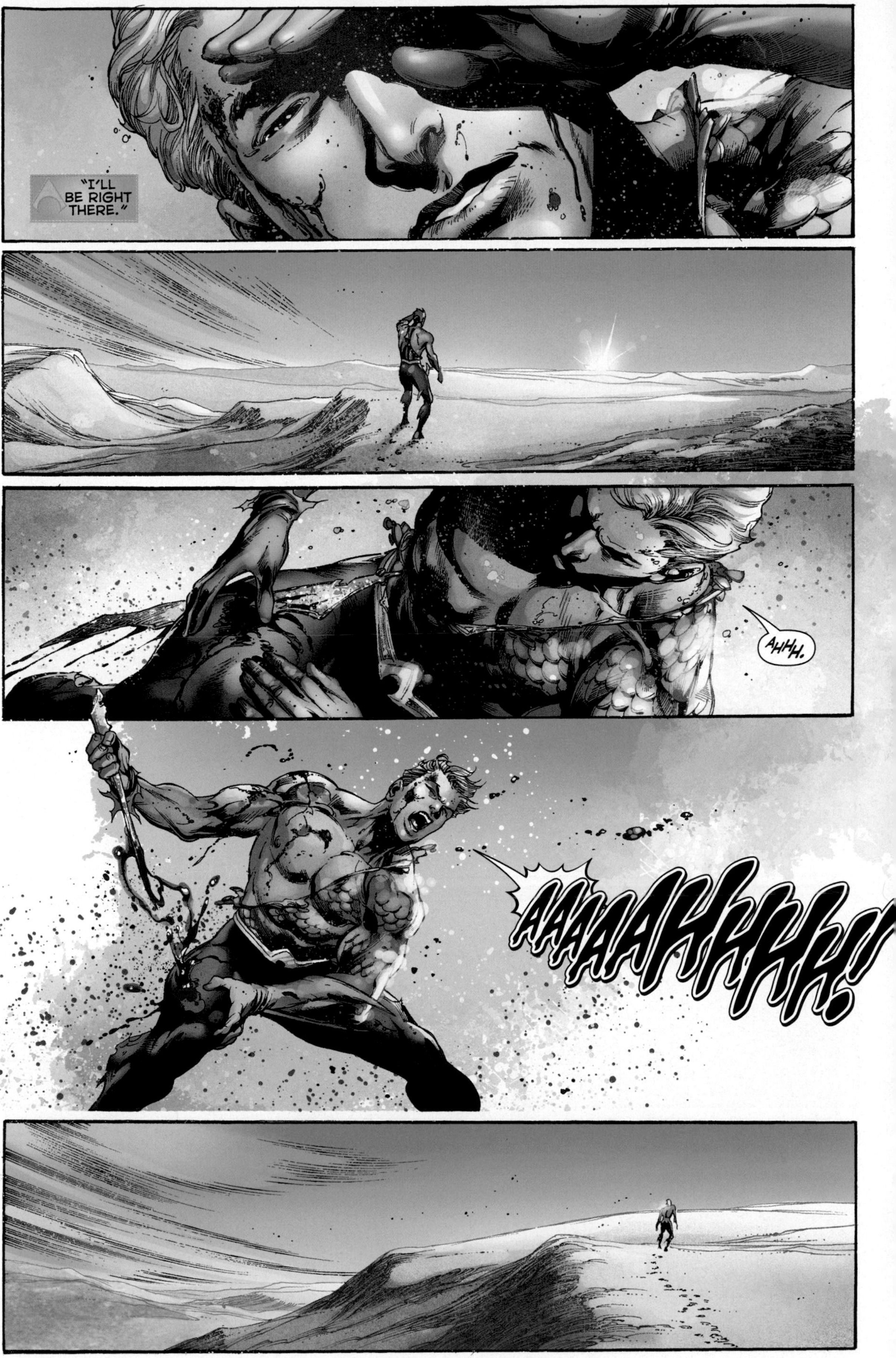
"I'LL BE RIGHT THERE."
AHHH.
AAAAAHHHHH!

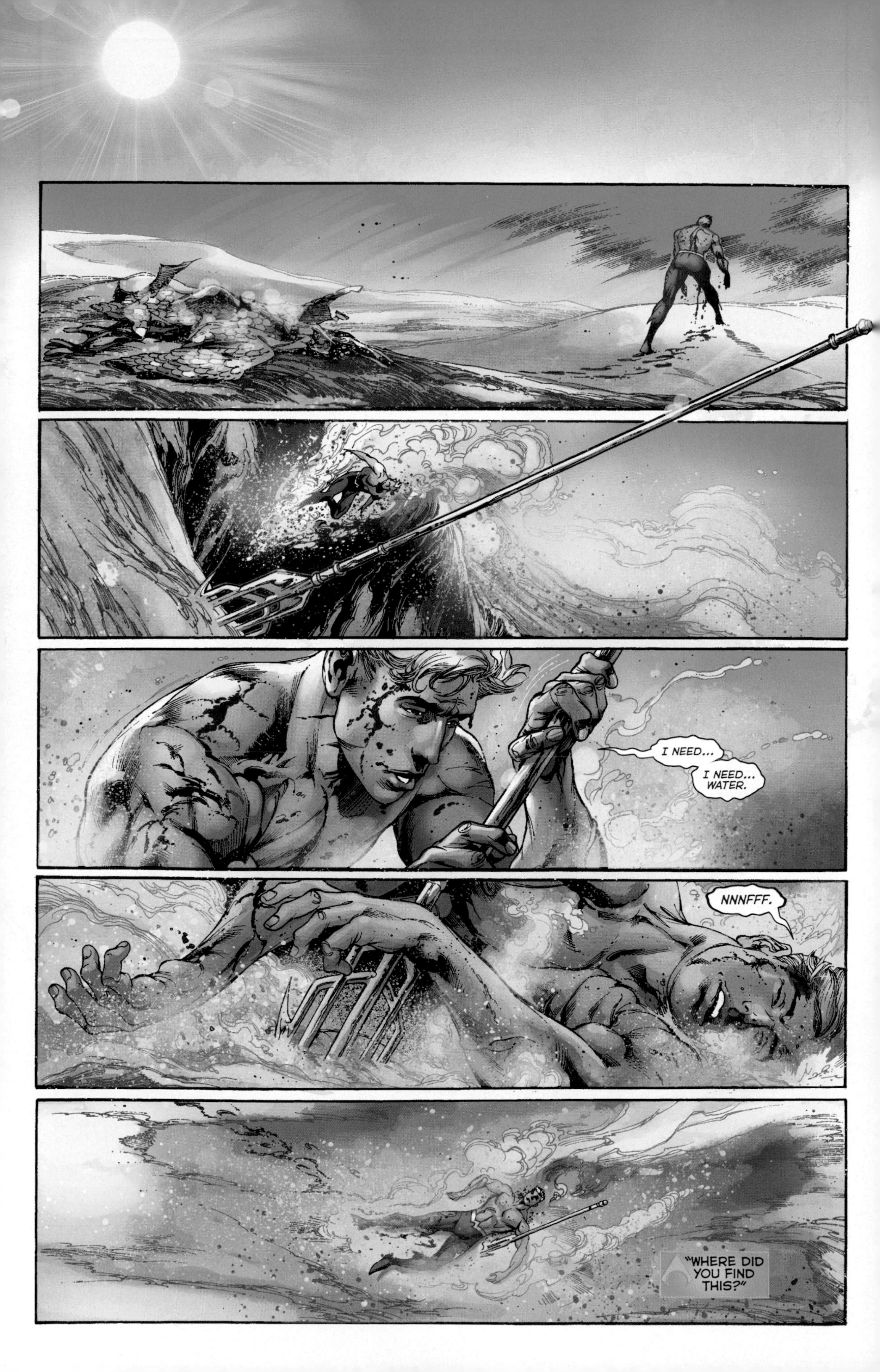
I NEED...
I NEED... WATER.
NNNFFF.
"WHERE DID YOU FIND THIS?"

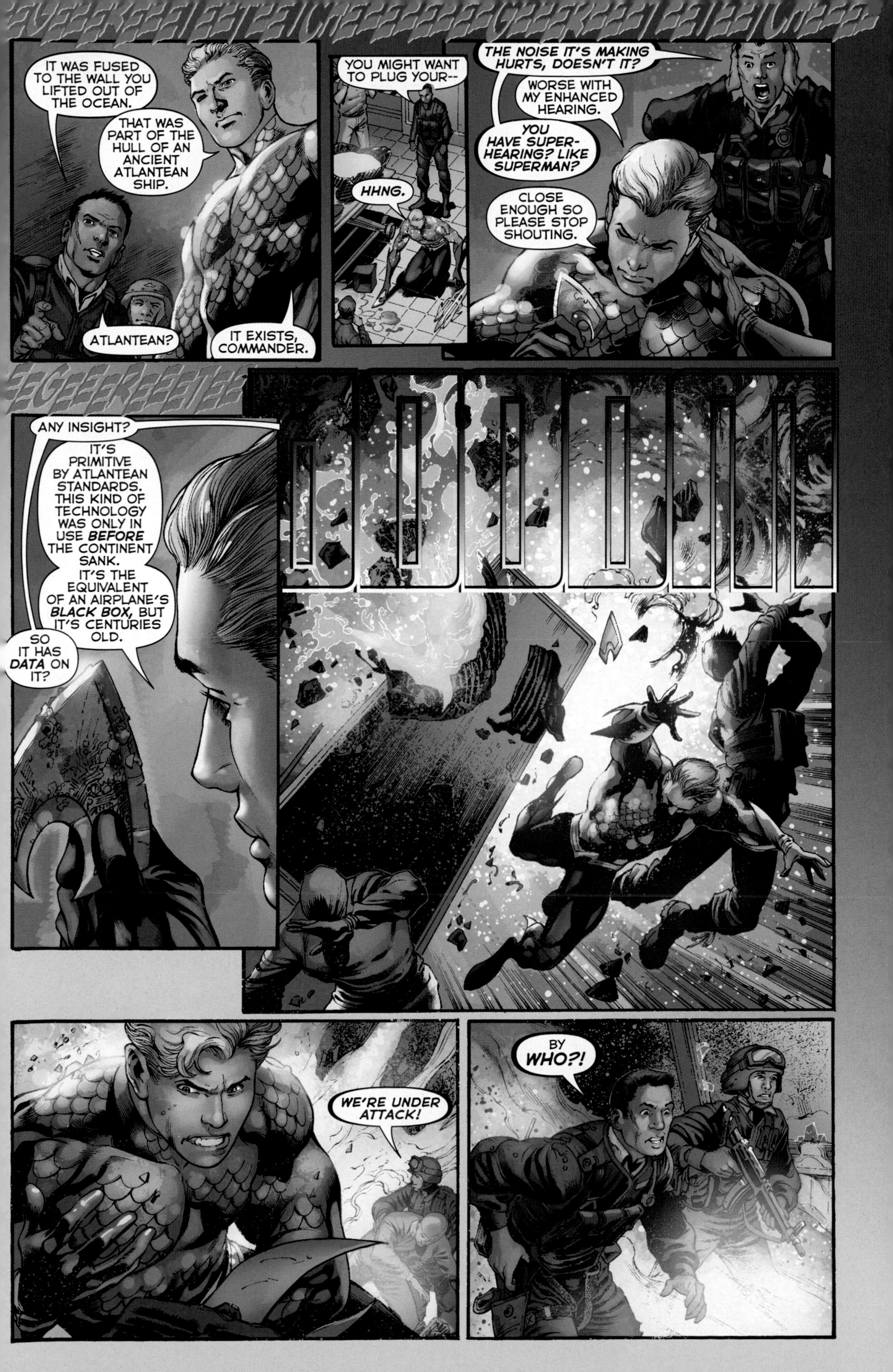

IT WAS FUSED TO THE WALL YOU LIFTED OUT OF THE OCEAN.
THAT WAS PART OF THE HULL OF AN ANCIENT ATLANTEAN SHIP.
ATLANTEAN?
IT EXISTS, COMMANDER.
YOU MIGHT WANT TO PLUG YOUR--
HHNG.
THE NOISE IT'S MAKING HURTS, DOESN'T IT?
WORSE WITH MY ENHANCED HEARING.
YOU HAVE SUPER-HEARING? LIKE SUPERMAN?
CLOSE ENOUGH SO PLEASE STOP SHOUTING.
ANY INSIGHT?
IT'S PRIMITIVE BY ATLANTEAN STANDARDS. THIS KIND OF TECHNOLOGY WAS ONLY IN USE BEFORE THE CONTINENT SANK.
IT'S THE EQUIVALENT OF AN AIRPLANE'S BLACK BOX, BUT IT'S CENTURIES OLD.
SO IT HAS DATA ON IT?
WE'RE UNDER ATTACK!
BY WHO?!

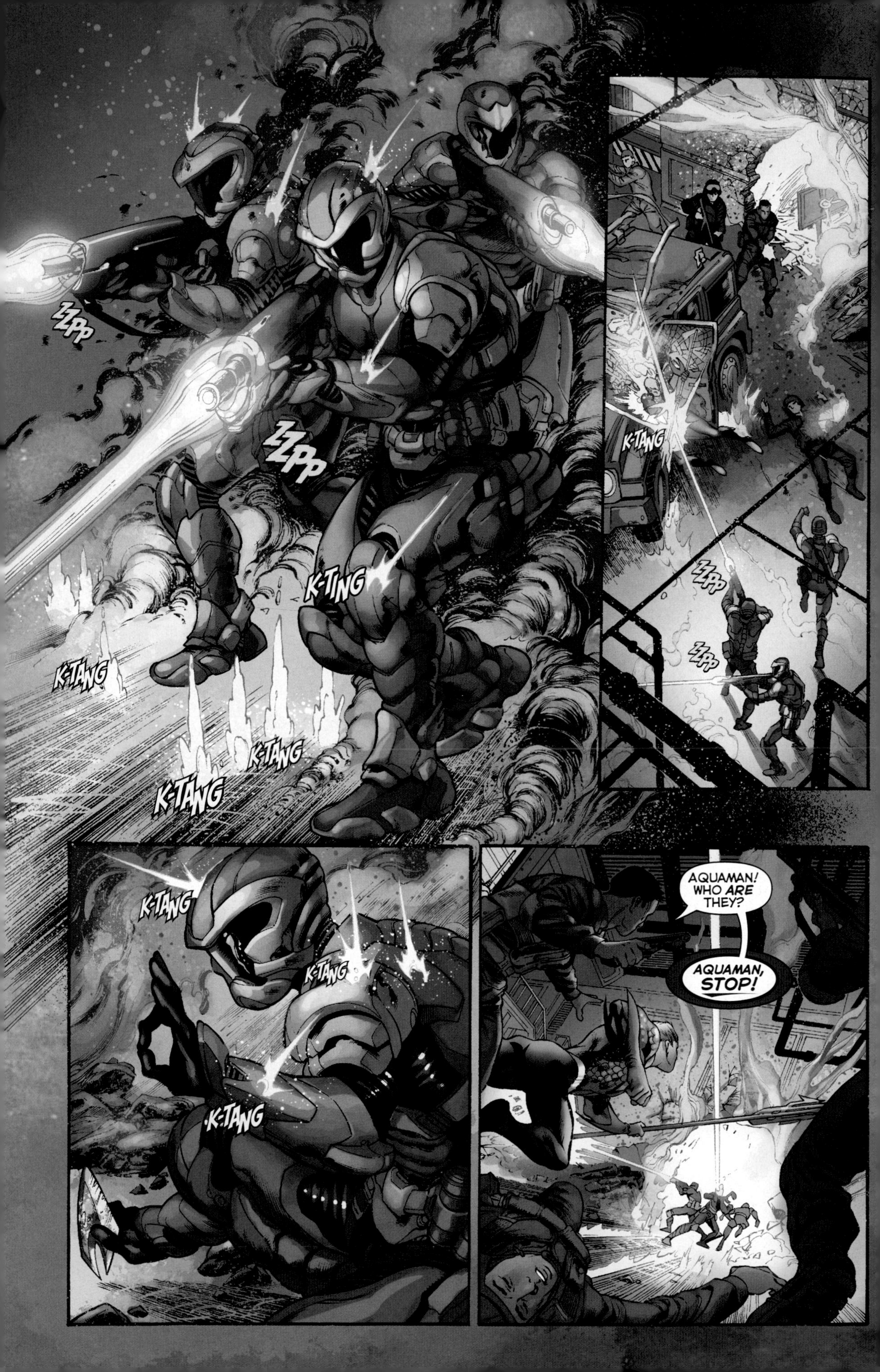
ZZPP
ZZPP
K-TING
K-TANG
K-TANG
K-TANG
K-TANG
ZZPP
ZZPP
K-TANG
K-TANG
K-TANG
AQUAMAN! WHO ARE THEY?
AQUAMAN, STOP!

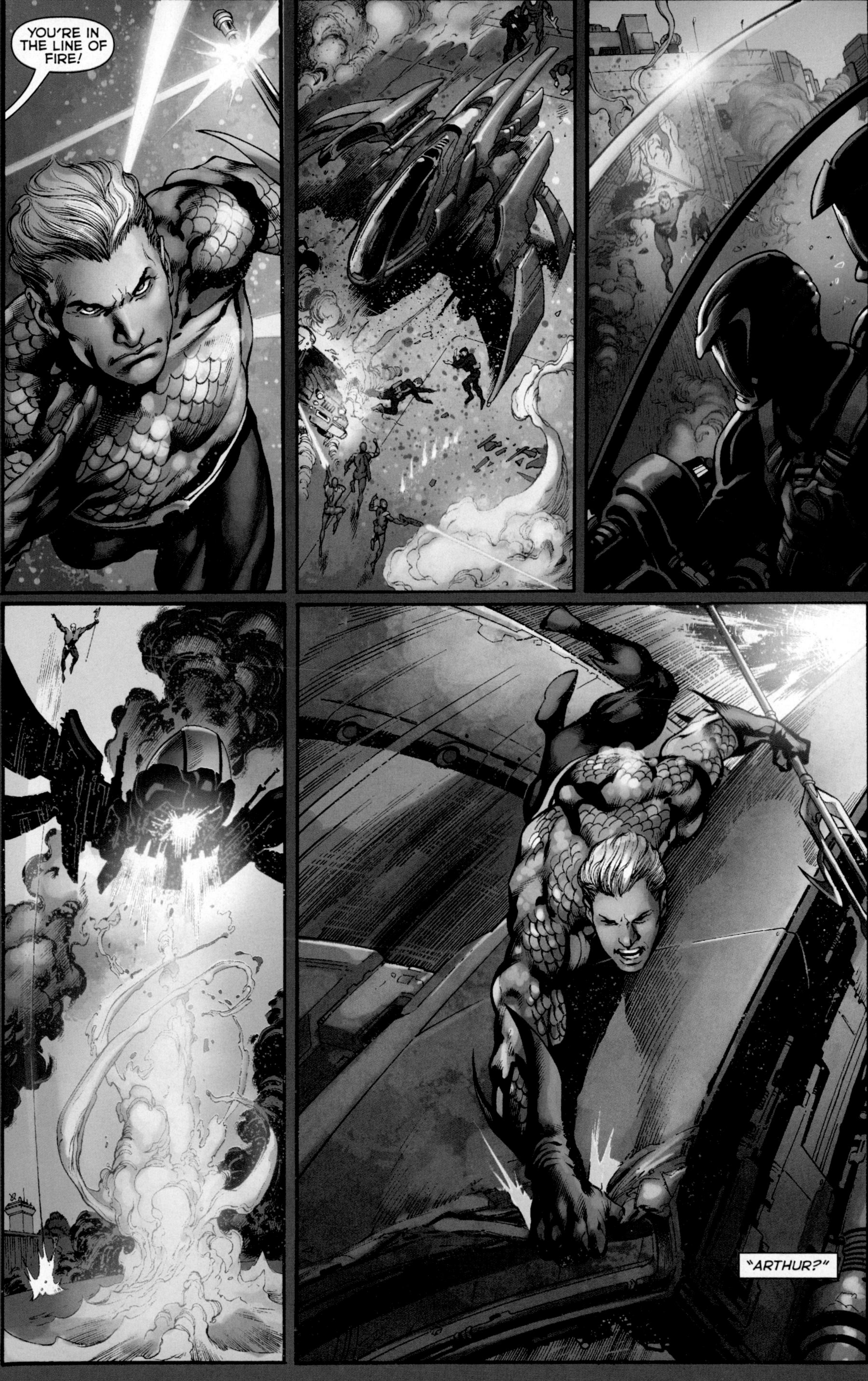
YOU'RE IN THE LINE OF FIRE!
"ARTHUR?"

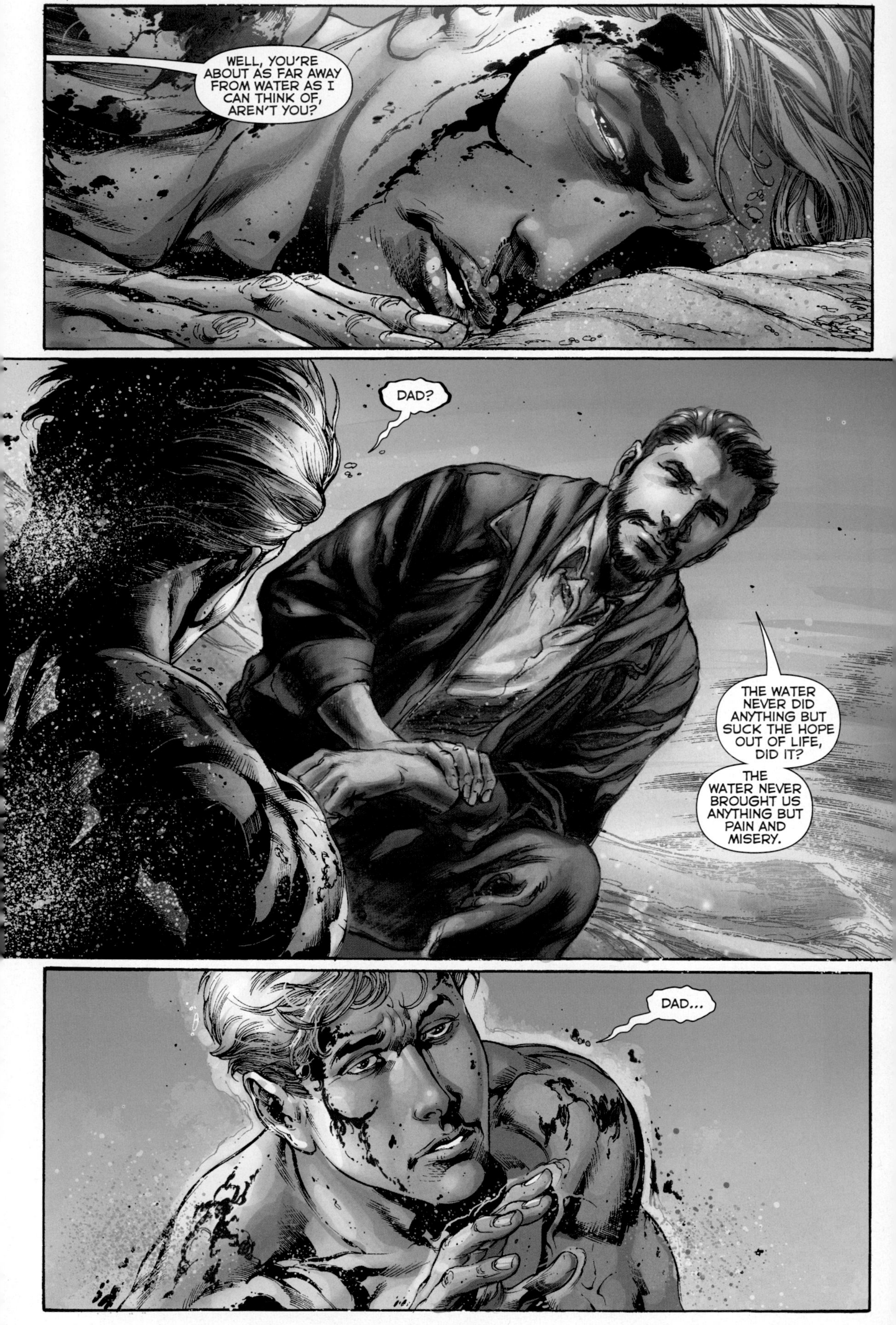
WELL, YOU'RE ABOUT AS FAR AWAY FROM WATER AS I CAN THINK OF, AREN'T YOU?
DAD?
THE WATER NEVER DID ANYTHING BUT SUCK THE HOPE OUT OF LIFE, DID IT?
THE WATER NEVER BROUGHT US ANYTHING BUT PAIN AND MISERY.
DAD...

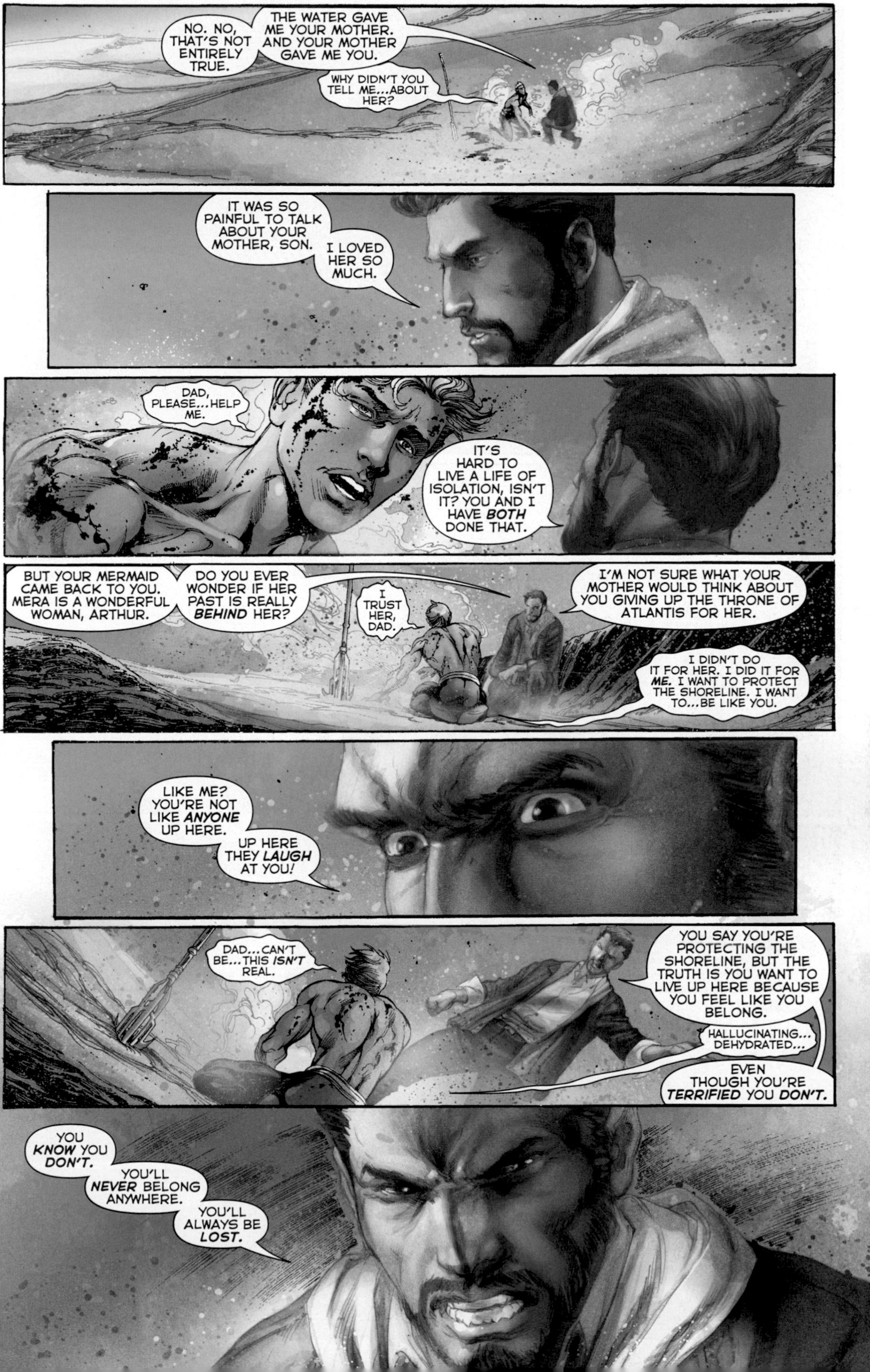

NO. NO, THAT'S NOT ENTIRELY TRUE.
THE WATER GAVE ME YOUR MOTHER. AND YOUR MOTHER GAVE ME YOU.
WHY DIDN'T YOU TELL ME...ABOUT HER?
IT WAS SO PAINFUL TO TALK ABOUT YOUR MOTHER, SON.
I LOVED HER SO MUCH.
DAD, PLEASE...HELP ME.
IT'S HARD TO LIVE A LIFE OF ISOLATION, ISN'T IT? YOU AND I HAVE BOTH DONE THAT.
BUT YOUR MERMAID CAME BACK TO YOU. MERA IS A WONDERFUL WOMAN, ARTHUR.
DO YOU EVER WONDER IF HER PAST IS REALLY BEHIND HER?
I TRUST HER, DAD.
I'M NOT SURE WHAT YOUR MOTHER WOULD THINK ABOUT YOU GIVING UP THE THRONE OF ATLANTIS FOR HER.
I DIDN'T DO IT FOR HER. I DID IT FOR ME. I WANT TO PROTECT THE SHORELINE. I WANT TO...BE LIKE YOU.
LIKE ME? YOU'RE NOT LIKE ANYONE UP HERE.
UP HERE THEY LAUGH AT YOU!
DAD...CAN'T BE...THIS ISN'T REAL.
YOU SAY YOU'RE PROTECTING THE SHORELINE, BUT THE TRUTH IS YOU WANT TO LIVE UP HERE BECAUSE YOU FEEL LIKE YOU BELONG.
HALLUCINATING... DEHYDRATED...
EVEN THOUGH YOU'RE TERRIFIED YOU DON'T.
YOU KNOW YOU DON'T.
YOU'LL NEVER BELONG ANYWHERE.
YOU'LL ALWAYS BE LOST.

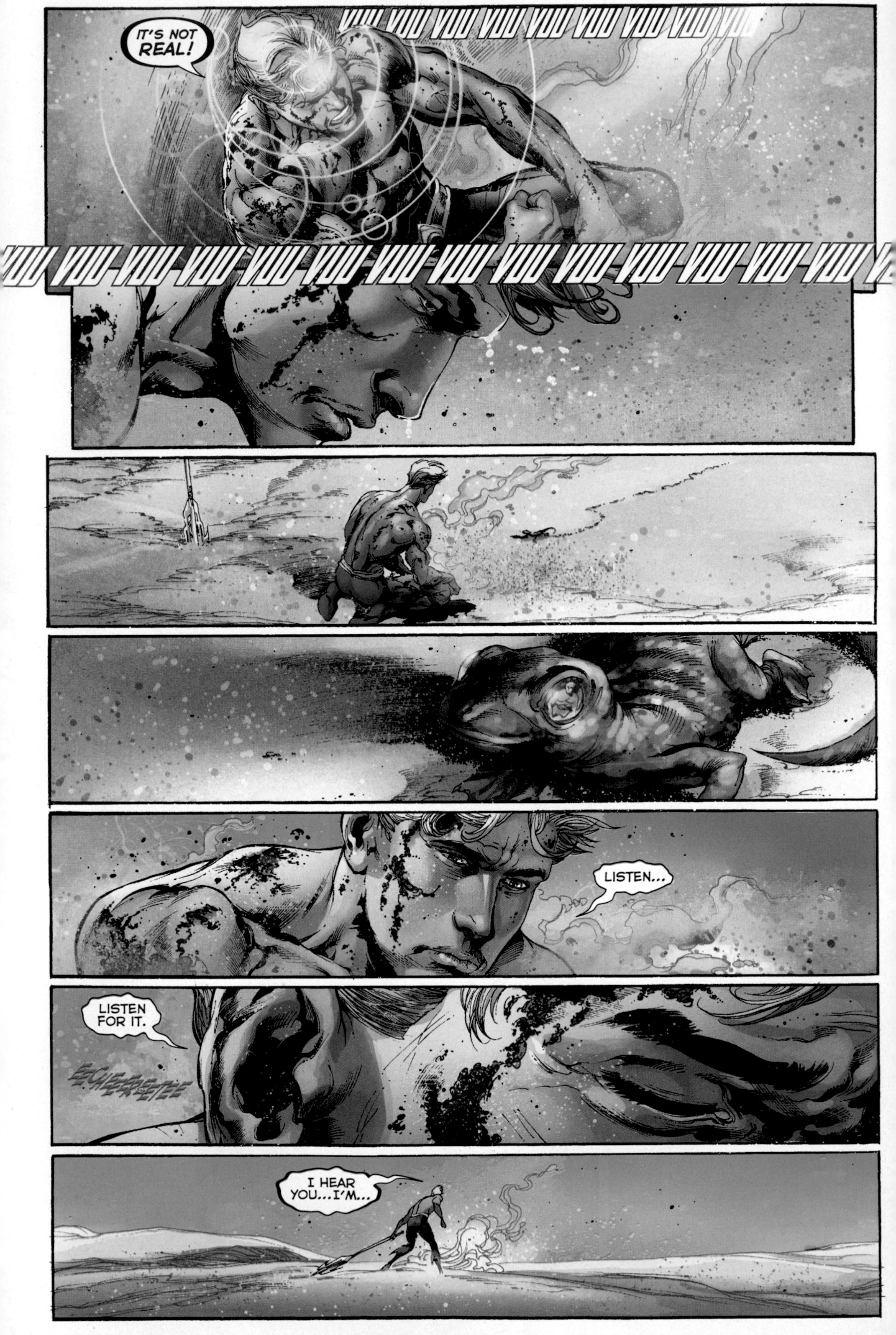
IT'S NOT REAL!
VUU VUU VUU VUU VUU VUU VUU VUU VUU VUU
VUU VUU VUU VUU VUU VUU VUU VUU VUU VUU VUU VUU VUU VUU VUU
LISTEN...
LISTEN FOR IT.
I HEAR YOU...I'M...

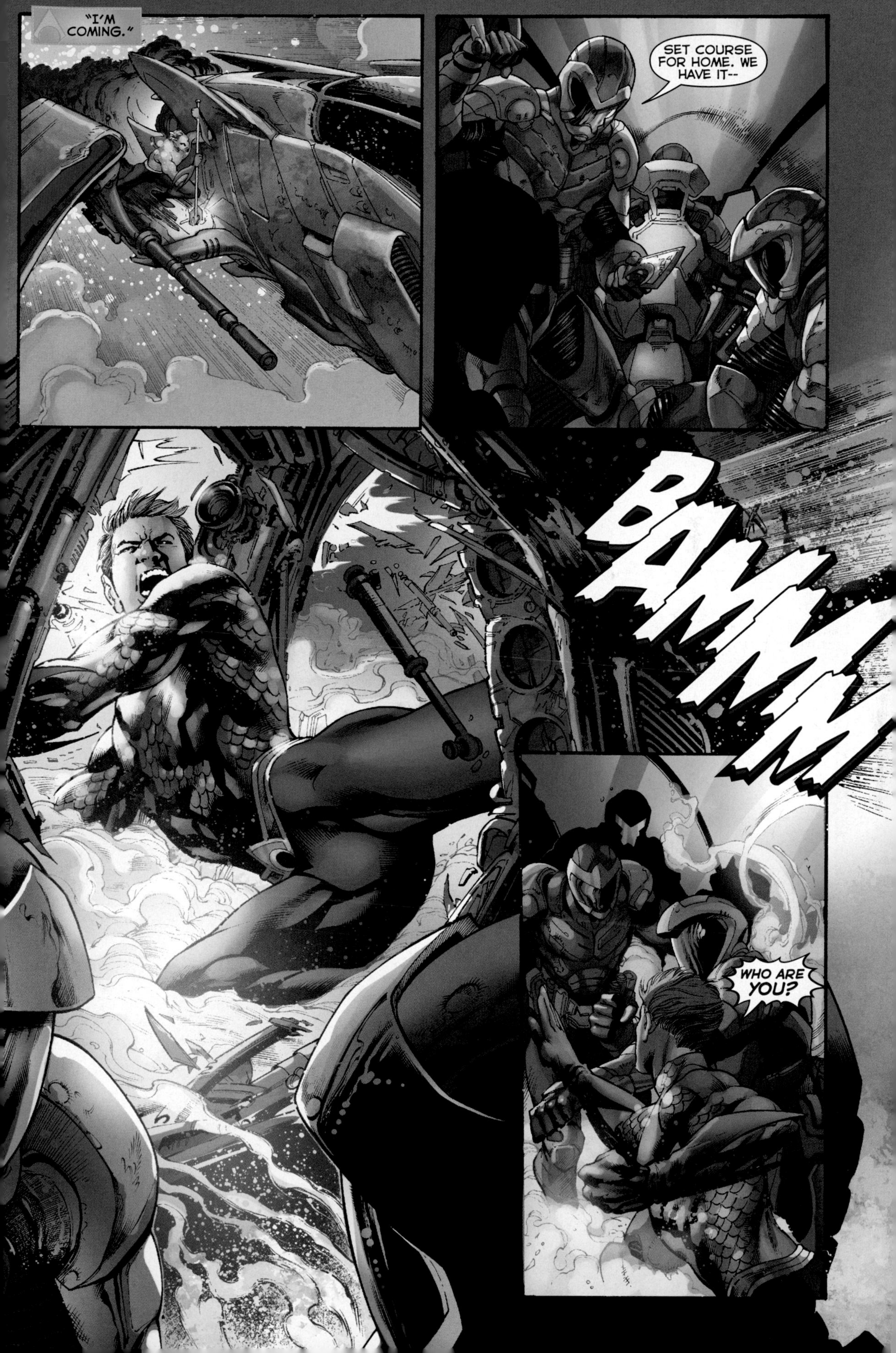
"I'M COMING."
SET COURSE FOR HOME. WE HAVE IT--
BAMMM
WHO ARE YOU?

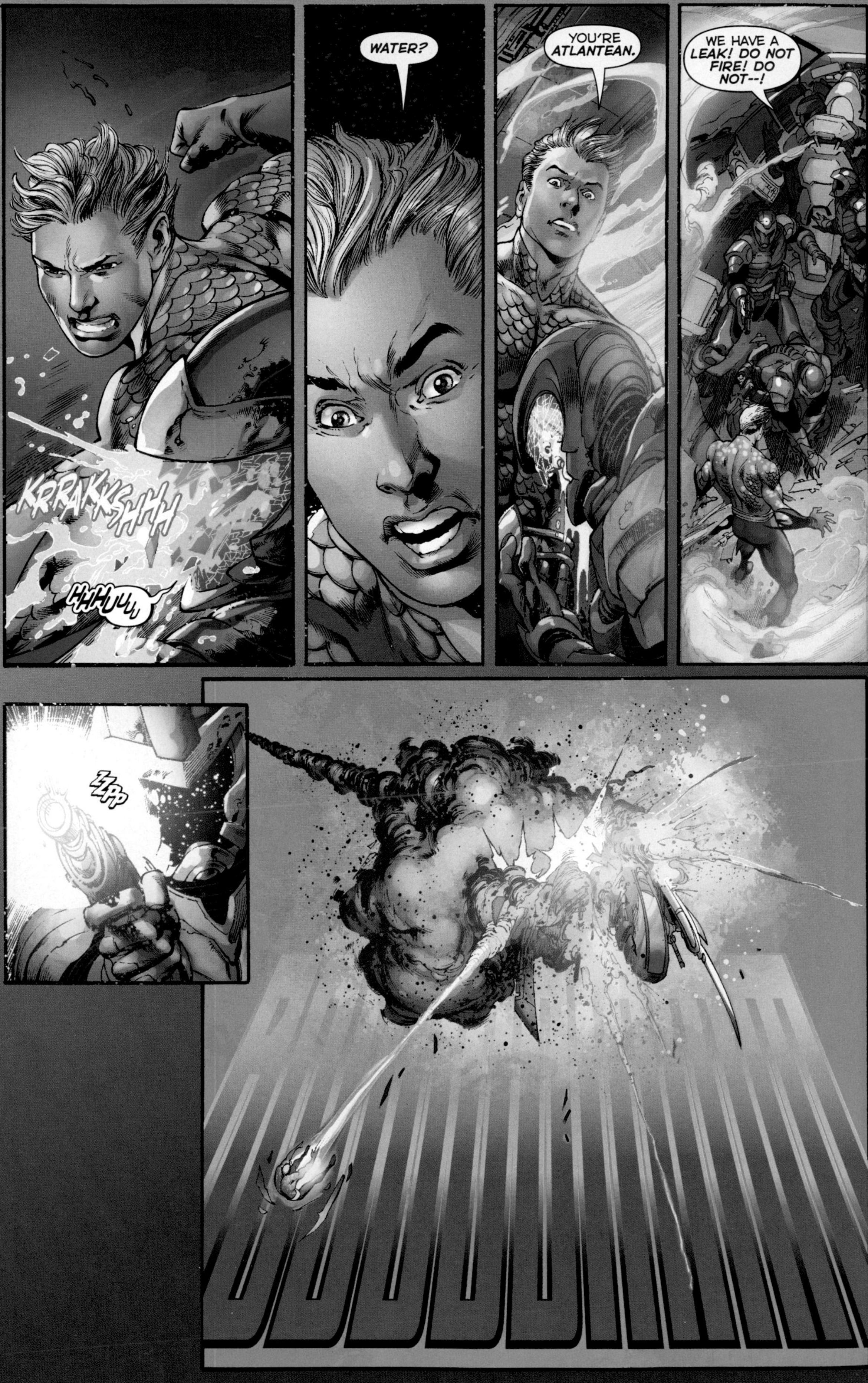
KRRAKKSHHH
HHHUUU
WATER?
YOU'RE ATLANTEAN.
WE HAVE A LEAK! DO NOT FIRE! DO NOT--!
ZZPP

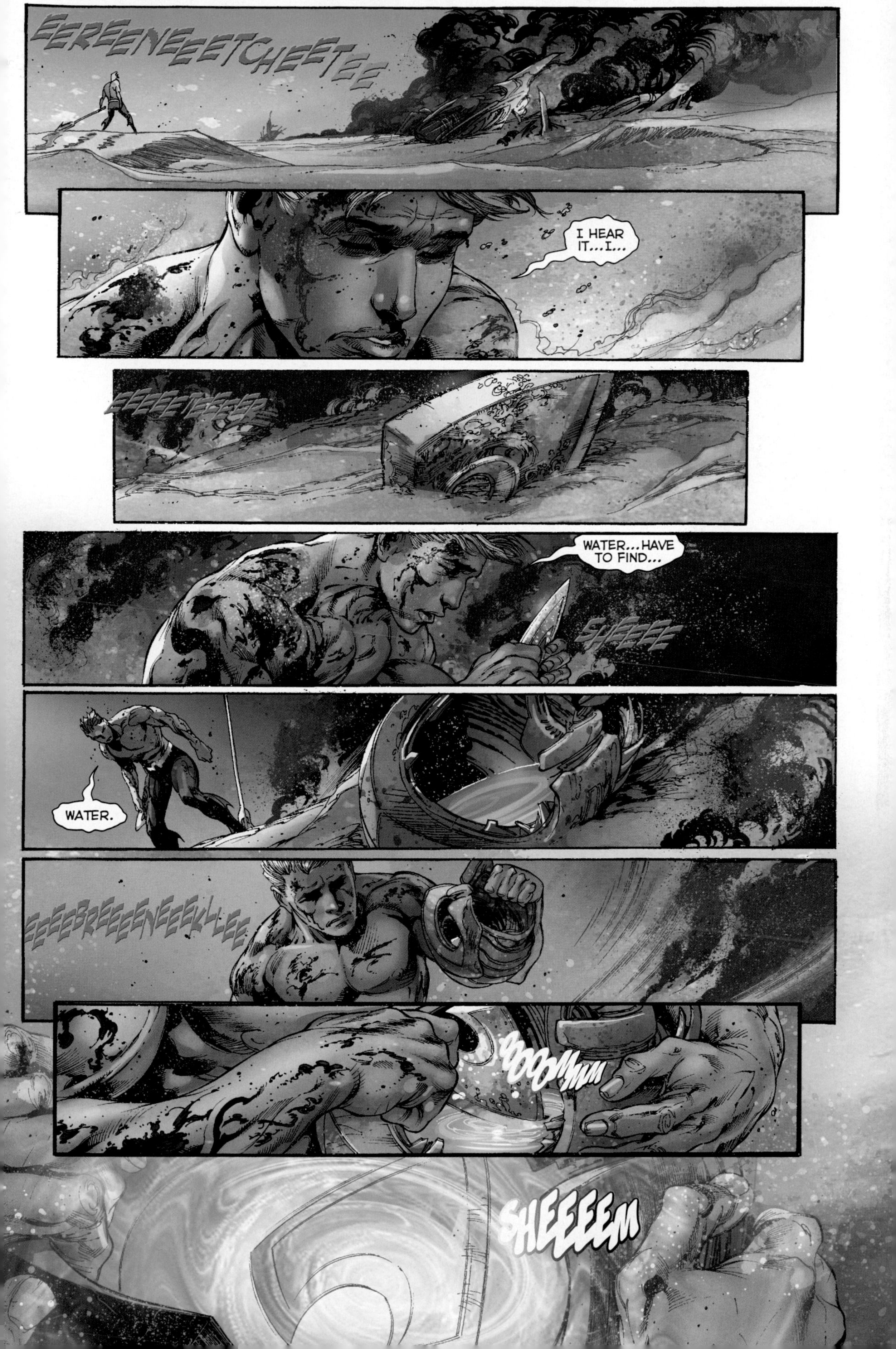
EEREEENEEEETCHEEETEE
I HEAR IT...I...
EEEEEETEEEEP
WATER...HAVE TO FIND...
SHEEEE
WATER.
EEEEBREEEENEEEKLLEE
OOOOMMM
SHEEEEM

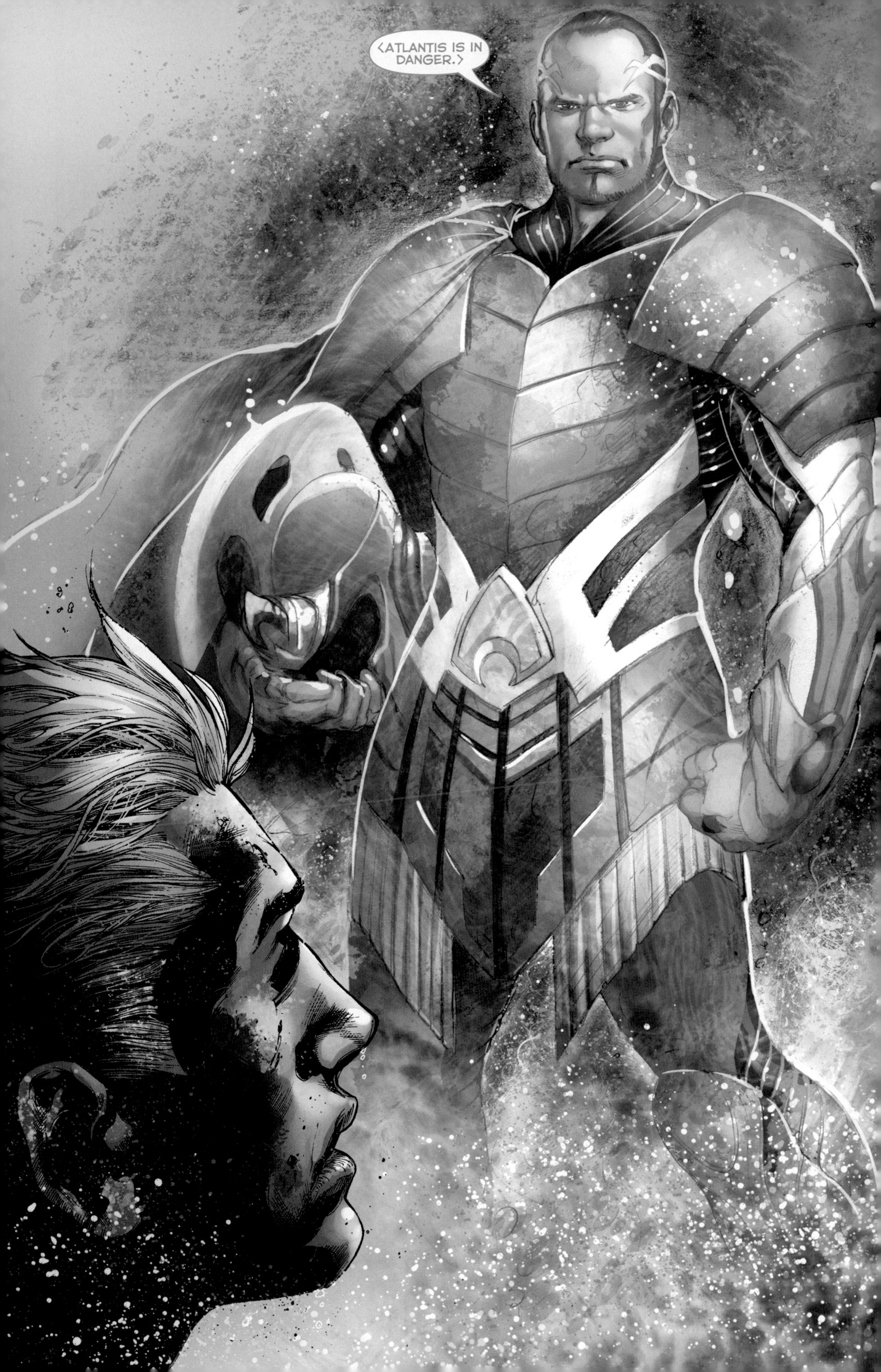

<ATLANTIS IS IN DANGER.>

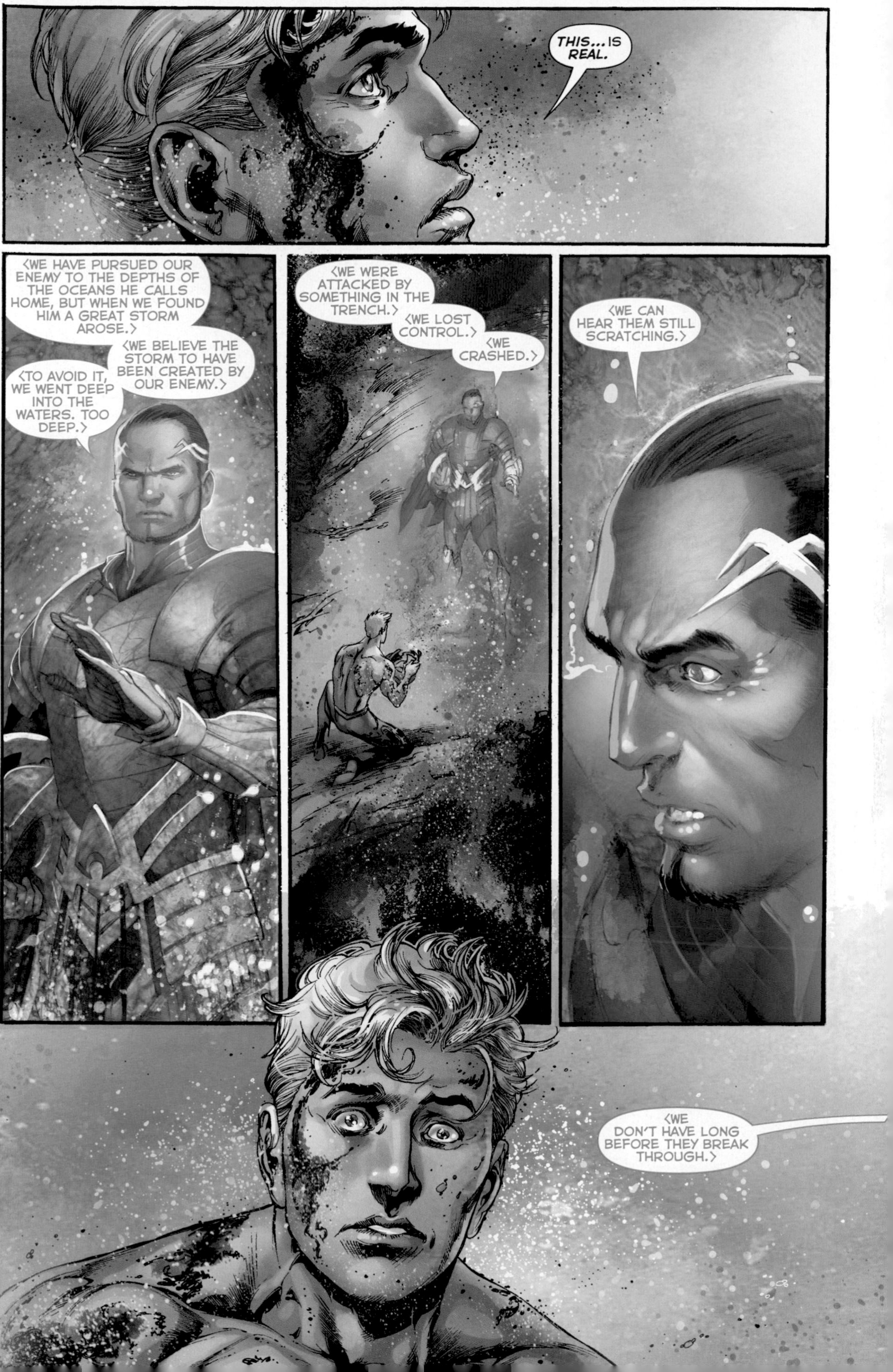
THIS... IS REAL.
<WE HAVE PURSUED OUR ENEMY TO THE DEPTHS OF THE OCEANS HE CALLS HOME, BUT WHEN WE FOUND HIM A GREAT STORM AROSE.>
<WE BELIEVE THE STORM TO HAVE BEEN CREATED BY OUR ENEMY.>
<TO AVOID IT, WE WENT DEEP INTO THE WATERS. TOO DEEP.>
<WE WERE ATTACKED BY SOMETHING IN THE TRENCH.>
<WE LOST CONTROL.>
<WE CRASHED.>
<WE CAN HEAR THEM STILL SCRATCHING.>
<WE DON'T HAVE LONG BEFORE THEY BREAK THROUGH.>

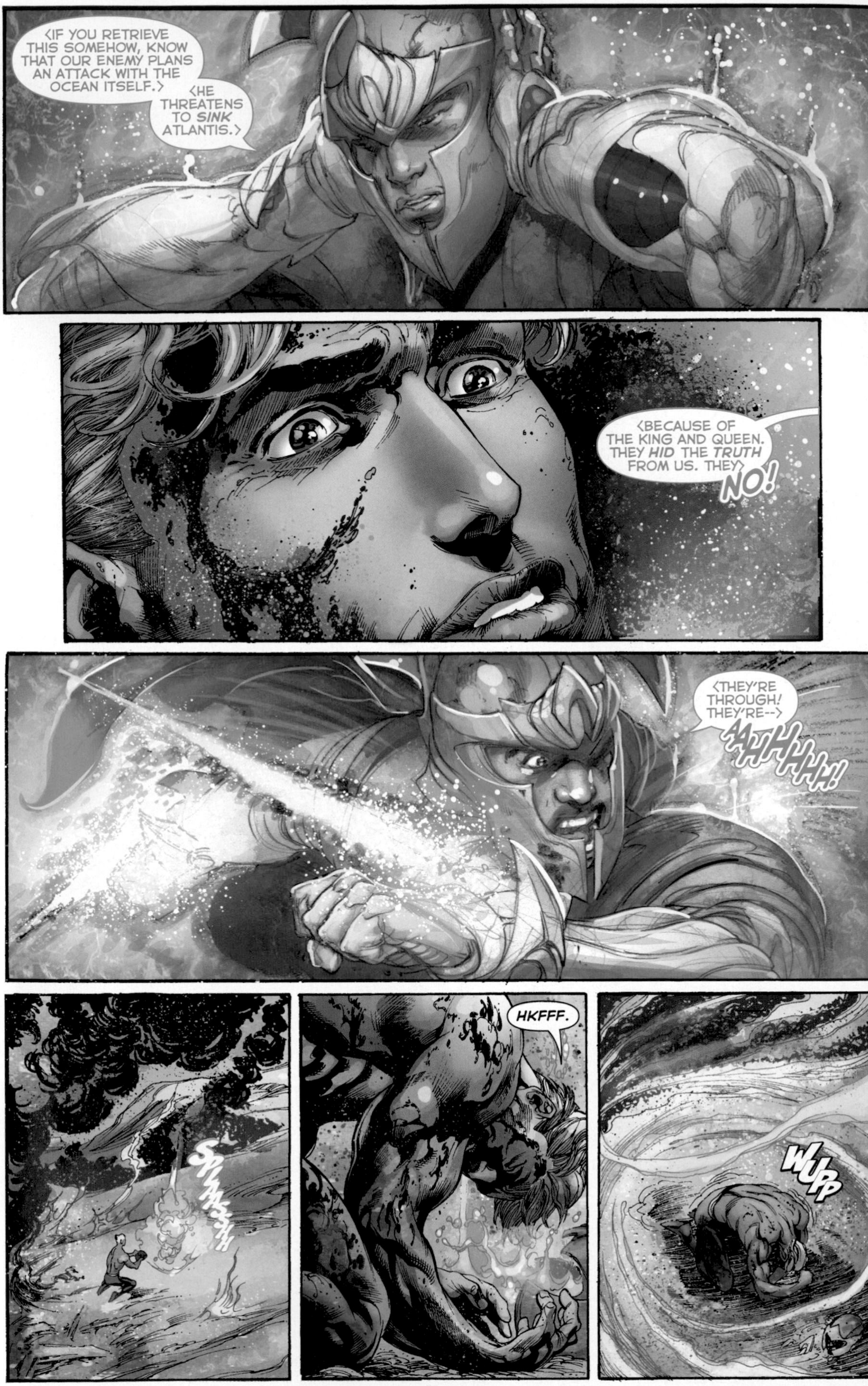

<IF YOU RETRIEVE THIS SOMEHOW, KNOW THAT OUR ENEMY PLANS AN ATTACK WITH THE OCEAN ITSELF.>
<HE THREATENS TO SINK ATLANTIS.>
<BECAUSE OF THE KING AND QUEEN. THEY HID THE TRUTH FROM US. THEY>
NO!
<THEY'RE THROUGH! THEY'RE-->
AAHHHHHH!
SPLASSHH
HKFFF.
WUPP

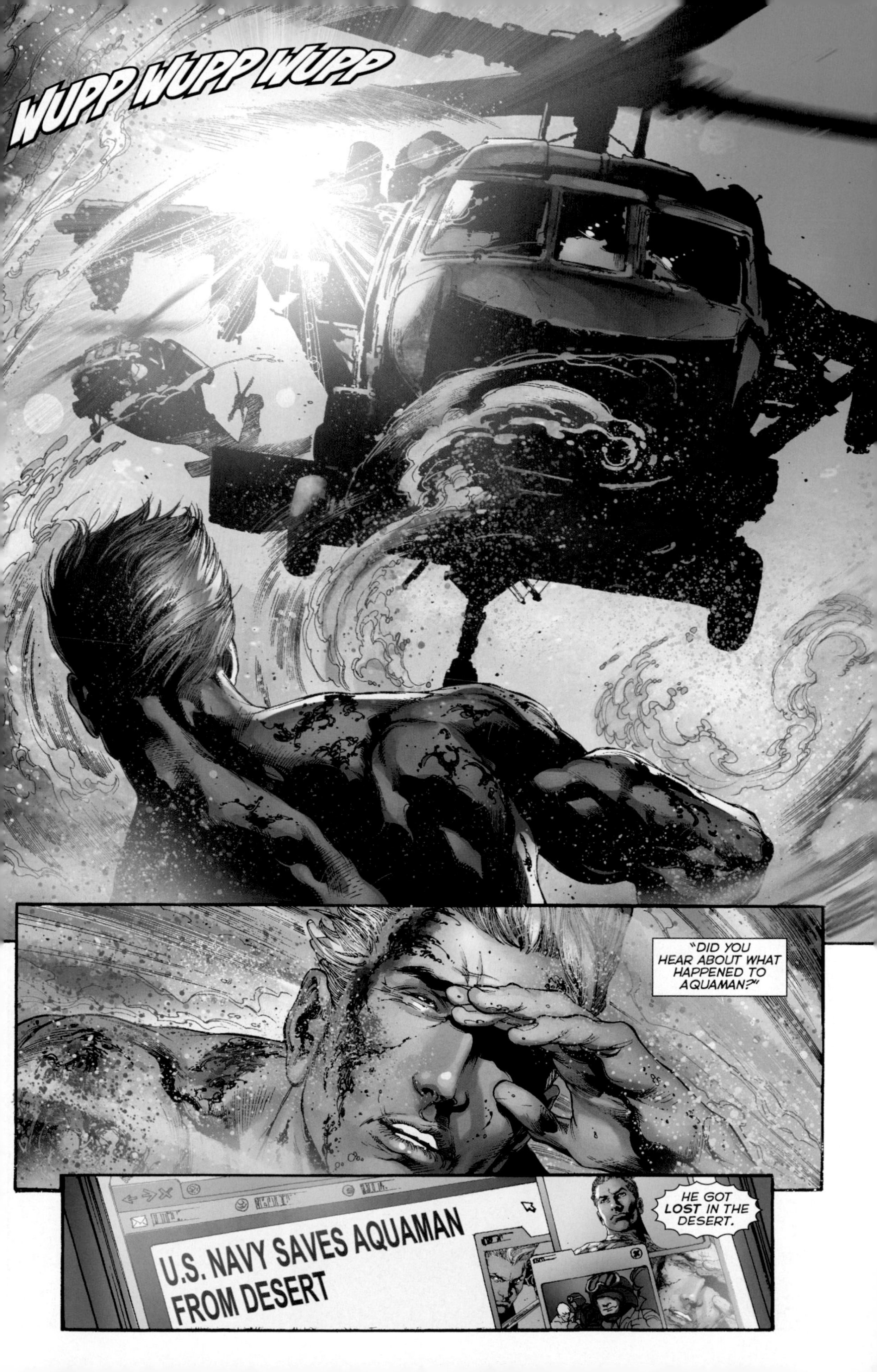
WUPP WUPP WUPP
"DID YOU HEAR ABOUT WHAT HAPPENED TO AQUAMAN?"
U.S. NAVY SAVES AQUAMAN FROM DESERT
HE GOT LOST IN THE DESERT.

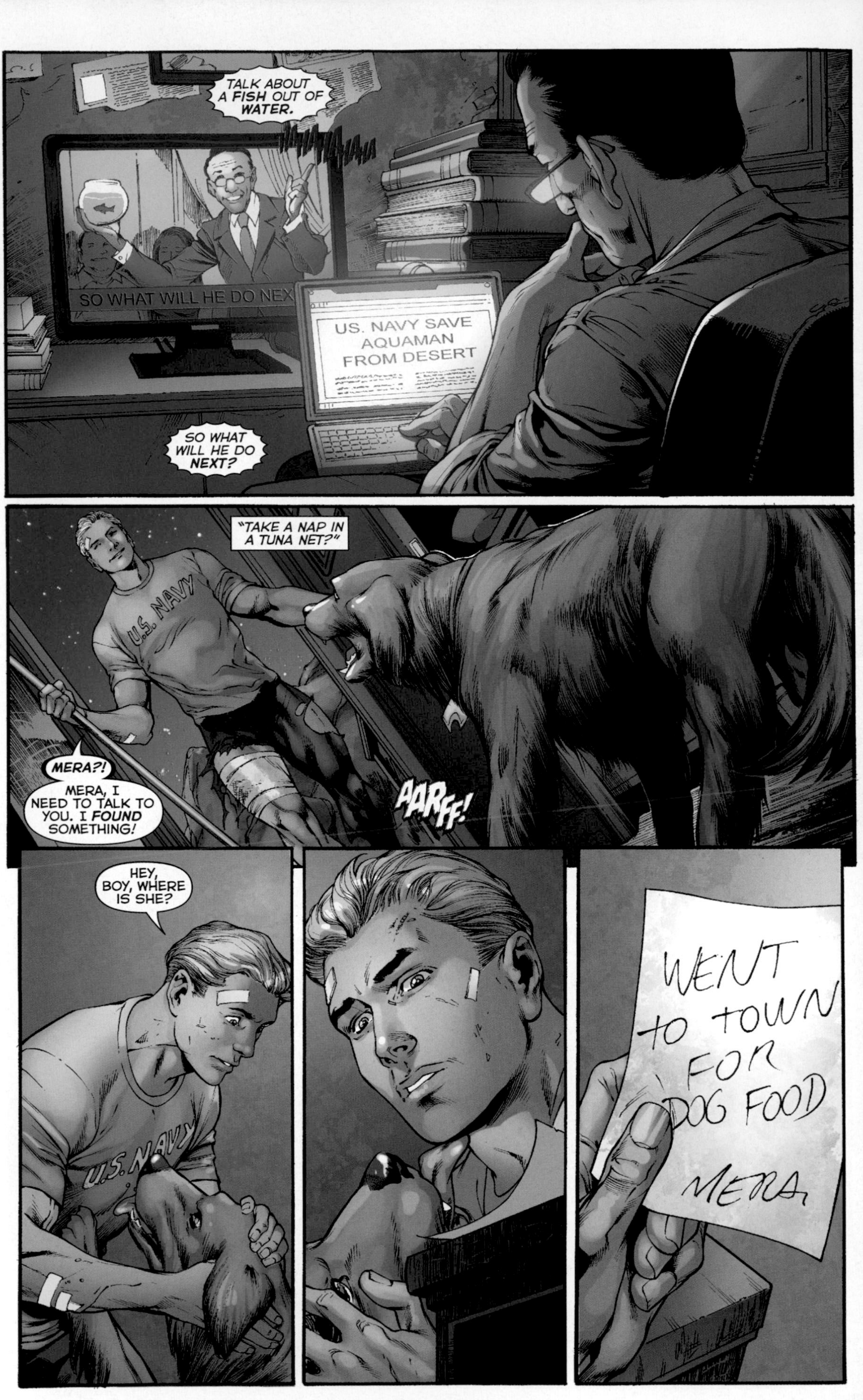
TALK ABOUT A FISH OUT OF WATER.
HAHAHAHAHA
SO WHAT WILL HE DO NEX
US. NAVY SAVE AQUAMAN FROM DESERT
SO WHAT WILL HE DO NEXT?
"TAKE A NAP IN A TUNA NET?"
MERA?!
MERA, I NEED TO TALK TO YOU. I FOUND SOMETHING!
AARFF!
HEY, BOY, WHERE IS SHE?
WENT TO TOWN FOR DOG FOOD
MERA

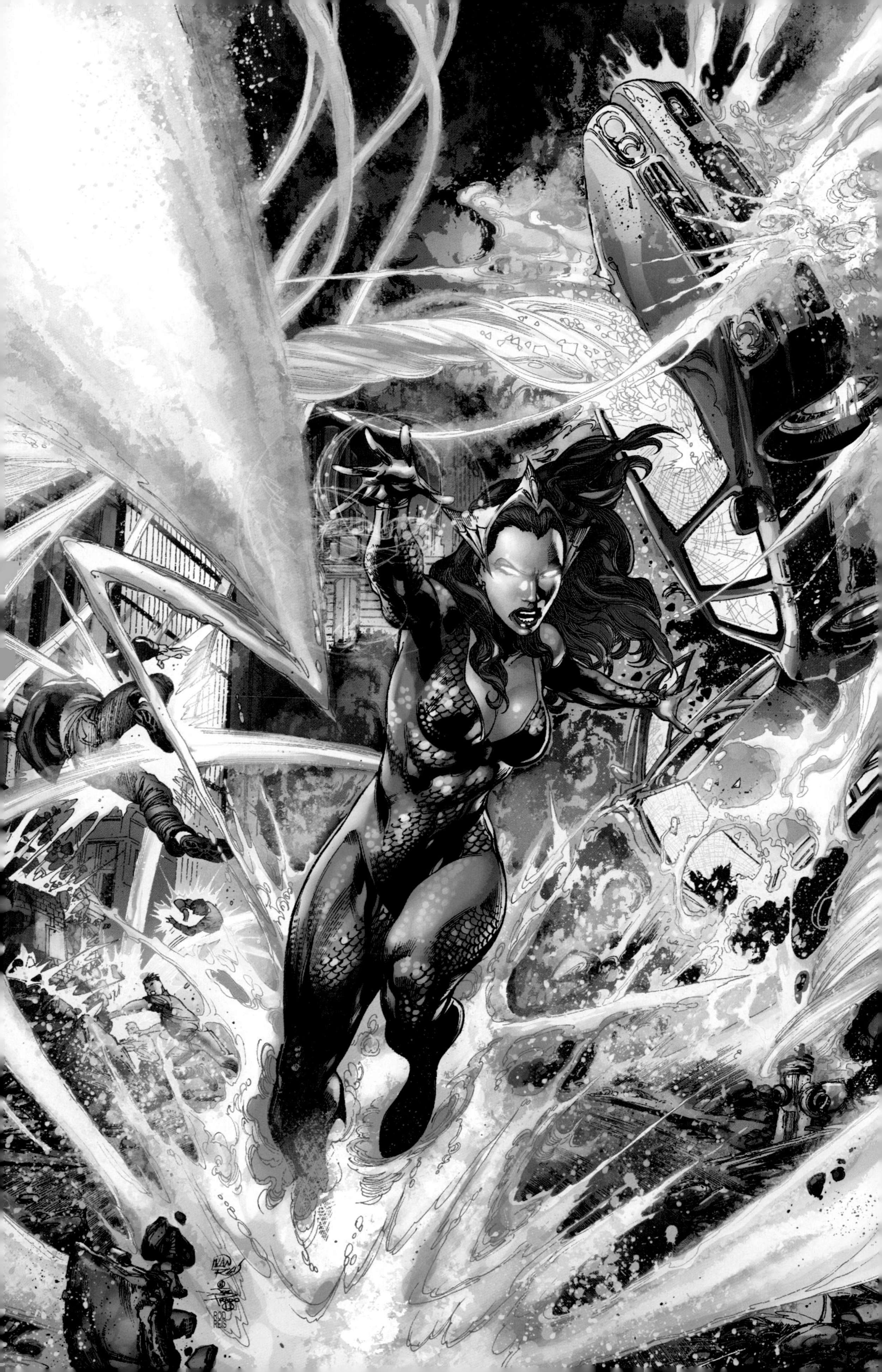
ROD REIS

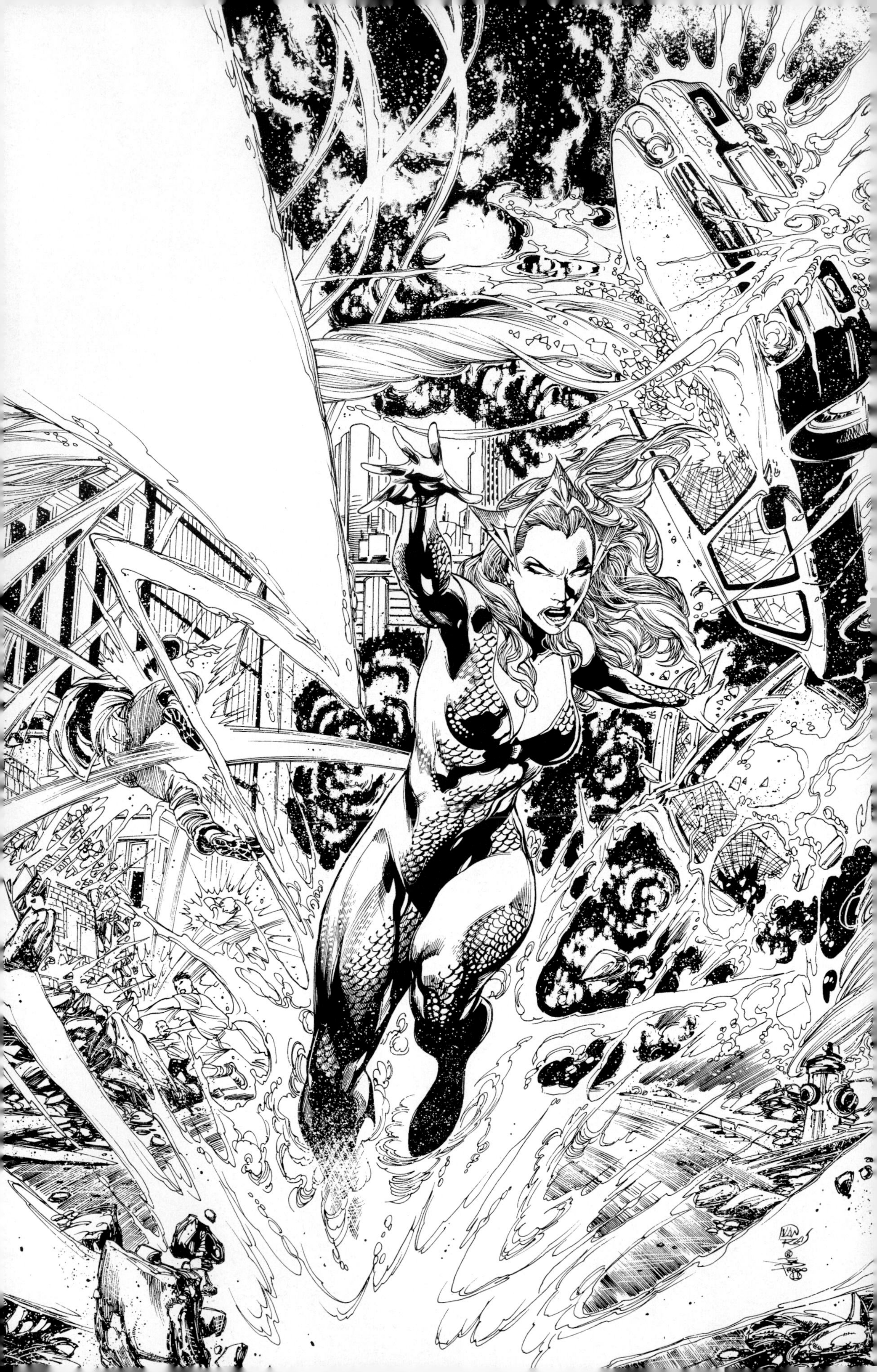

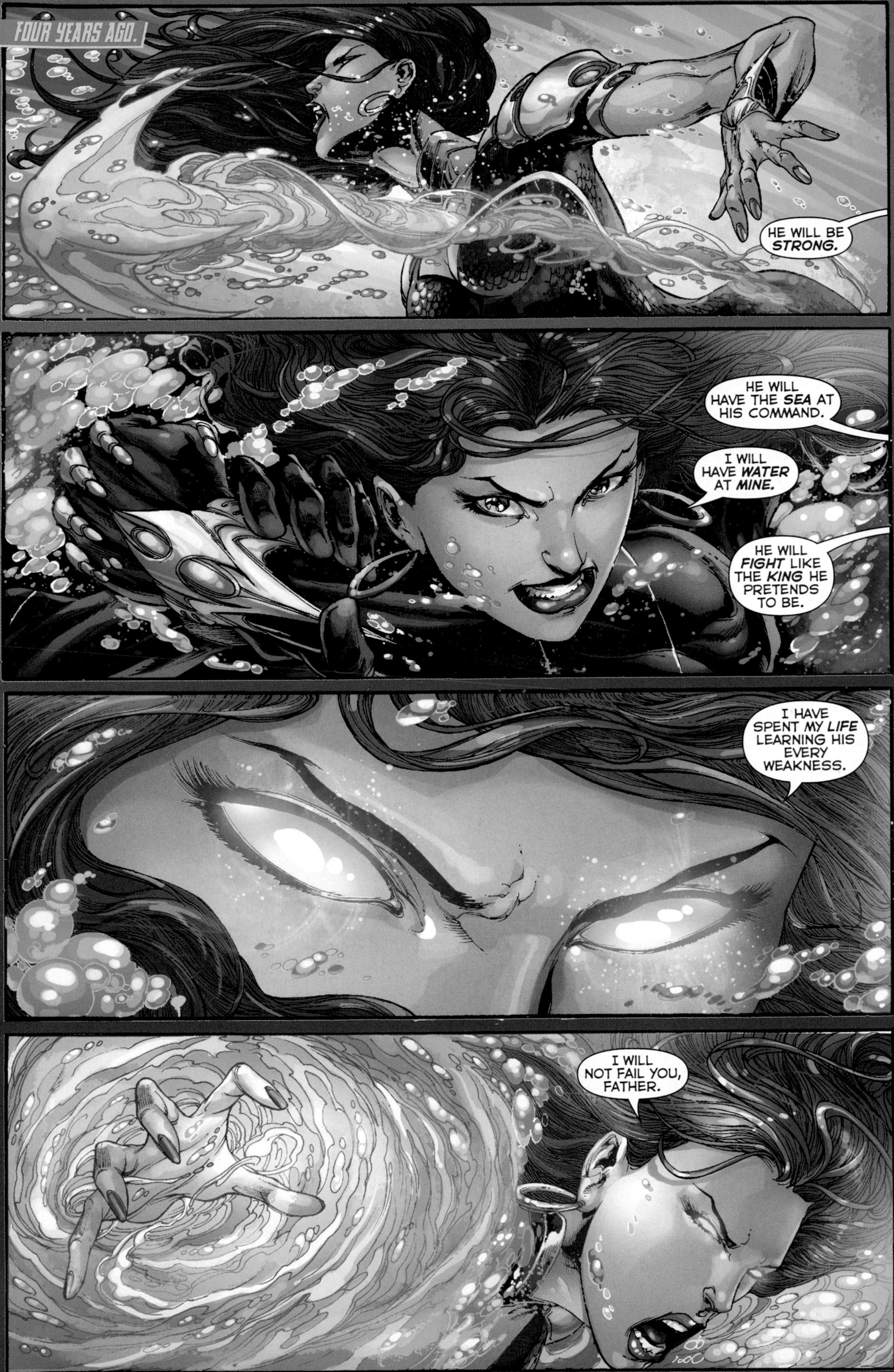
FOUR YEARS AGO.
HE WILL BE STRONG.
HE WILL HAVE THE SEA AT HIS COMMAND.
I WILL HAVE WATER AT MINE.
HE WILL FIGHT LIKE THE KING HE PRETENDS TO BE.
I HAVE SPENT MY LIFE LEARNING HIS EVERY WEAKNESS.
I WILL NOT FAIL YOU, FATHER.

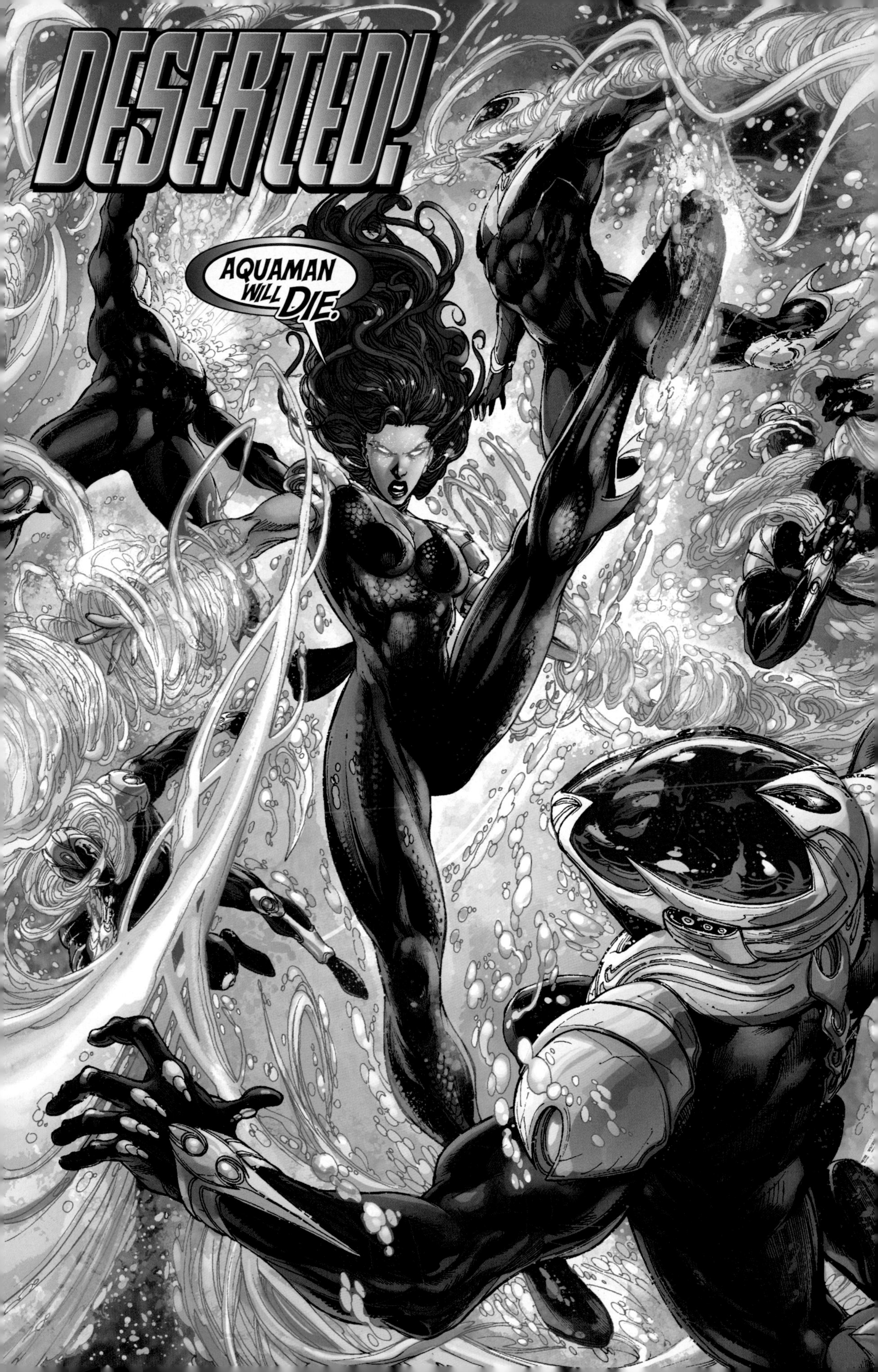
DESERTED!
AQUAMAN WILL DIE.

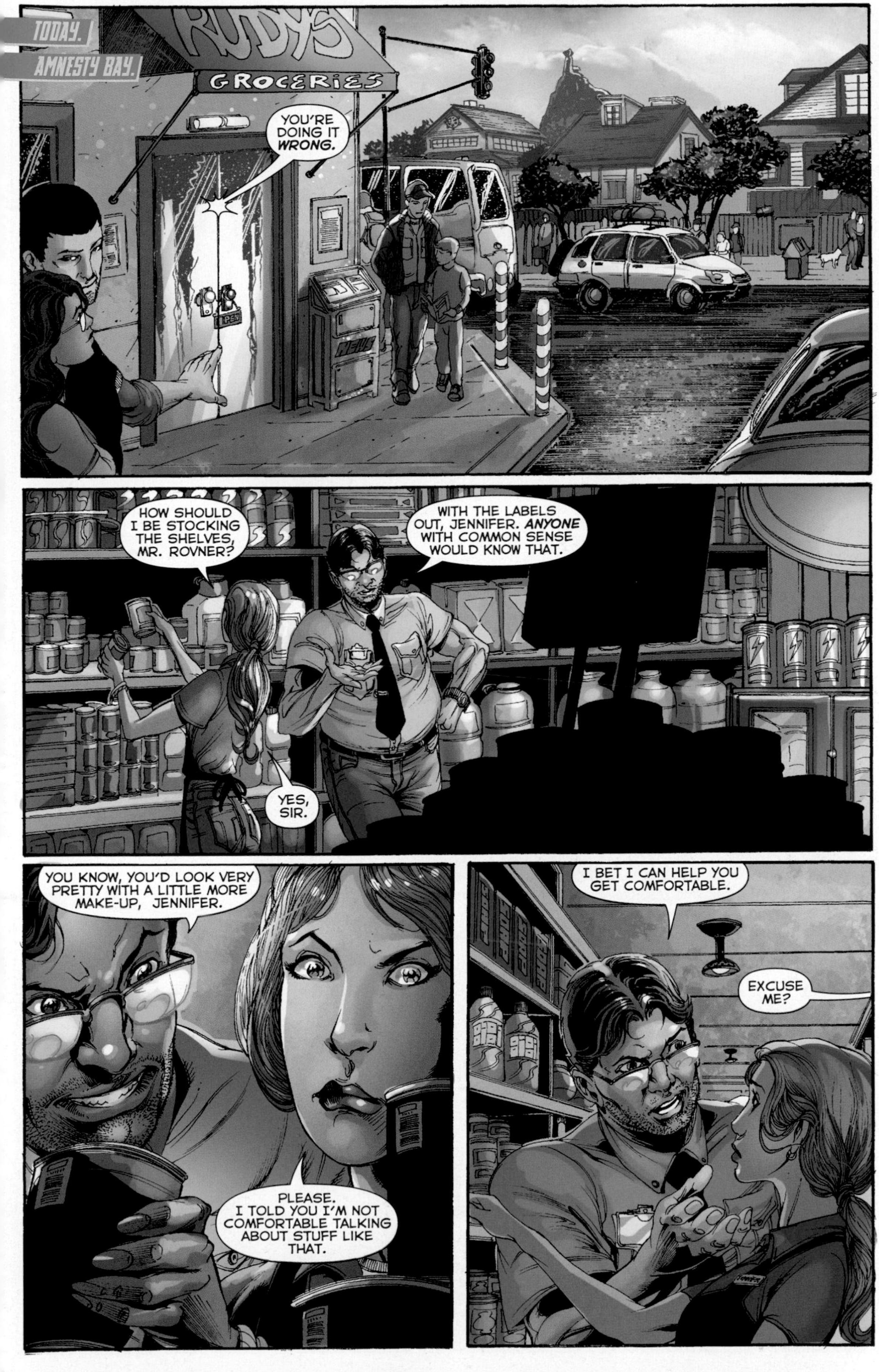
TODAY.
AMNESTY BAY.
RUDY'S
GROCERIES
YOU'RE DOING IT WRONG.
NEWS
HOW SHOULD I BE STOCKING THE SHELVES, MR. ROVNER?
WITH THE LABELS OUT, JENNIFER. ANYONE WITH COMMON SENSE WOULD KNOW THAT.
YES, SIR.
YOU KNOW, YOU'D LOOK VERY PRETTY WITH A LITTLE MORE MAKE-UP, JENNIFER.
PLEASE. I TOLD YOU I'M NOT COMFORTABLE TALKING ABOUT STUFF LIKE THAT.
I BET I CAN HELP YOU GET COMFORTABLE.
EXCUSE ME?

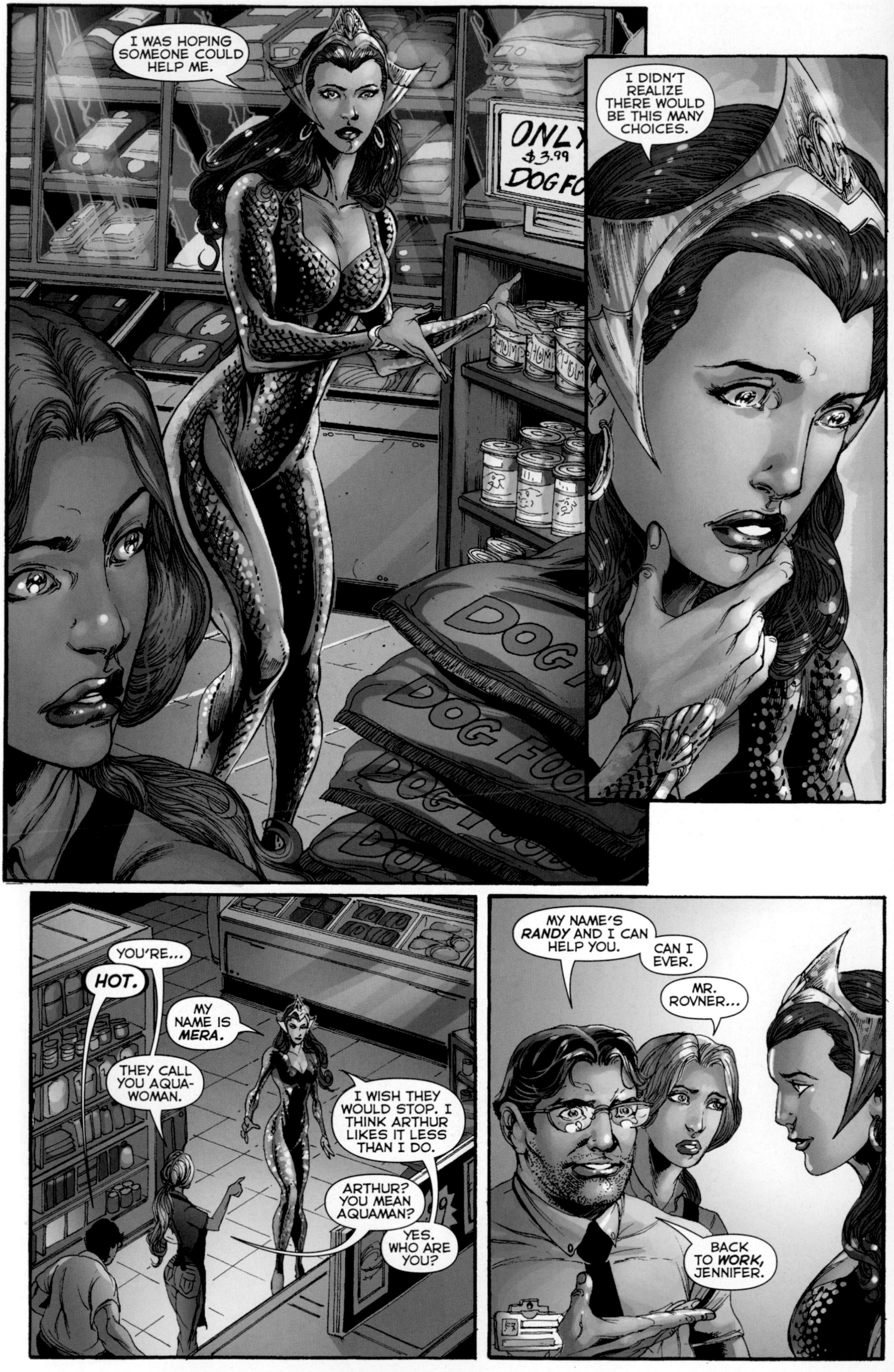
I WAS HOPING SOMEONE COULD HELP ME.
ONLY $3.99 DOG FO
I DIDN'T REALIZE THERE WOULD BE THIS MANY CHOICES.
DOG F
DOG FOOD
DOG FOO
YOU'RE... HOT.
MY NAME IS MERA.
THEY CALL YOU AQUA-WOMAN.
I WISH THEY WOULD STOP. I THINK ARTHUR LIKES IT LESS THAN I DO.
ARTHUR? YOU MEAN AQUAMAN?
YES. WHO ARE YOU?
MY NAME'S RANDY AND I CAN HELP YOU.
CAN I EVER.
MR. ROVNER...
BACK TO WORK, JENNIFER.

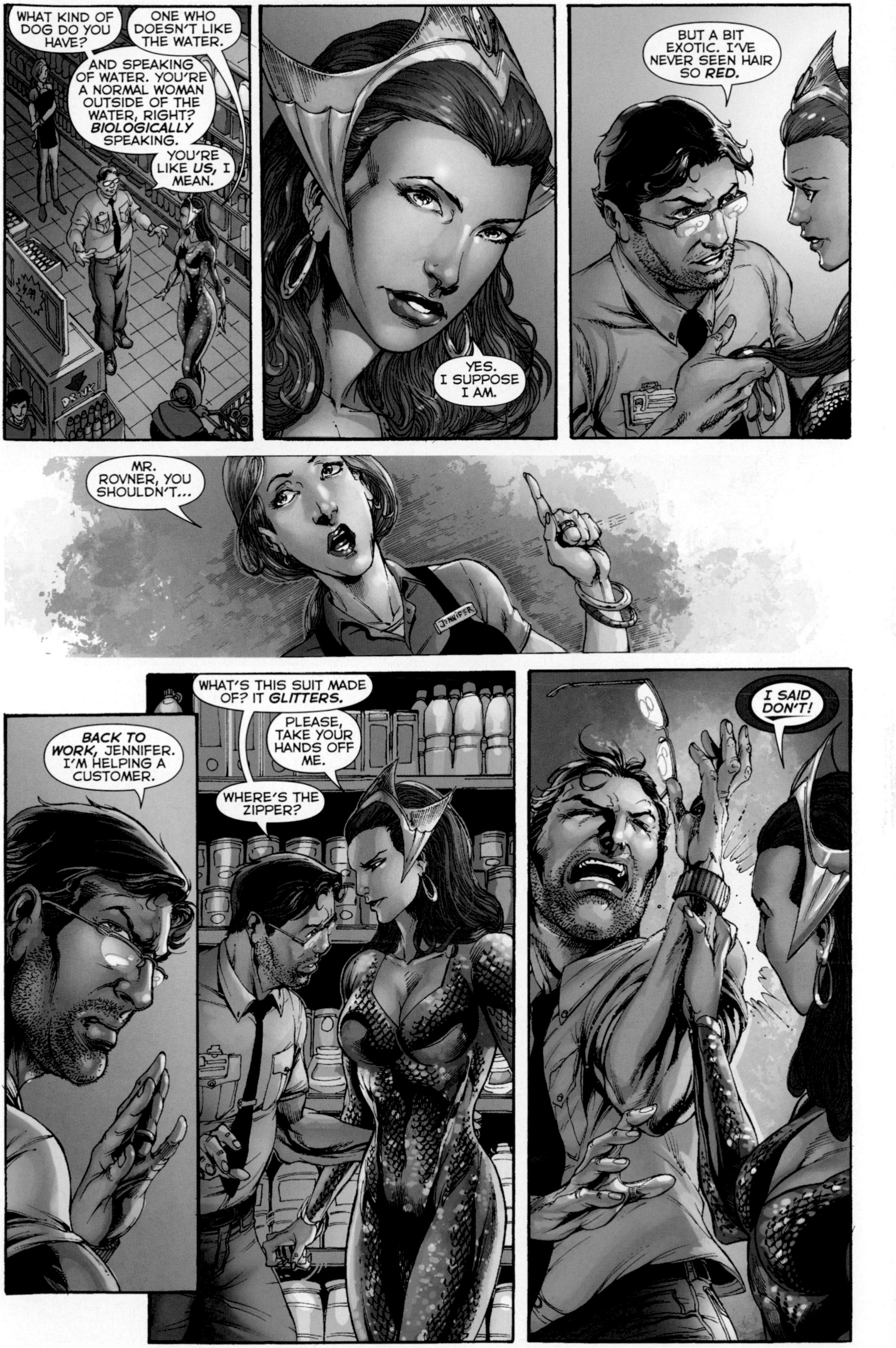
WHAT KIND OF DOG DO YOU HAVE?
ONE WHO DOESN'T LIKE THE WATER.
AND SPEAKING OF WATER. YOU'RE A NORMAL WOMAN OUTSIDE OF THE WATER, RIGHT? *BIOLOGICALLY* SPEAKING.
YOU'RE LIKE *US,* I MEAN.
YES. I SUPPOSE I AM.
BUT A BIT EXOTIC. I'VE NEVER SEEN HAIR SO *RED.*
MR. ROVNER, YOU SHOULDN'T...
JENNIFER
BACK TO WORK, JENNIFER. I'M HELPING A CUSTOMER.
WHAT'S THIS SUIT MADE OF? IT *GLITTERS.*
PLEASE, TAKE YOUR HANDS OFF ME.
WHERE'S THE ZIPPER?
I SAID DON'T!

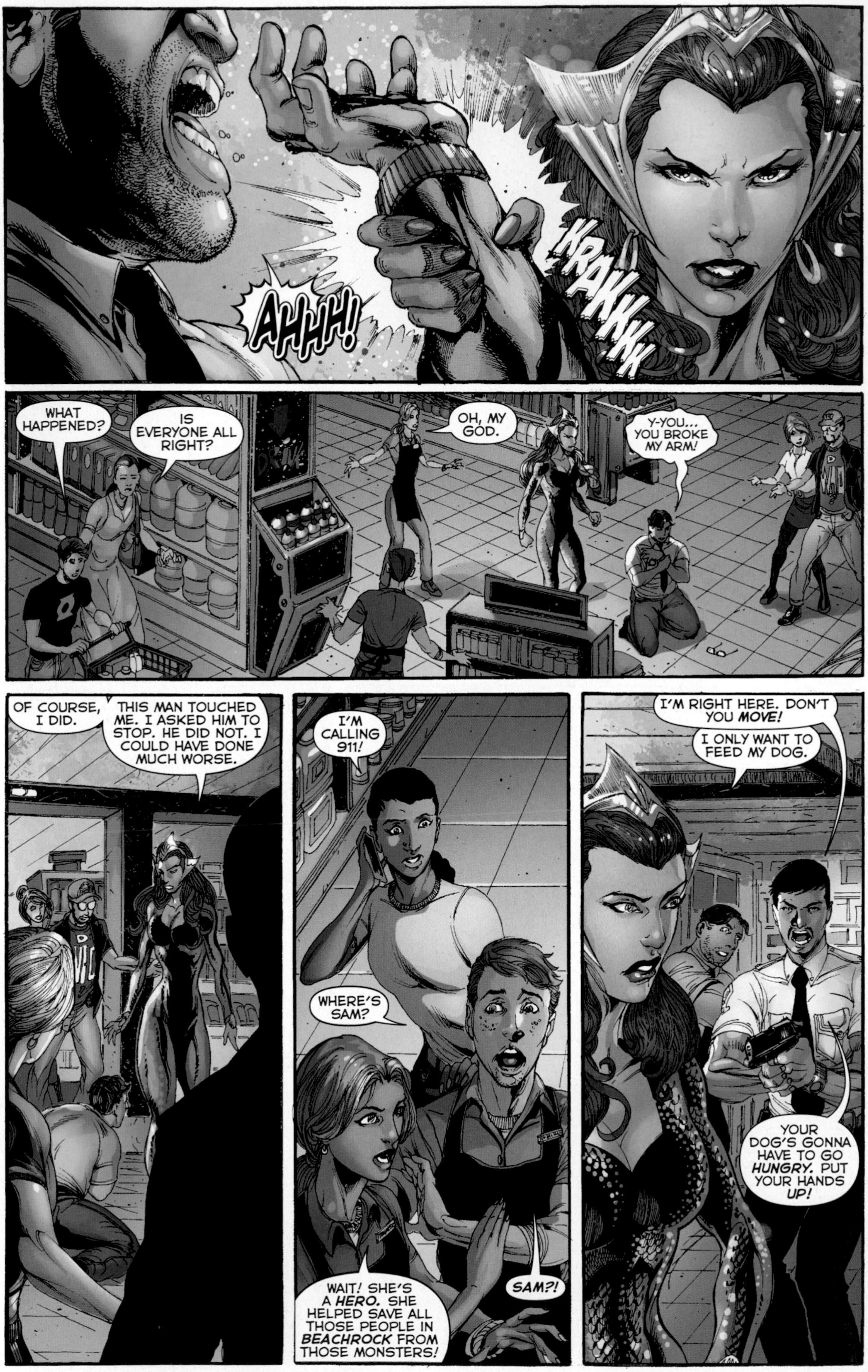

AHHH!
KRAKKKK
WHAT HAPPENED?
IS EVERYONE ALL RIGHT?
OH, MY GOD.
Y-YOU... YOU BROKE MY ARM!
OF COURSE, I DID.
THIS MAN TOUCHED ME. I ASKED HIM TO STOP. HE DID NOT. I COULD HAVE DONE MUCH WORSE.
I'M CALLING 911!
WHERE'S SAM?
WAIT! SHE'S A HERO. SHE HELPED SAVE ALL THOSE PEOPLE IN BEACHROCK FROM THOSE MONSTERS!
SAM?!
I'M RIGHT HERE. DON'T YOU MOVE!
I ONLY WANT TO FEED MY DOG.
YOUR DOG'S GONNA HAVE TO GO HUNGRY. PUT YOUR HANDS UP!

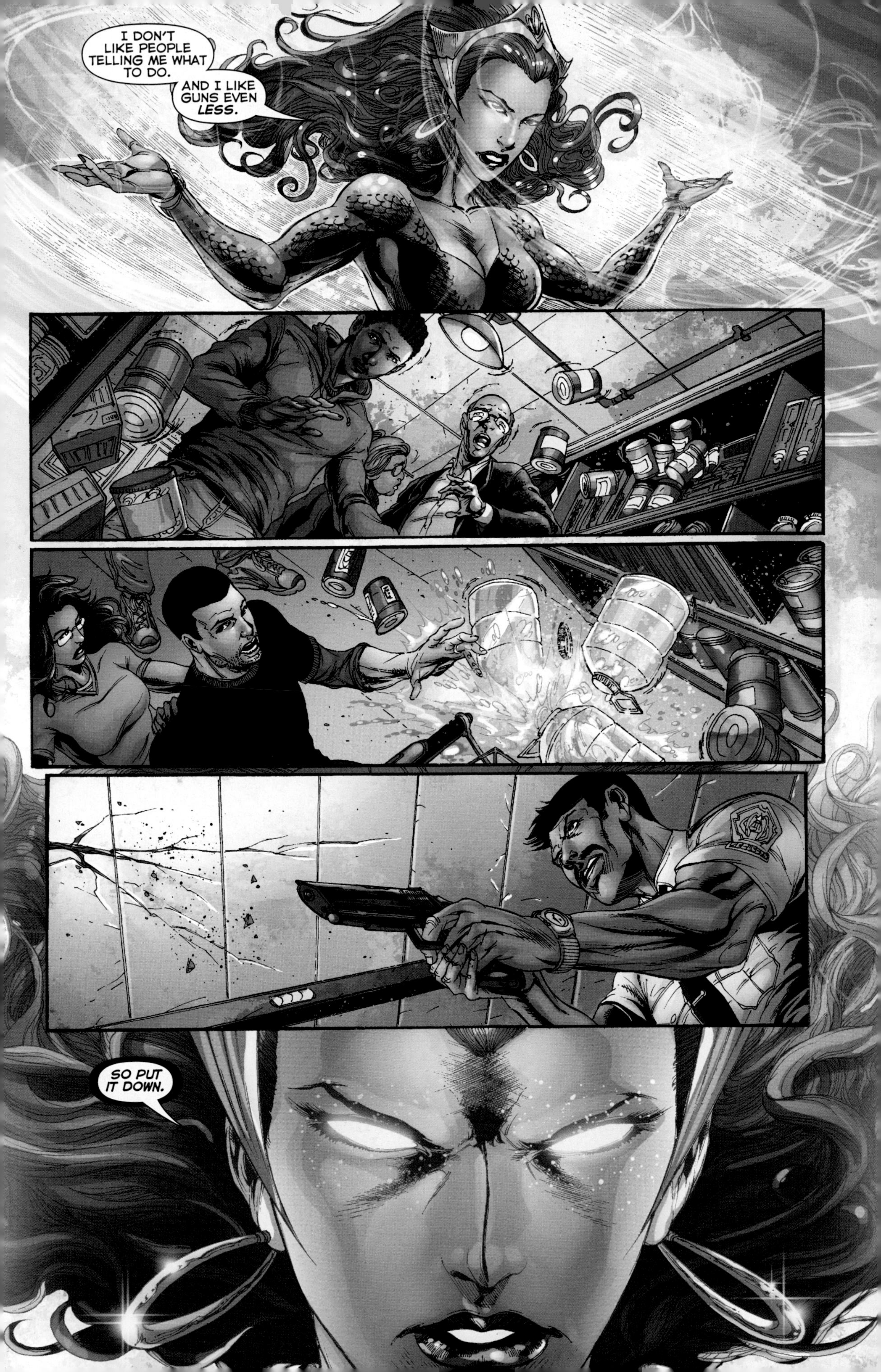
I DON'T LIKE PEOPLE TELLING ME WHAT TO DO.
AND I LIKE GUNS EVEN LESS.
SO PUT IT DOWN.

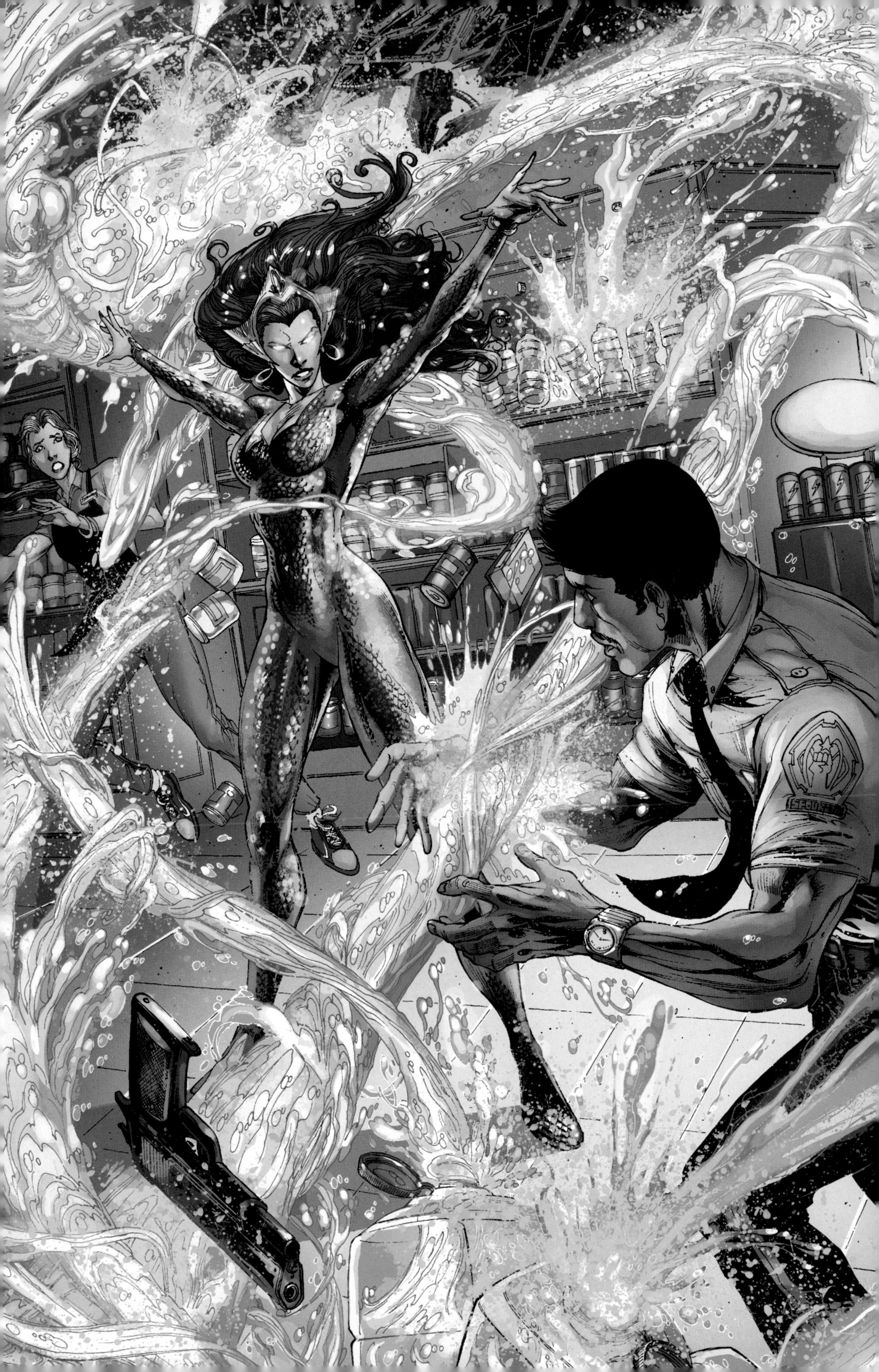

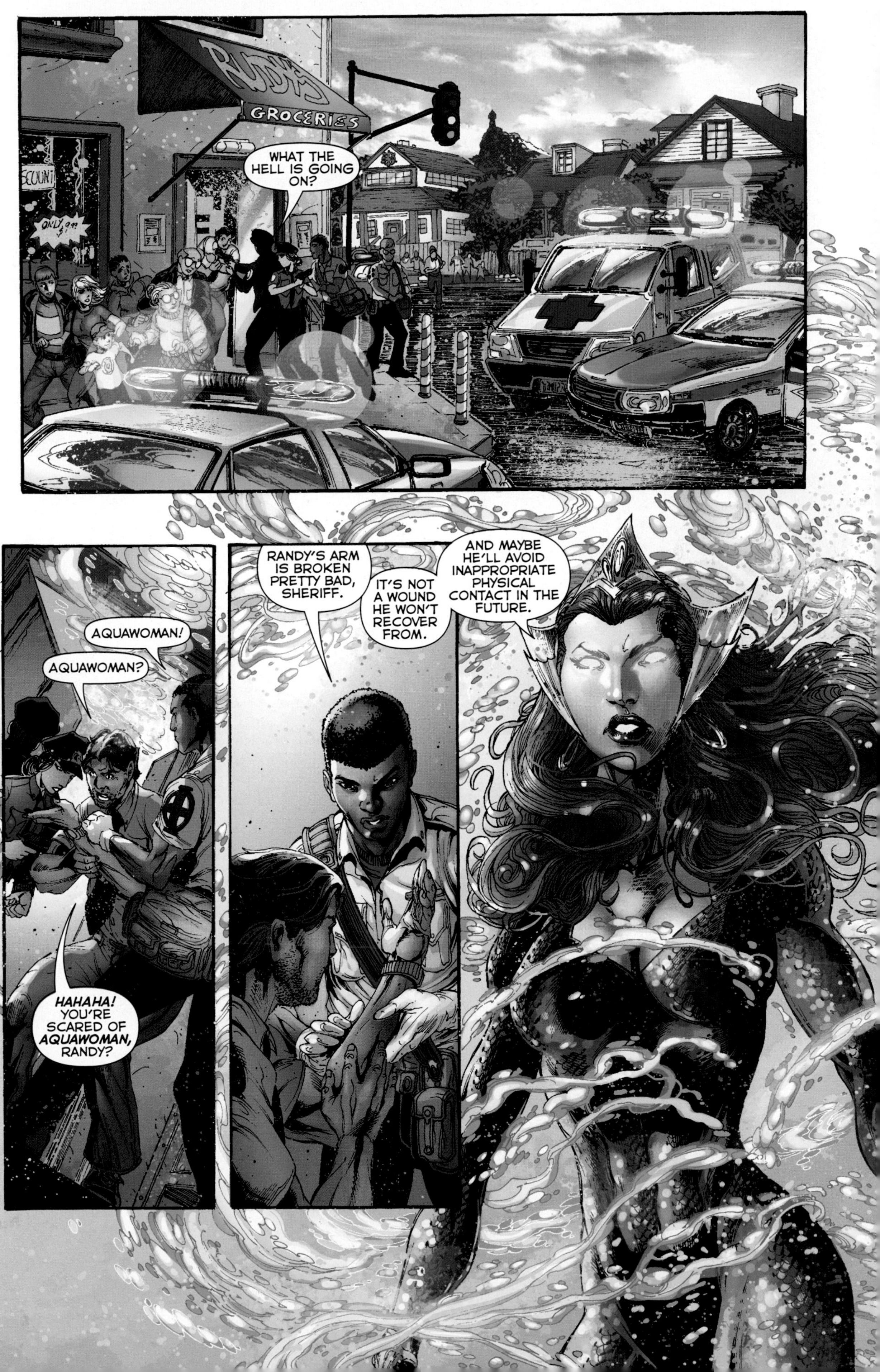
RUDY'S
GROCERIES
DISCOUNT
ONLY $9.99
WHAT THE HELL IS GOING ON?
AQUAWOMAN!
AQUAWOMAN?
HAHAHA! YOU'RE SCARED OF AQUAWOMAN, RANDY?
RANDY'S ARM IS BROKEN PRETTY BAD, SHERIFF.
IT'S NOT A WOUND HE WON'T RECOVER FROM.
AND MAYBE HE'LL AVOID INAPPROPRIATE PHYSICAL CONTACT IN THE FUTURE.

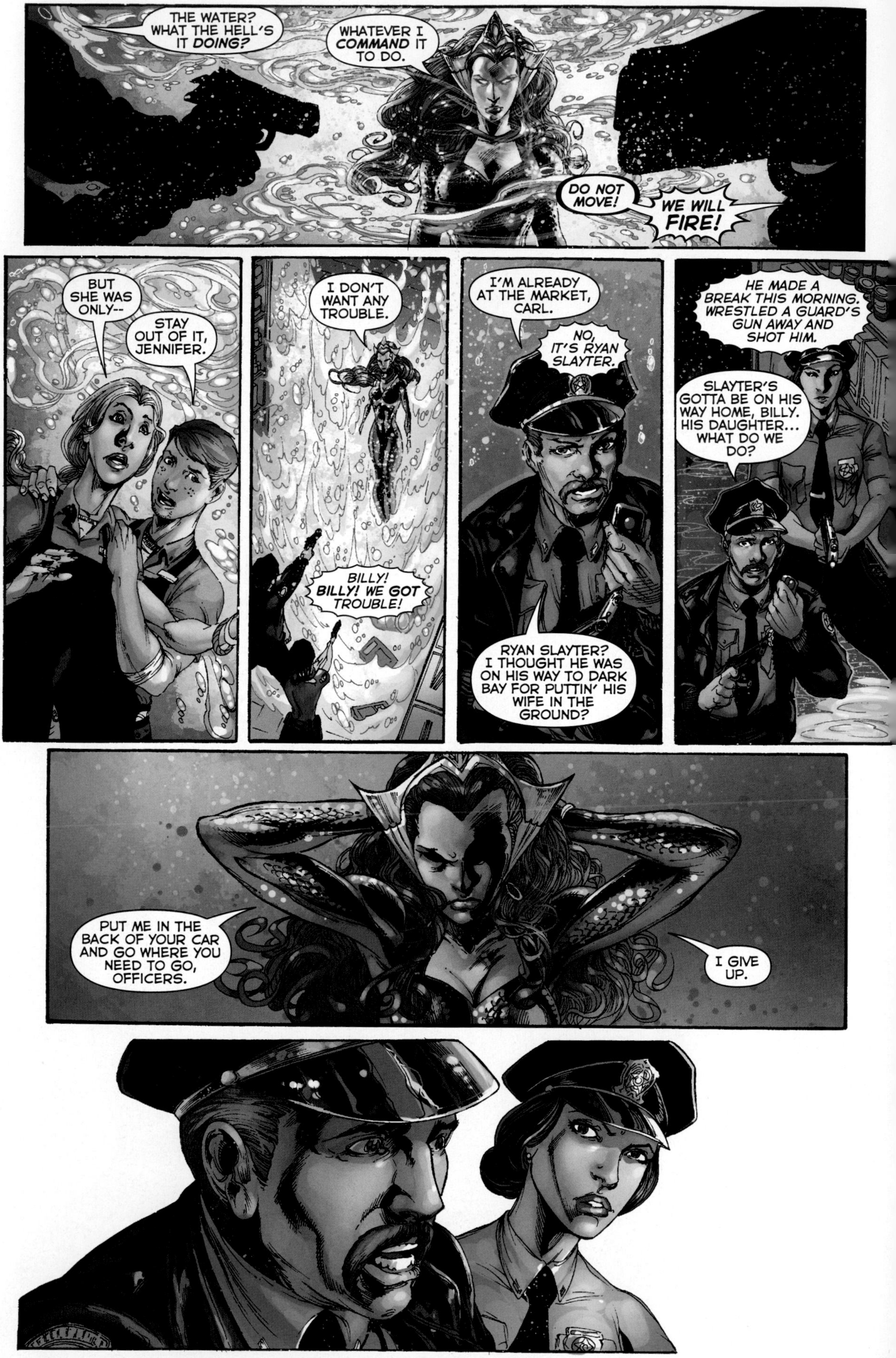
THE WATER? WHAT THE HELL'S IT *DOING?*
WHATEVER I *COMMAND* IT TO DO.
DO NOT MOVE!
WE WILL *FIRE!*
BUT SHE WAS ONLY--
STAY OUT OF IT, JENNIFER.
I DON'T WANT ANY TROUBLE.
BILLY! BILLY! WE GOT TROUBLE!
I'M ALREADY AT THE MARKET, CARL.
NO, IT'S RYAN SLAYTER.
RYAN SLAYTER? I THOUGHT HE WAS ON HIS WAY TO DARK BAY FOR PUTTIN' HIS WIFE IN THE GROUND?
HE MADE A BREAK THIS MORNING. WRESTLED A GUARD'S GUN AWAY AND SHOT HIM.
SLAYTER'S GOTTA BE ON HIS WAY HOME, BILLY. HIS DAUGHTER... WHAT DO WE DO?
PUT ME IN THE BACK OF YOUR CAR AND GO WHERE YOU NEED TO GO, OFFICERS.
I GIVE UP.

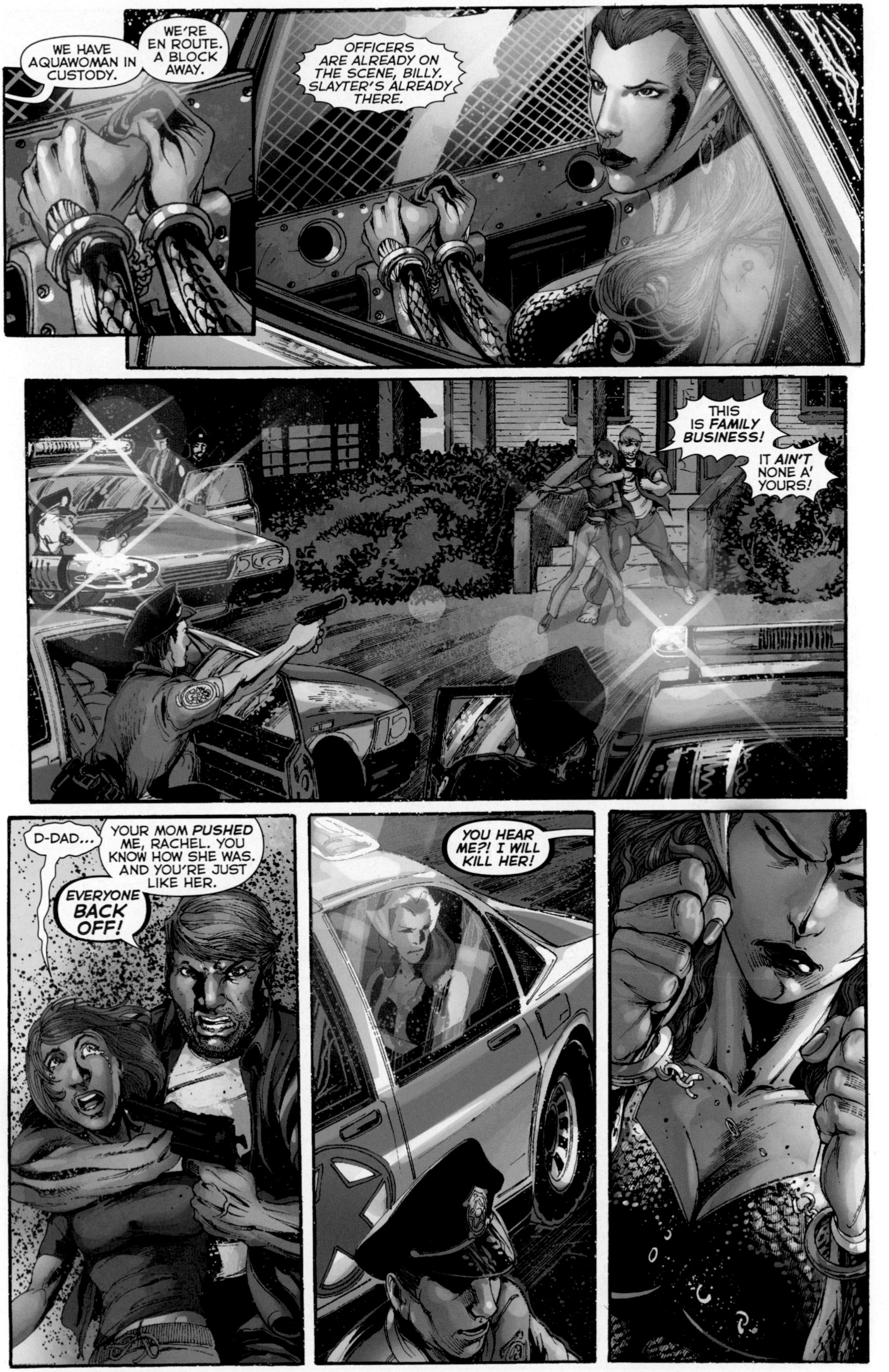
WE HAVE AQUAWOMAN IN CUSTODY.
WE'RE EN ROUTE. A BLOCK AWAY.
OFFICERS ARE ALREADY ON THE SCENE, BILLY. SLAYTER'S ALREADY THERE.
THIS IS FAMILY BUSINESS!
IT AIN'T NONE A' YOURS!
D-DAD...
YOUR MOM PUSHED ME, RACHEL. YOU KNOW HOW SHE WAS. AND YOU'RE JUST LIKE HER.
EVERYONE BACK OFF!
YOU HEAR ME?! I WILL KILL HER!

WHAT ARE YOU DOING?

I THOUGHT YOU SURRENDERED?

OBVIOUSLY NOT. I'LL DEAL WITH THIS.

DID YOU MURDER YOUR WIFE?

HEY... HEY...

STAY BACK!

DAMMIT, YOU HEARD HIM. STAY BACK!

THAT'S AQUAWOMAN, CHARLIE.

I DON'T CARE WHO IT IS. WE'RE HANDLING THIS. GET OUT OF THERE!

YOU'RE AQUAWOMAN?

HAHAHAHAHA!

YOU'RE REALLY AQUAWOMAN?

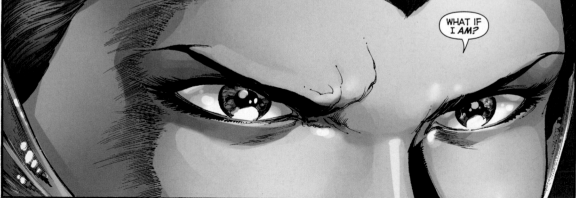

WHAT IF I AM?

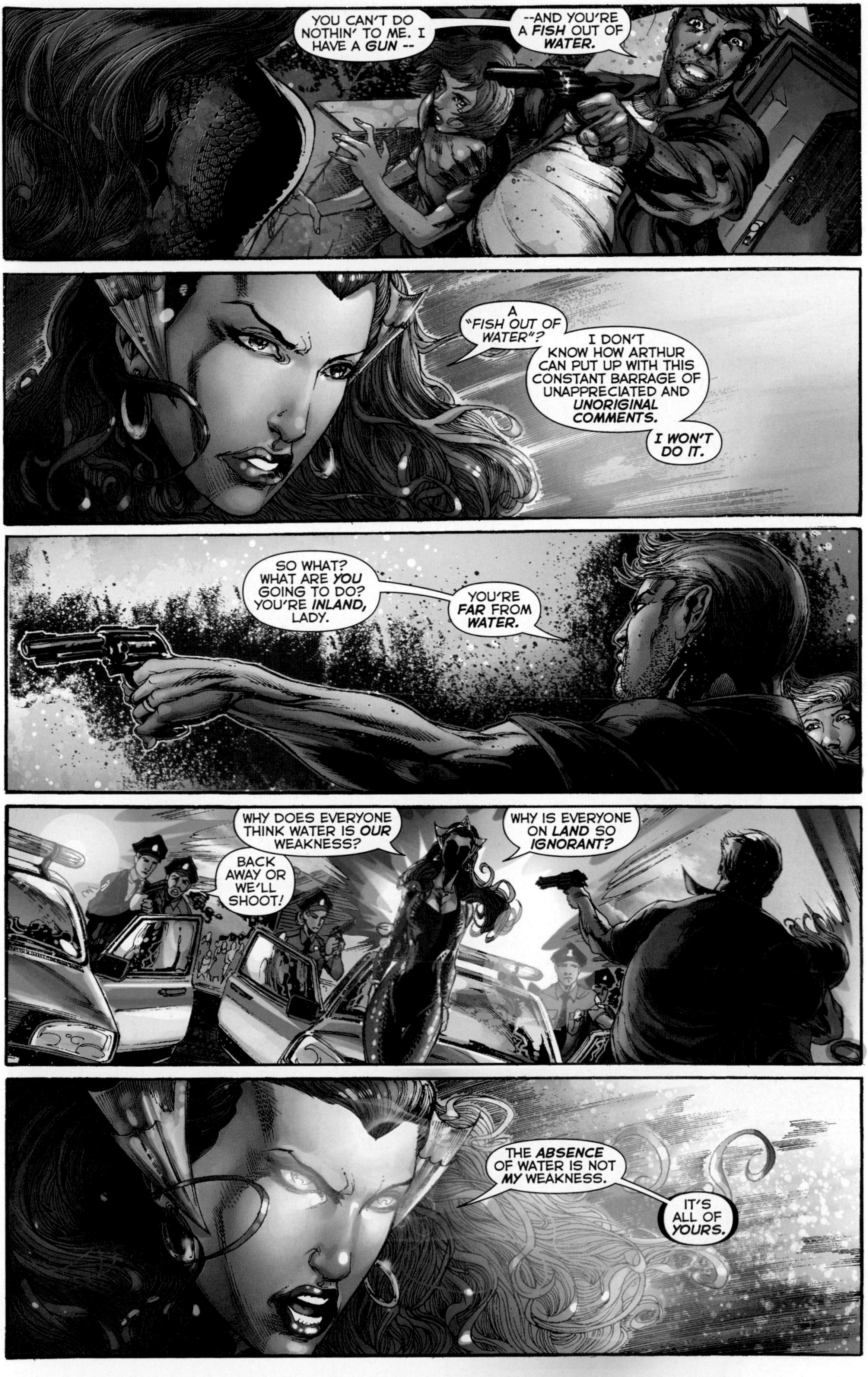
YOU CAN'T DO NOTHIN' TO ME. I HAVE A GUN --
--AND YOU'RE A FISH OUT OF WATER.
A "FISH OUT OF WATER"?
I DON'T KNOW HOW ARTHUR CAN PUT UP WITH THIS CONSTANT BARRAGE OF UNAPPRECIATED AND UNORIGINAL COMMENTS.
I WON'T DO IT.
SO WHAT? WHAT ARE YOU GOING TO DO? YOU'RE INLAND, LADY.
YOU'RE FAR FROM WATER.
WHY DOES EVERYONE THINK WATER IS OUR WEAKNESS?
BACK AWAY OR WE'LL SHOOT!
WHY IS EVERYONE ON LAND SO IGNORANT?
THE ABSENCE OF WATER IS NOT MY WEAKNESS.
IT'S ALL OF YOURS.

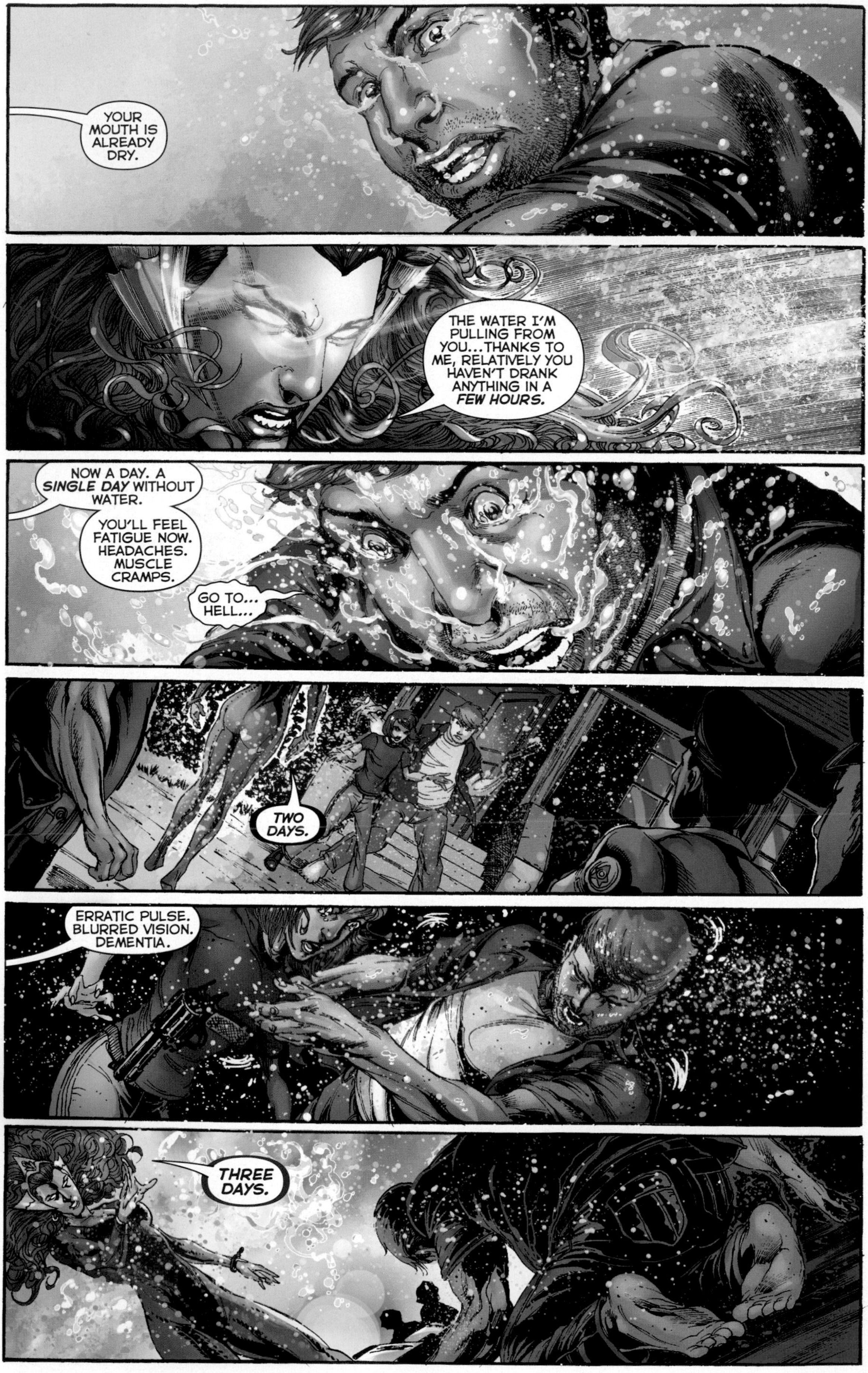
YOUR MOUTH IS ALREADY DRY.
THE WATER I'M PULLING FROM YOU...THANKS TO ME, RELATIVELY YOU HAVEN'T DRANK ANYTHING IN A *FEW HOURS.*
NOW A DAY. A *SINGLE DAY* WITHOUT WATER.
YOU'LL FEEL FATIGUE NOW. HEADACHES. MUSCLE CRAMPS.
GO TO... HELL...
TWO DAYS.
ERRATIC PULSE. BLURRED VISION. DEMENTIA.
THREE DAYS.

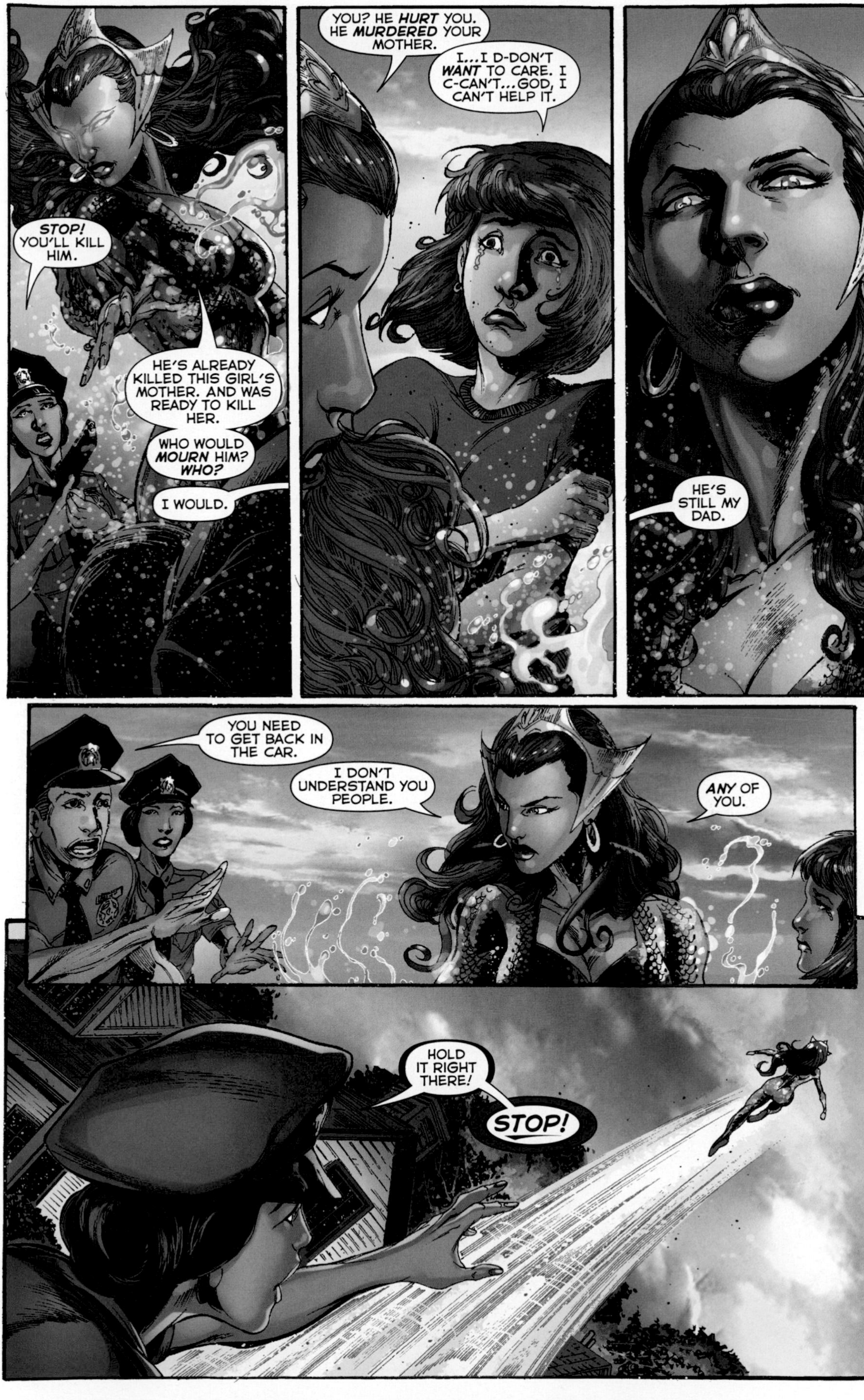
STOP! YOU'LL KILL HIM.
HE'S ALREADY KILLED THIS GIRL'S MOTHER. AND WAS READY TO KILL HER.
WHO WOULD MOURN HIM? WHO?
I WOULD.
YOU? HE HURT YOU. HE MURDERED YOUR MOTHER.
I...I D-DON'T WANT TO CARE. I C-CAN'T...GOD, I CAN'T HELP IT.
HE'S STILL MY DAD.
YOU NEED TO GET BACK IN THE CAR.
I DON'T UNDERSTAND YOU PEOPLE.
ANY OF YOU.
HOLD IT RIGHT THERE!
STOP!

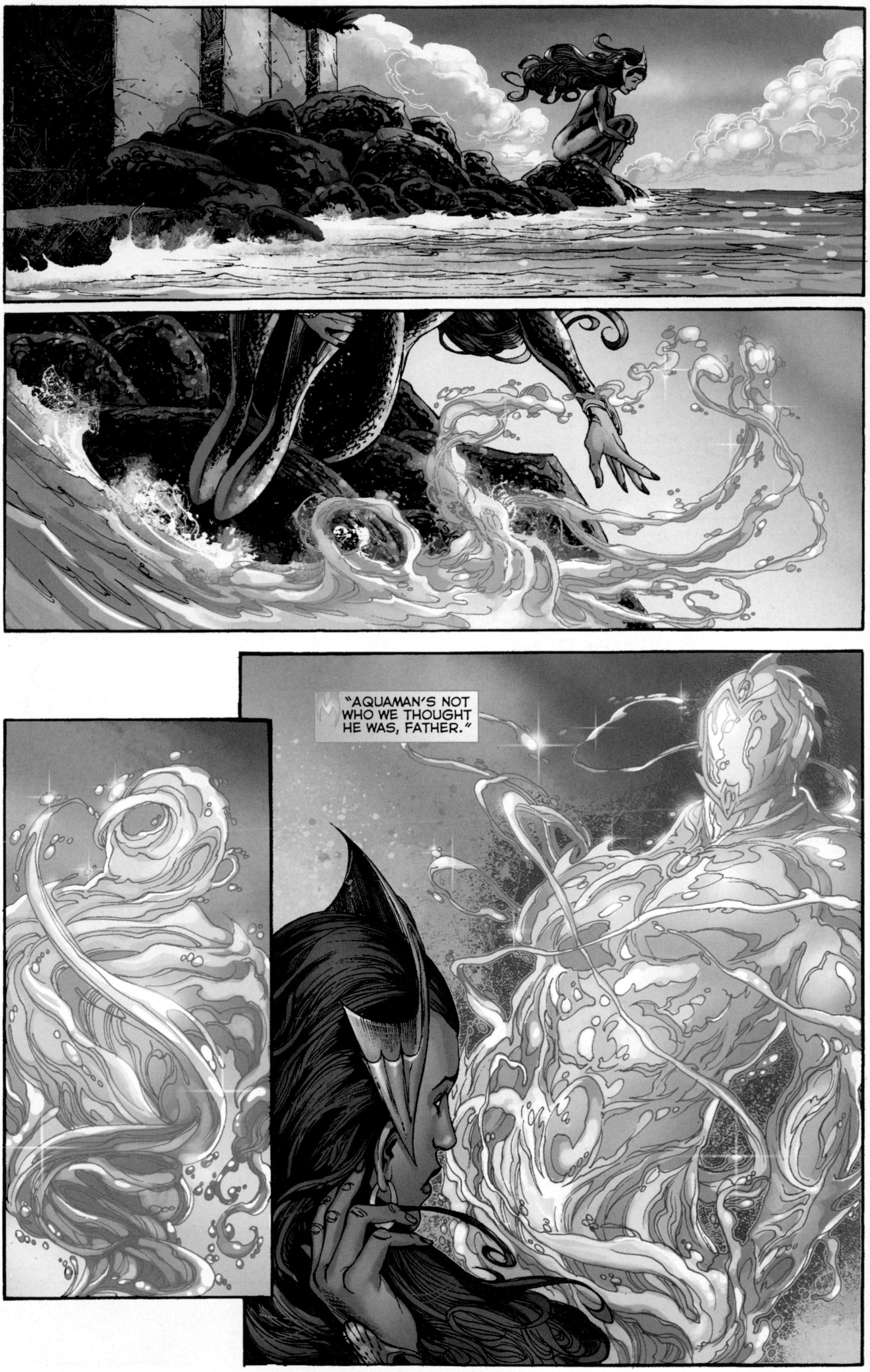
"AQUAMAN'S NOT WHO WE THOUGHT HE WAS, FATHER."

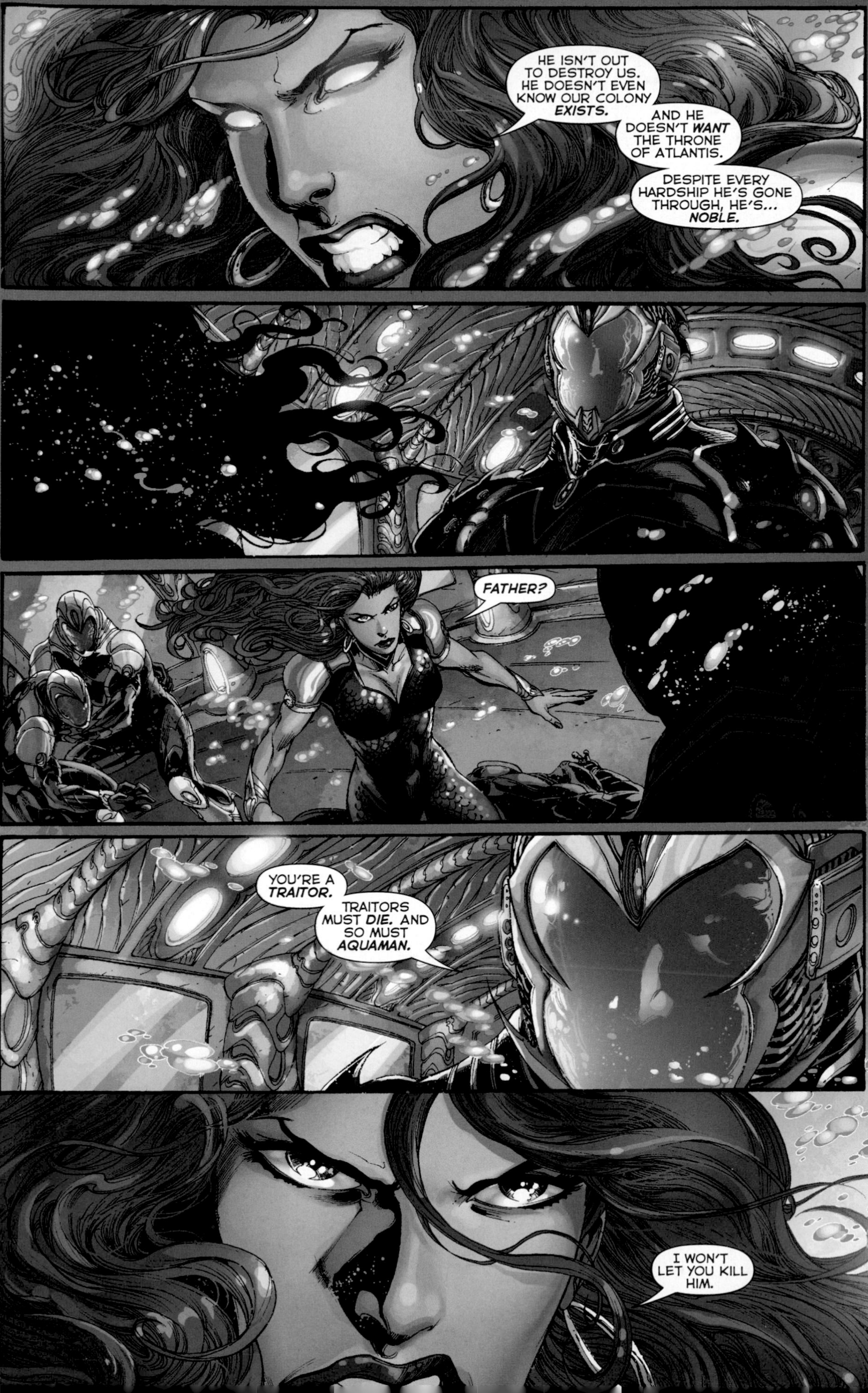
HE ISN'T OUT TO DESTROY US. HE DOESN'T EVEN KNOW OUR COLONY EXISTS.
AND HE DOESN'T WANT THE THRONE OF ATLANTIS.
DESPITE EVERY HARDSHIP HE'S GONE THROUGH, HE'S... NOBLE.
FATHER?
YOU'RE A TRAITOR.
TRAITORS MUST DIE. AND SO MUST AQUAMAN.
I WON'T LET YOU KILL HIM.

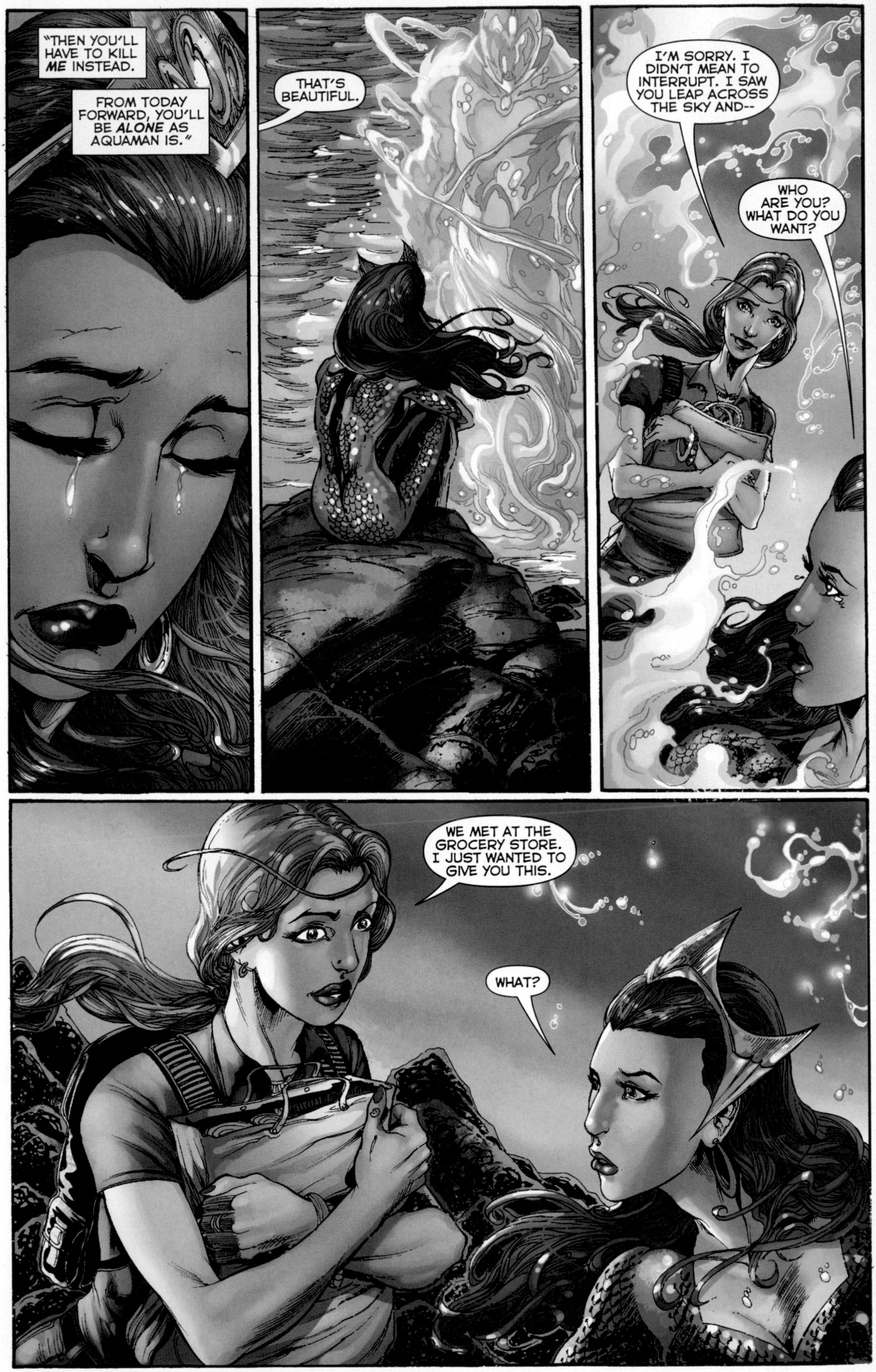
"THEN YOU'LL HAVE TO KILL *ME* INSTEAD.
FROM TODAY FORWARD, YOU'LL BE *ALONE* AS AQUAMAN IS."
THAT'S BEAUTIFUL.
I'M SORRY. I DIDN'T MEAN TO INTERRUPT. I SAW YOU LEAP ACROSS THE SKY AND--
WHO ARE YOU? WHAT DO YOU WANT?
WE MET AT THE GROCERY STORE. I JUST WANTED TO GIVE YOU THIS.
WHAT?

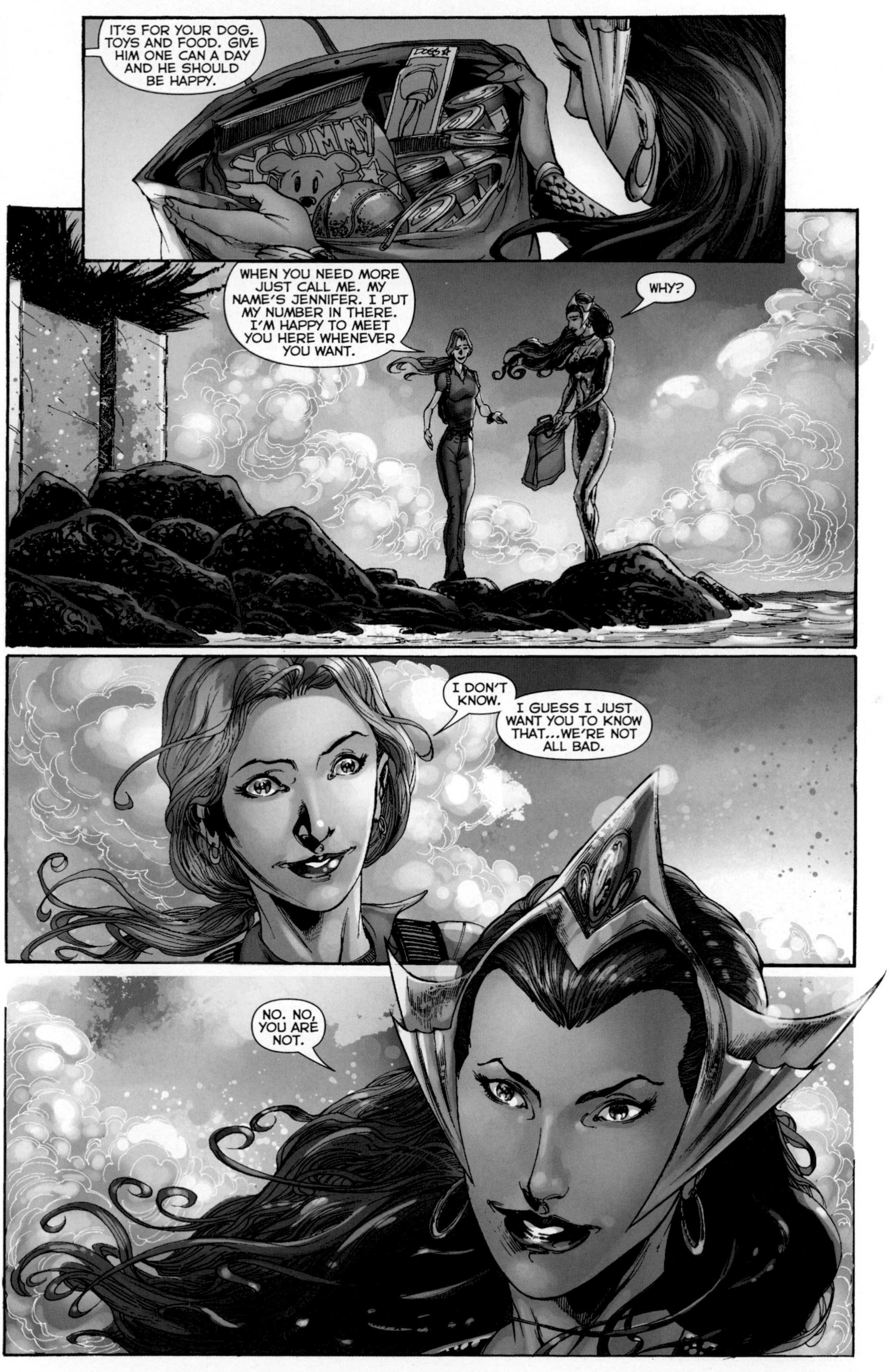
IT'S FOR YOUR DOG. TOYS AND FOOD. GIVE HIM ONE CAN A DAY AND HE SHOULD BE HAPPY.
YUMMY
WHEN YOU NEED MORE JUST CALL ME. MY NAME'S JENNIFER. I PUT MY NUMBER IN THERE. I'M HAPPY TO MEET YOU HERE WHENEVER YOU WANT.
WHY?
I DON'T KNOW.
I GUESS I JUST WANT YOU TO KNOW THAT...WE'RE NOT ALL BAD.
NO. NO, YOU ARE NOT.

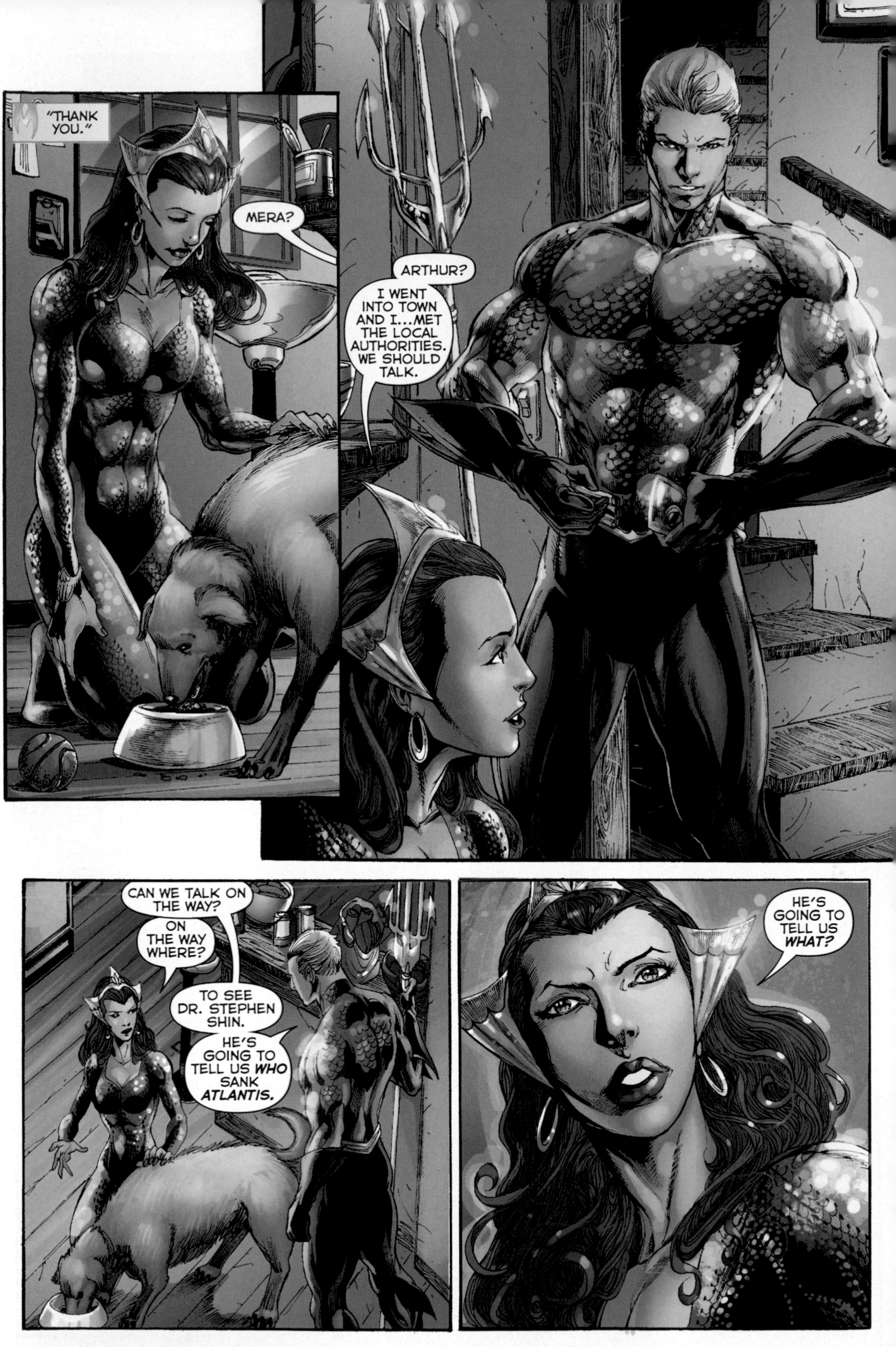
"THANK YOU."
MERA?
ARTHUR?
I WENT INTO TOWN AND I...MET THE LOCAL AUTHORITIES. WE SHOULD TALK.
CAN WE TALK ON THE WAY?
ON THE WAY WHERE?
TO SEE DR. STEPHEN SHIN.
HE'S GOING TO TELL US *WHO* SANK *ATLANTIS.*
HE'S GOING TO TELL US *WHAT?*

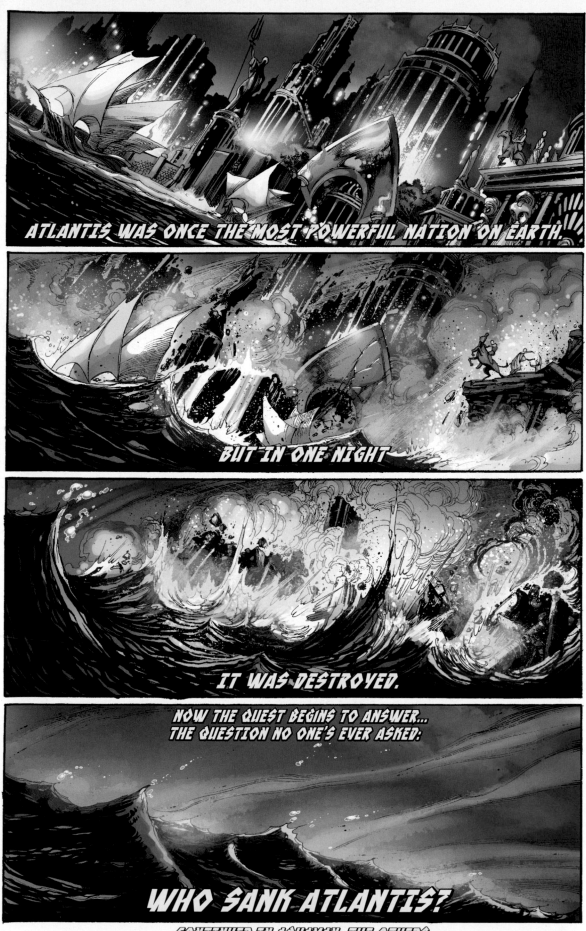

ATLANTIS WAS ONCE THE MOST POWERFUL NATION ON EARTH.

BUT IN ONE NIGHT

IT WAS DESTROYED.

NOW THE QUEST BEGINS TO ANSWER...
THE QUESTION NO ONE'S EVER ASKED:

WHO SANK ATLANTIS?

CONTINUED IN AQUAMAN: THE OTHERS

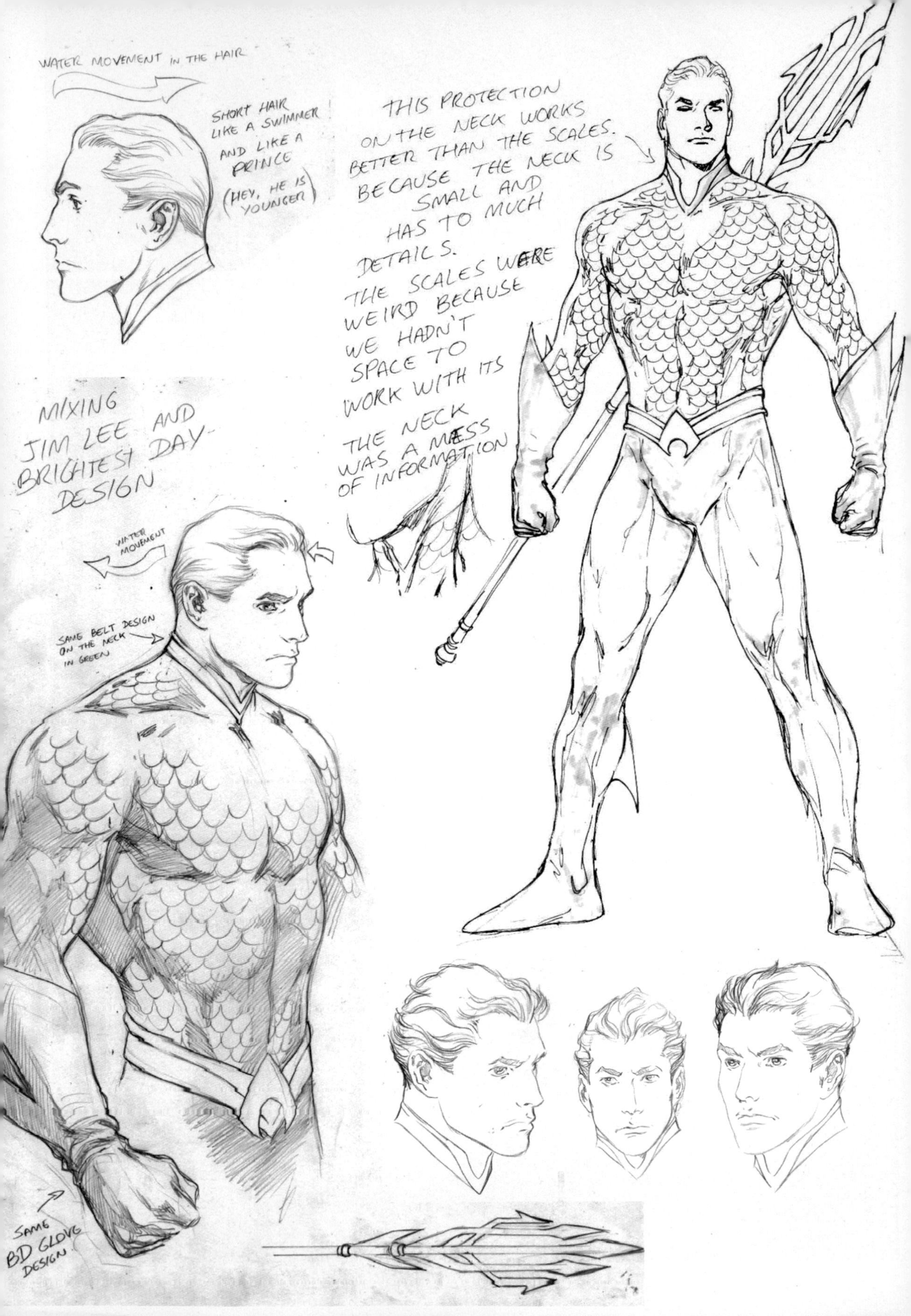
WATER MOVEMENT IN THE HAIR
SHORT HAIR LIKE A SWIMMER AND LIKE A PRINCE (HEY, HE IS YOUNGER)
THIS PROTECTION ON THE NECK WORKS BETTER THAN THE SCALES. BECAUSE THE NECK IS SMALL AND HAS TO MUCH DETAILS. THE SCALES WERE WEIRD BECAUSE WE HADN'T SPACE TO WORK WITH ITS
THE NECK WAS A MESS OF INFORMATION
MIXING JIM LEE AND BRIGHTEST DAY DESIGN
WATER MOVEMENT
SAME BELT DESIGN ON THE NECK IN GREEN
SAME BD GLOVE DESIGN

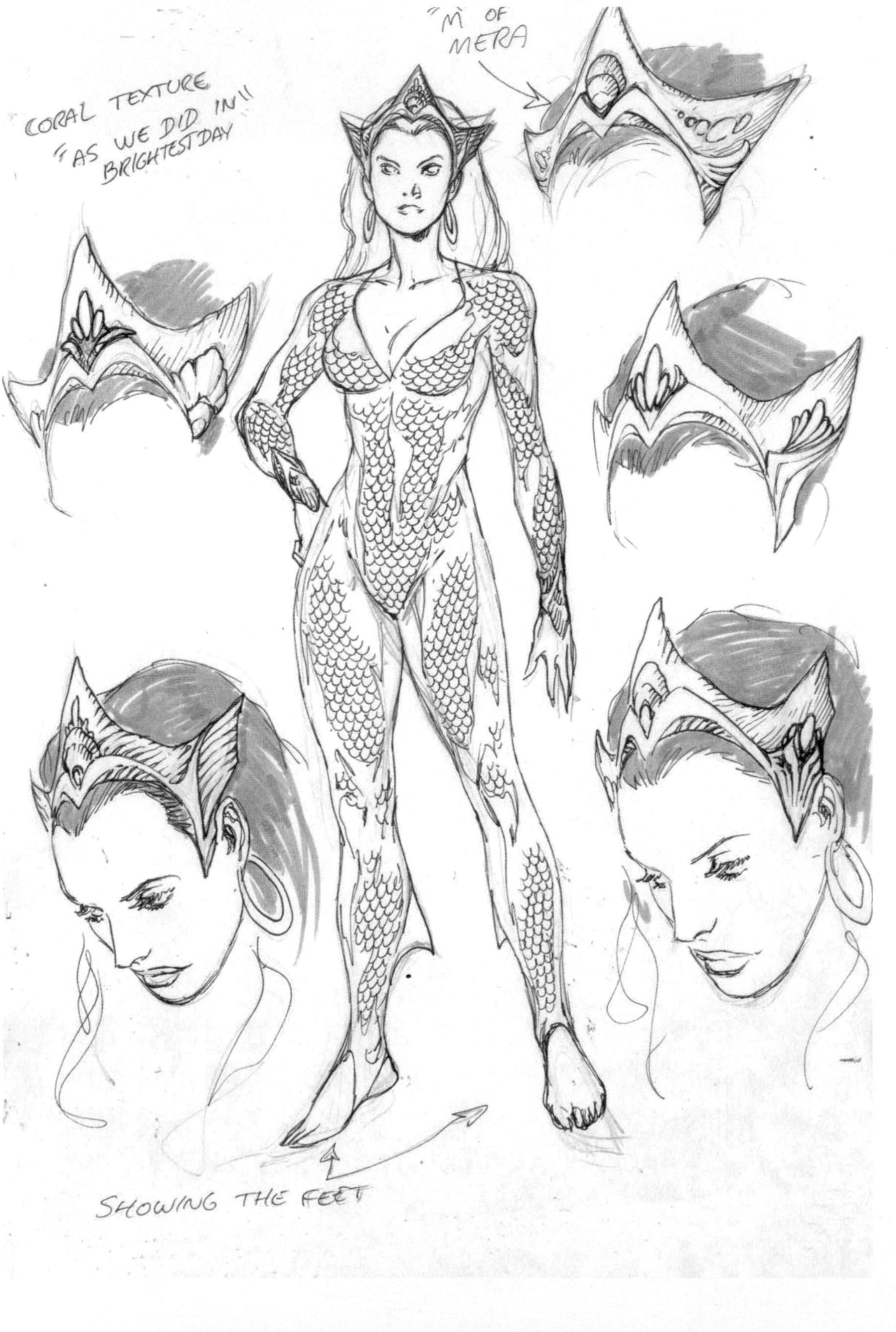

"M" OF MERA
CORAL TEXTURE "AS WE DID IN" BRIGHTEST DAY
SHOWING THE FEET

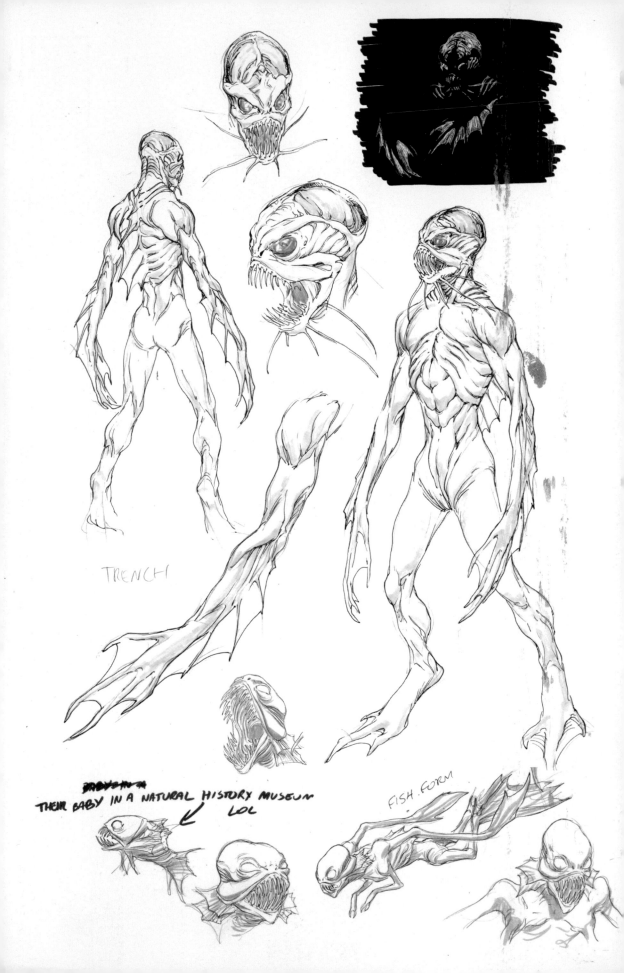

TRENCH

THEIR BABY IN A NATURAL HISTORY MUSEUM
LOL

FISH FORM